The FLORIDA INVESTOR

The FLORIDA INVESTOR

*How to find solid values in stocks, real estate,
fixed income, and tax-free investments in one
of America's most dynamic markets*

J. W. Dicks

BOB ADAMS, INC.
Holbrook, Massachusetts

Published by Bob Adams, Inc.
260 Center Street, Holbrook, MA 02343

ISBN: 1-55850-366-8

Printed in the United States of America.

J   I   H   G   F   E   D   C   B   A

Library of Congress Cataloging-in-Publication Data
Dicks, J.W. (Jack William), 1949-.
    The Florida investor : how to find solid values in stocks, real estate, fixed income, and
tax-free investments in one of America's most dynamic markets / J.W. Dicks.
        p.   cm.
    Includes bibliographical references and index.
    ISBN 1-55850-366-8
    1. Investments—Florida. 2. Stocks—Florida. 3. Real estate investment—Florida. 4. Tax
sales—Florida. I. Title.
    HG4910.D52   1994
    332.6'09759—dc20   94-8684
                                                             CIP

COVER DESIGN: Marshall Henrichs

This book is available at quantity discounts for bulk purchases.
For information, call 1-800-872-5627.

To Bert Rodgers
for his friendship and the opportunity he gave me
and to
David Edmunds who taught me so much
of what I know about real estate and business.

Acknowledgments

It is amazing the many people who touch the life of a book. To the following people, my thanks for their contribution.

Jim Paris for believing in the project enough to find a publisher.

Dick Staron, of Bob Adams, Inc. who recognized the value of producing the first book of its kind.

Ted Black, Sean Casterline, James Dicks, and John Tangri for their research assistance.

Buddy Smith for saying yes to yet another of my projects.

Debi McDade for all of her help on this and other works.

Table of Contents

Chapter 1

Florida—the Investor's State

When it comes to investment lore, Florida stands alone. Unfortunately, most of the publicity has centered on the swamp land swindles of the forties and fifties, or the penny stock boilerrooms of the early eighties. Whatever the flim or the flam, Florida has seen it.

Needless to say, there is another side to the Florida investment story. Florida's periodic land booms have made far more instant millionaires than its famous lottery. The state's size, climate, and favorable tax structure have made Florida a magnet to new businesses, businesses that have often taken root and prospered where elsewhere they might have struggled. It is on this Florida, the Florida of promise, that this book focuses.

Peter Lynch, perhaps the most successful mutual fund manager of all time, believes that people should put their money in things they know about. In his first book, *One up on Wall Street*, he cites numerous examples of investments he selected because his wife, children, or friends brought them to his attention. L'eggs, the company that makes hosiery, was one such example—selected not so much because of its financial fundamentals but because of its new product in the little egg marketing package. A recommendation of Mr. Lynch's wife.

In many ways, the role of this book will be the one played by Mr. Lynch's family. As your advisor, I will point out to you opportunities I see in our "backyard," the state of Florida. It is my goal to present all of the many options open to you. Although stocks take up a lot of room in this book, don't assume I think they are for everyone. I don't. I will present both conservative and aggressive investments, but I will try to point out the risk associated with each. I will try to be fair in my reporting, but I admit in advance to certain biases in the investment arena. You will see, for example, that certain so-called "conservative" investments, such as CDs, are not conservative at all, in my opinion. This position may not endear me to the banking industry, but being totally independent does allow me an objectivity not available to others. I'm not saying all other advisors lack objectivity. It's just that if you go to an insurance salesman, what's he going to sell you? Insurance. If you go to a stock broker, he'll sell you—stocks. If you go to a real estate broker, he'll sell you—real estate. If you go to a mortgage broker, he'll sell you—a mortgage. There's nothing *wrong* with that. People work in the industries they believe in; they wouldn't be worth their salt if they tried to sell you what they didn't believe in. But remember, not every investment is right for everyone.

Investors can be divided into certain broad groupings. Earlier I mentioned conservative and aggressive. Another grouping is active or passive. An investor can be active, meaning he or she likes to get involved directly with the investment. This category includes people who want to buy real estate and manage it. A passive investor is just the opposite. Because of his life style or state of mind, he wants little to do with his investments other than collect the highest yield someone will send him. Clearly there are few investments that would satisfy both types of investors.

In today's world, unlike in the past, there are no good long-term investments. By that I mean that today's investors must be more flexible. There used to be certain investments whose yields stayed relatively constant. You could invest in bonds or CDs and not think about change. This is no longer the case. In only thirteen years we have seen interest rates fluctuate from high double digits in 1980 to the low single digits as of this writing. During the same period real estate has boomed, busted, and popped. Where it is going to stop, few will try to predict. The stock market has also had a roller coaster ride. It boomed in the early eighties, crashed in 1987, and is back to making all-time highs again even as many professionals worry about where it is going. To remain constant in any investment today takes deep pockets and nerves of steel. Even if it were good for you, the practicality is that there aren't many people like that. That is why I say you must be flexible and move with the trends. No, I'm not suggesting you jump from one product to the next. Just make sure you understand the rules for each investment and place your money when the odds are in your favor. For example, if you are an income investor and bonds are normally your game, you learn to seek other options when the economy shifts to a rising interest rate environment. Why? Because no matter what you do, it is a fact that when interest rates rise, lower-yielding bonds will lose value as investors seek higher yields. If you have to sell your lower-yielding bond, you will lose money, so why take that risk? When the economy changes and rates begin to fall, you can return to your favorite bond investment with an additional opportunity of capital gain.

In summary, I want to convey three principles in this book.

1. Invest in what you know.

2. No single investment is the "right" investment.

3. There is no good "long-term" investment for all times.

In the upcoming chapters, we will explore many different kinds of investments. This is your opportunity to think about and, ultimately, to select those that best fit your investment profile. Next, within the investment categories laid out, we will look at specific selections—investments you can watch on a regular basis as you continue to make investment decisions. In short, this book will become a handbook of Florida investment opportunity.

Throughout this book I have listed hundreds of phone numbers and other reference points. Each has been rechecked prior to printing and confirmed for accuracy. Unfortunately, as investments change, so do people and businesses. Occasionally you will find a number that has been changed or is no longer working. I apologize for the inconvenience; it is one of the realities of trying to give the specific details that will make this book useful to you. So please mentally jump over these changes and use what remains for your success.

To make sure you get the most current information, I will gladly send you a copy of the current month's edition of *The Florida Investor Newsletter*. To get your free copy, call 1-800-333-3700.

Chapter 2

Investing in Florida's Best Companies

If you believe that "backyard" investing makes a lot of sense, you're in luck, because Florida is a hotbed for growth-oriented companies.

There are several reasons Florida attracts so many good companies, not the least of which is its size. The fourth-largest state, its current population base is around 13,196,855 (1992 census estimate). Other factors that make Florida an attractive place to start a business are its favorable state corporate statutes, relatively low filing fees, and lack of a state income tax–a feature that saves relocating corporate executives big bucks.

At this point it's easy to accept the fact that Florida is a good place to run a business and that there are probably some pretty good companies in Florida. I say "at this point," because so far the only thing you've actually invested in is the price of this book and a little time. By the time you have finished reading, I'm going to try and convince you that Florida is the place to put your serious money. To go along with that you are going to want more than platitudes about the size of the state and its corporate laws. You will want to know specifically why a company we talk about has any real chance of making any money. After all, that is what investment analysis is all about.

To begin with, we are going to look at Florida's stocks from the point of view of industry. That means that we, as investors, can pick an industry that we like and quickly compare the performances of all the public companies in the state, as well as the general trend of the industry as a whole. We may see that the general trend in an industry nationwide is booming, while Florida's companies are lagging. This could be caused by many factors, including such unusual events as Hurricane Andrew, which had a disproportionate impact on insurance companies doing business primarily in Florida. The opposite trend might also be true. Florida companies may lead the way, outperforming companies in other parts of the country.

Once you have selected an industry, compare the individual companies available–their earnings, profit, and return on equity. Does the stock show a consistent pattern of growth in these areas, or is this year just an aberration? Of course, important as such financial information is, the data itself does not assure you of making money, as any experienced investor knows. A stock can have great earnings and growth but be out of favor for any number of reasons. To determine how it is viewed by others, we will look to the market itself and analyze the price trend over a certain time period. Where a stock's price is today is determined by the collective group of investors who are presently making the market by buying and selling.

Our analysis of Florida companies will thus be based on three factors:

- Current industry performance and trend
- Individual corporate fundamentals
- Technical market indicators

Each of these three components of stock analysis information will be presented in a concise fashion. The trick, of course, is ultimately deciding what to do with all of the information.

It is not within the scope of this book to attempt a detailed analysis of the advantages of fundamental analysis over technical. This topic has been well covered elsewhere. My task is simply to present as much information as possible so that you can make an informed decision about which company is right for you. The beauty of investing is that you don't have to be right all the time. You must simply be right more times than not.

You will see quite a selection of companies throughout. I have tried to cover most Florida companies. We have omitted those carried only in the "pink sheets" circulated at brokerage houses and those stocks priced under one dollar. Some of the companies have tremendous growth potential; others are on the verge of bankruptcy. Using this book, you'll be able to tell the difference between them at a glance. How? Take a look at the way the company information is formatted (see examples in chapter 3).

The first set of boxes on each page contains the current price at the time of report, the hi-low range, price to earnings ratios, current dividend payout, the yield earned, and the beta of the stock. The second set of boxes contains financial data on the company using the last four quarters available. This may or may not be a calendar quarter since companies report at different times. This information may not directly correlate with the annual data on the bottom of the page which is calculated using full completed years. While this is somewhat confusing, it does allow us to use the latest data on all companies.

The bottom third of the page contains a summary of information about the fundamentals of the company. This data is often difficult for investors to put together, because it requires securing the company's financial information and poring over endless dry figures. By seeing the information summarized in this fashion, you can quickly recognize whether a company's revenues, net income, and return on equity are growing. For the investor who buys on fundamentals, this chart will be a joy.

The middle third of the page contains a one-year price chart on the company in question, the kind of chart frequently used by investors following technical analysis. It can be helpful in spotting companies whose prices have a strong positive trend and eliminating those whose prices are falling dramatically. The price line chart is also extremely useful in making buy and sell decisions. Here's how.

Stock prices tend to move in patterns. A company begins to make money, people get interested and buy stock, and the price begins to move up, not in a straight line, but trending up. After a while, the price you pay for the stock is too high relative to the underlying value of the company. At that point the price retreats to a more comfortable level for new buyers as they compare various investment alternatives.

If a company falls out of favor, the reverse happens. Fewer and fewer people are willing to pay the current price of the stock, and it begins to fall in value, seeking a new balance between price and perceived value of the company.

Historically, all of the performance I just described can be charted on a price chart. On each of our company charts you will recognize the price line as the most irregular one. The more irregular the line, the more volatile the price of the stock.

In addition to the price line, each chart displays two moving average lines. The line that most closely follows the path of the price line is the short-term (65-day) moving average line, while the slower curving line is the long-term (195-day) moving average.

These lines tell us "on average" the price direction of the stock. They take out some of the fluctuations within daily prices and attempt to show us a more blended view of where the stock price is heading. You will note that the shorter the moving average, the closer the line follows the path of the actual price.

Over the years, a tremendous amount of study has been done about the relationship between these lines. The most exhaustive work is *Technical Analysis of Stock Trends* by Robert D. Edwards and John Magee. If you desire to become a technical analyst, I highly recommend this book.

The lines appear on each chart in order to simplify analysis. When the price line of a company falls through the short-term moving average, you will see that the price of that company is now lower than its most recent average price for that period (sixty-five days). This moving average line is like an early warning system. Historically, if a price line continues to fall and subsequently crosses its long-term moving average, this is a bad indication of the direction of the price ahead.

The reverse pattern is also true. A company's price crossing both its short-term and long-term trend and moving upward tends to continue in that direction. This is particularly true of companies with lower volatility, because they are now breaking a pattern.

If you are reading this carefully you will note that I have used the words "indication" and "tends" to describe what will happen to a stock's price once it crosses our indicated lines. This is because moving averages are only indicators; they are not perfect. If they were, it would take all the excitement out of investing. Nevertheless, I recommend them highly. The moving average crossover points are excellent places to put stop/loss orders, which will protect your downside risk on stock selections. In addition, when used in conjunction with the fundamentals of a company that we list, they are an excellent confirmation that the market is currently looking at this stock the same way you are.

There are no guaranteed ways to make money in stocks. There are, however, definite indicators that anyone can use to aid in the selection of a good company to invest in. Each of these indicators is founded on logical conclusions.

Key Elements to "Market Logic" Stock Selections

- It is better to invest in stocks when the stock market as a whole is performing well. This is not a necessity, but it is logical.

- It is better to invest in a company whose industry is performing well. Again, not a necessity, but logical. If all of the major institutional buyers are favoring an industry, its performance will tend to be better.

- It is better to invest in a company whose fundamentals show a pattern of steady growth. This is another nonemotional guide. Either it is or it isn't, and wishing it were otherwise won't make it so.

- It is better to invest in a company that has established a positive price-trend moving above its short-term and long-term moving averages. There is greater profit potential if you can invest as the price line approaches the moving average lines in a clear upward trend. There also tends to be greater risk until the price line actually crosses.

- It is better to sell a company when its price line drops below its moving average. When the price line reverses and crosses its short-term moving average (moving down), you can take this as an early warning. When it crosses its long-term average, it's time to sell.

The keys I have just presented are elements of a logical approach to stock market investing. They are not guarantees, but logical affirmations that will help you make the best selections.

How Do You Buy a Stock You Like?

There are three ways to buy stocks:

- Through a full-service broker

- Through a discount broker
- Directly from the company (limited to those that have such a program)

Which of the three methods you choose will depend on how active you are as an investor. If you are picking your own stocks and can buy directly without paying a commission, why use a full service or even a discount broker? On the other hand, although buying direct is a new trend, it limits your selection of companies to those that allow this option. Until they do, your most economical course is to use a discount brokerage firm and try to negotiate the best commission rate available. Yes, they will negotiate, so ask for the best rate. In Florida, the major discount brokerage firms are:

Charles Schwab & Company, 1-800-435-4000
Jack White & Company, 1-800-909-6777
Olde Discount, 1-800-448-8221

If you can't spend the time to pick your own stocks, then you might consider hiring a service broker to make recommendations for you. It's not hard to decide whether he's doing a good job. If he makes you money, he is. If he doesn't make you money, he's not. To select a broker in the beginning, I would seek opinions from friends and business associates you consider to be successful. Don't rely on the opinion of anyone who hasn't invested and made money. If they knew what they were talking about, they would be making money.

When you finally find a broker you like, start off small. Don't give him all of your account until he has proven his worth. It won't hurt to let him know that there is more to come if he produces, but make him earn the privilege. This is your hard-earned money, so control the decisions.

Entering the Investment Cycle
When you start an investment program, you are entering the investment cycle — of both the market and the individual stocks whose shares you have purchased — after the cycle has already begun. You may enter (unknowingly) just as things are beginning to slow.

To counter that possibility, I recommend that you buy your stocks in incremental investments. If you have $12,000 to invest, you might invest in three equal increments. Your first investment would be $4,000. After waiting a week or two, if the stock's trend continued up, you would invest your next $4,000. Wait a week or two and repeat with your final $4,000. If at any time the stock's upward trend stalled or reversed, you would wait until it resumed. Meanwhile, to protect your downside, your enter a stop/loss order when you make your first buy. The stop/loss order calls for the stock to be sold automatically at a predetermined price should its price begin to fall. It should be used whenever you purchase stock. A comfortable price for most people is 10 percent below your original purchase price. If the price rises, you raise your stop/loss order to an amount 10 percent below the new price.

The advantage to incremental investing is clear: You don't dive into unknown waters. The disadvantages are that you will pay slightly higher commissions and you will have paid more for your second and third buy if the trend continues. The advantages of protecting your downside, however, outweigh these negatives.

Chapter 3

Florida Headline Companies

Things aren't always as they seem. In this chapter we'll be breaking out of their industry listing the companies that you hear about most frequently—the ones that get the "headlines" in Florida newspapers. We'll also be bending the rules a little along the way and listing some companies that might not be technically Florida-based. That's okay, because this book is about investing; it's not a road atlas. Consequently, I am including companies that I consider strongly Florida influenced, such as Disney and Home Depot.

The fact that these companies have been called headline stocks does **not** mean they are necessarily good investments. In fact, just because a company is well known and maybe even well liked does not mean it is a good investment. This is where the novice investor has historically gone wrong. He hears of a hot company (old or new) and makes his investment precisely during the inevitable price pull back. Then he watches his hot tip fall 5 to 10 percent in a short period of time, panics, and decides to sell. Shortly thereafter, the company's price recovers—the company was fundamentally sound—and the price moves up again. Our uneducated investor now remains frustrated, or worse yet, watches the price continue to rise, waits till he can stand it no longer, and places another order for the stock. Guess what happens? It takes a breather and falls back some, and our hapless investor swears off investing in the stock market forever.

Some company's stock is extremely volatile. The company's price will have wide swings up and down in value. This is particularly true of lower-capitalized companies and new public companies. The price swings are not necessarily bad, but most investors don't have the temperament for it. If you fit that mold, don't invest in these companies, or all too often you'll find yourself with an upset stomach when you read the morning paper.

You can easily see how volatile a company is by looking at the price chart accompanying each listing. The more up and down the price line is, the more volatile the prices have been historically. Although the pattern may change at some point in the future, your personal digestive system may not be willing to wait that long.

Investing should be fun. If the stock market's not comfortable for you, don't invest in it. You'll find many other options in this book that fit your investment style better.

In addition to appearing in this chapter, these stocks will also be listed in chapters relating to their appropriate industry for ease of reference.

BLOCKBUSTER ENTERTAINMENT CORPORATION

Symbol: BV   Exchange: NYS

PRICE 3/4/94	RANGE	P-E RATIO	DIVIDEND	YIELD	BETA
27	27 - 13¼	30.68	0.03	0	0.7

LAST FOUR QUARTERS REPORTED

REVENUES	% CHANGE	NET INCOME	% CHANGE	RETURN ON EQUITY	% CHANGE
2227.003	69.25	243.646	64.33	18.24	- 15.03

Corporate Summary

Blockbuster Entertainment Corporation's principal areas of business are home video and music retailing. Through its Domestic and International Home Video Divisions, the company is the largest home video retailer in the world, with over 30 million members and 3,127 video stores in the Blockbuster system. The company is also a partner with the Virgin Retail Group in the ownership and operation of fifteen music "Megastores" in Australia, the United States, and six European countries.

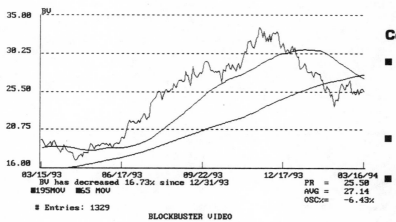

BLOCKBUSTER VIDEO

BV has decreased 16.73% since 12/31/93
■195MOV ■65 MOV
PR = 25.50
AVG = 27.14
OSC%= -6.43%
Entries: 1329

Commentary

- Good company with great potential but takes risks.
- Price trend is negative.
- Fundamentals are positive.

YEAR	REVENUES	% CHANGE	NET INCOME	% CHANGE	RETURN ON EQUITY	% CHANGE
89	402.538	194.053	44.152	184.888	21.2	39.3
90	632.670	57.170	68.654	55.495	21.8	2.8
91	868.003	37.197	93.681	36.454	19.4	- 11.2
92	1200.494	38.305	142.034	51.615	18.1	- 6.4

CARNIVAL CRUISE LINES INCORPORATED

Symbol: CCL   Exchange: NYS

PRICE 3/4/94	RANGE	P-E RATIO	DIVIDEND	YIELD	BETA
49½	32¾ - 49½	22.00	.14	0	1.6

LAST FOUR QUARTERS REPORTED

REVENUES	% CHANGE	NET INCOME	% CHANGE	RETURN ON EQUITY	% CHANGE
1556.899	5.65	318.131	12.90	19.93	- 3.75

Corporate Summary

Carnival Cruise Lines Incorporated, together with its subsidiaries, is the world largest multiple-night cruise line. The company offers a broad range of cruise products, serving the contemporary cruise market through Carnival Cruise Lines, the premium market through Holland America Line, and the luxury market through Windstar Cruises and the company's joint venture, Seabourn Cruise Line.

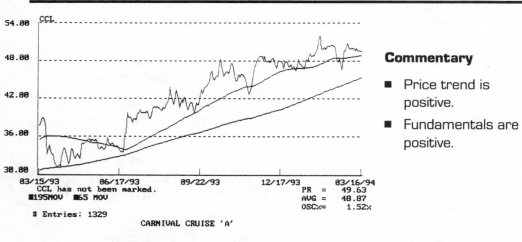

CCL has not been marked.
■19SMOV ■65 MOV
PR = 49.63
AVG = 48.87
OSC%= 1.52%

Entries: 1329

CARNIVAL CRUISE 'A'

Commentary

- Price trend is positive.

- Fundamentals are positive.

YEAR	REVENUES	% CHANGE	NET INCOME	% CHANGE	RETURN ON EQUITY	% CHANGE
89	1147.675	91.365	193.605	- 1.420	21.7	- 17.0
90	1391.332	21.230	206.202	6.507	19.9	- 8.2
91	1404.704	0.961	253.824	23.095	21.7	8.9
92	1473.614	4.906	281.773	11.011	20.3	- 6.1

CHECKERS DRIVE-IN RESTAURANTS

Symbol: CHKR   Exchange: NMS

PRICE 3/4/94	RANGE	P-E RATIO	DIVIDEND	YIELD	BETA
$11\frac{3}{8}$	$10\frac{7}{8}$ - $15\frac{3}{16}$	36.34	0	0	0.6

LAST FOUR QUARTERS REPORTED

REVENUES	% CHANGE	NET INCOME	% CHANGE	RETURN ON EQUITY	% CHANGE
162.624	89.23	15.059	47.55	14.18	4.34

Corporate Summary

Checkers Drive-In Restaurants develops, produces, owns, operates, and franchises "double drive-thru" quick-service hamburger restaurants under the name "Checkers." The restaurants are designed around a distinctive 1950's diner and art deco theme that permits service of more than one automobile simultaneously from opposite sides of the restaurant.

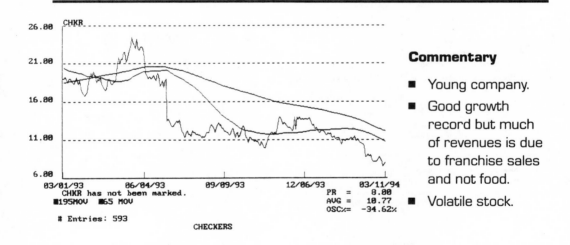

Commentary

- Young company.
- Good growth record but much of revenues is due to franchise sales and not food.
- Volatile stock.

YEAR	REVENUES	% CHANGE	NET INCOME	% CHANGE	RETURN ON EQUITY	% CHANGE
89	NA	NA	NA	NA	NA	NA
90	22.925	NA	1.213	NA	106.1	NA
91	42.151	83.865	3.680	203.380	11.5	- 89.1
92	88.577	110.142	10.693	190.571	13.6	18.3

DISCOUNT AUTO PARTS

Symbol: DAP   Exchange: NYS

PRICE 3/4/94	RANGE	P-E RATIO	DIVIDEND	YIELD	BETA
$27\frac{1}{2}$	$23\frac{5}{8}$ - $29\frac{1}{4}$	29.25	0	0	NA

LAST FOUR QUARTERS REPORTED

REVENUES	% CHANGE	NET INCOME	% CHANGE	RETURN ON EQUITY	% CHANGE
191.174	18.71	13.179	-2.70	14.65	-16.78

Corporate Summary

Discount Auto Parts operates one of the nation's largest chains of automotive products and accessories retail stores. The retail outlets offer a number of high quality, name brand automotive parts for auto repair and servicing as well as a number of automotive accessories and options.

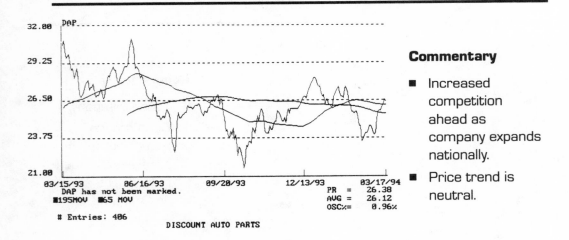

DISCOUNT AUTO PARTS

Commentary

- Increased competition ahead as company expands nationally.

- Price trend is neutral.

YEAR	REVENUES	% CHANGE	NET INCOME	% CHANGE	RETURN ON EQUITY	% CHANGE
89	NA	NA	NA	NA	NA	NA
90	NA	NA	NA	NA	NA	NA
91	NA	NA	NA	NA	NA	NA
92	141.206	NA	12.226	NA	34.5	NA

DISNEY (WALT) COMPANY

Symbol: DIS   Exchange: NYS

PRICE 3/4/94	RANGE	P-E RATIO	DIVIDEND	YIELD	BETA
47$\frac{1}{4}$	37$\frac{1}{2}$ - 47$\frac{1}{4}$	33.75	.06	0	1.3

LAST FOUR QUARTERS REPORTED

REVENUES	% CHANGE	NET INCOME	% CHANGE	RETURN ON EQUITY	% CHANGE
8865.129	11.10	764.764	- 13.46	15.20	- 19.07

Corporate Summary

Disney (Walt) Company currently operates a number of theme parks including Disneyland (CA), Walt Disney World (FL), Epcot Center, Disney MGM Studios, and EuroDisney (the company owns a 49% stake in EuroDisney). Additionally Disney supplies entertainment for theaters, TV, and video as well as publishes books and records music, the majority of which is marketed towards children. The company also owns and operates the Disney Channel.

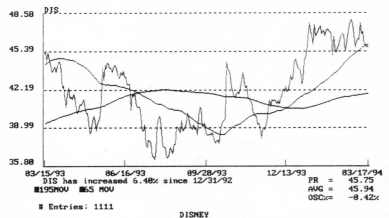

```
48.58  DIS
45.39
42.19
38.99
35.88
      03/15/93      06/16/93      09/20/93      12/13/93      03/17/94
         DIS has increased 6.40% since 12/31/92      PR  =  45.75
      ■195MOV  ■65 MOV                               AVG =  45.94
                                                     OSC%=  -0.42%
      # Entries: 1111
                         DISNEY
```

COMMENTARY

- Price trend is positive.
- Fundamentals are neutral.

YEAR	REVENUES	% CHANGE	NET INCOME	% CHANGE	RETURN ON EQUITY	% CHANGE
89	4594.296	33.625	703.300	34.732	23.1	4.4
90	5843.699	27.195	824.000	17.162	23.6	2.2
91	6182.398	5.796	636.600	- 22.743	16.4	- 30.4
92	7504.000	21.377	816.700	28.291	17.36	5.6

ECKERD (JACK) CORPORATION

Symbol: ECK   Exchange: NYS

PRICE 3/4/94	RANGE	P-E RATIO	DIVIDEND	YIELD	BETA
19.75	19.75 -13.88	NA	0	0	NA

LAST FOUR QUARTERS REPORTED

REVENUES	% CHANGE	NET INCOME	% CHANGE	RETURN ON EQUITY	% CHANGE
4190.021	9.30	13.873	219.90	NA	NA

Corporate Summary

Eckerd Corporation operates a retail chain of stores offering a diverse range of items, mainly nationally-known name brand items, as well as their own generic "Eckerd" brand items. The company directs its stores towards family-style, value-oriented consumers. Eckerd Corporation operates retail chains throughout the United States and became public in the third quarter of 1993.

Entries: 139

ECKERD CORPORATION

Commentary

- Price trend is positive.

- Fundamentals are improving.

YEAR	REVENUES	% INCREASE	NET INCOME	% INCREASE	RETURN ON EQUITY	% INCREASE
89	3170.608	10.252	- 7.977	NA	3.8	961.5
90	3367.259	6.202	- 32.569	NA	12.9	237.9
91	3562.197	5.789	- 1.278	NA	0.5	- 96.2
92	3695.436	3.740	- 9.476	NA	3.3	590.3

FLORIDA ROCK INDUSTRIES INCORPORATED

Symbol: FRK   Exchange: ASE

PRICE 3/4/94	RANGE	P-E RATIO	DIVIDEND	YIELD	BETA
32⅛	24¼ - 32⅛	27.93	0.25	0	0.7

LAST FOUR QUARTERS REPORTED

REVENUES	% CHANGE	NET INCOME	% CHANGE	RETURN ON EQUITY	% CHANGE
303.480	13.46	10.661	235.46	6.21	229.38

Corporate Summary

Florida Rock Industries Incorporated, and its subsidiaries, are principally engaged in the production and sale of ready mixed concrete and the mining, processing, and sale of sand, gravel, and crushed stone. The company also produces and sells concrete block and prestressed concrete as well as other building materials. Overall, the majority of the company's business is conducted within the southeastern United States.

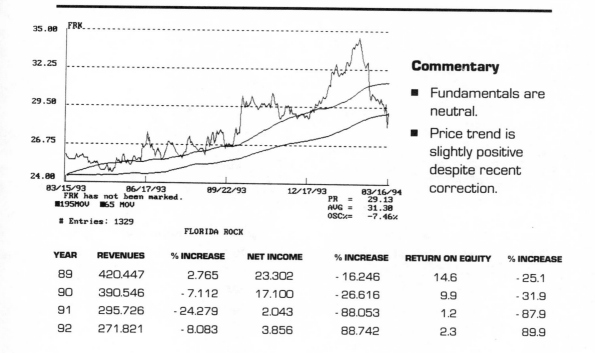

Commentary

- Fundamentals are neutral.
- Price trend is slightly positive despite recent correction.

FRK has not been marked.
■195MOV ■65 MOV
PR = 29.13
AVG = 31.30
OSC% = -7.46%

Entries: 1329

FLORIDA ROCK

YEAR	REVENUES	% INCREASE	NET INCOME	% INCREASE	RETURN ON EQUITY	% INCREASE
89	420.447	2.765	23.302	- 16.246	14.6	- 25.1
90	390.546	- 7.112	17.100	- 26.616	9.9	- 31.9
91	295.726	- 24.279	2.043	- 88.053	1.2	- 87.9
92	271.821	- 8.083	3.856	88.742	2.3	89.9

HOME DEPOT INCORPORATED

Symbol: HD   Exchange: NYSE

PRICE 3/4/94	RANGE	P-E RATIO	DIVIDEND	YIELD	BETA
39	38½ - 48⅞	38.61	0.30	0	1.4

LAST FOUR QUARTERS REPORTED

REVENUES	% CHANGE	NET INCOME	% CHANGE	RETURN ON EQUITY	% CHANGE
9238.763	29.24	457.401	26.053	17.06	1.969

Corporate Summary

Home Depot Incorporated operates a chain of retail "warehouse" building supply/home improvement stores in the eastern seaboard states, ranging from Connecticut to Florida, and in the states of Texas, Arizona, and California. The retail outlets average 97,000 sq. ft. in size and carry about 30,000 items.

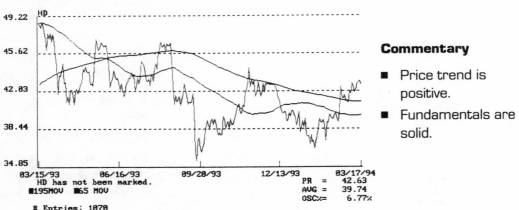

```
49.22  HD
45.62
42.03
38.44
34.85
       03/15/93      06/16/93      09/20/93      12/13/93      03/17/94
       HD has not been marked.                          PR  =   42.63
       ■195MOV  ■65 MOV                                 AVG =   39.74
                                                        OSC%=    6.77%
       # Entries: 1070
                         HOME DEPOT
```

Commentary

- Price trend is positive.
- Fundamentals are solid.

YEAR	REVENUES	% CHANGE	NET INCOME	% CHANGE	RETURN ON EQUITY	% CHANGE
89	2785.5	39.3	112.0	45.8	80.8	22.3
90	3815.4	36.9	163.4	45.9	51.7	- 36.0
91	5136.7	34.6	249.2	52.5	162.1	213.5
92	7148.4	39.2	362.9	45.6	50.52	- 68.8

HOME SHOPPING NETWORK INCORPORATED

Symbol: HSN   Exchange: NYS

PRICE 3/4/94	RANGE	P-E RATIO	DIVIDEND	YIELD	BETA
14¼	6⅛ - 14⅞	712.50	0	0	1.0

LAST FOUR QUARTERS REPORTED

REVENUES	% CHANGE	NET INCOME	% CHANGE	RETURN ON EQUITY	% CHANGE
SF	SF	SF	NA	SF	SF

Corporate Summary

Home Shopping Network is a holding company, the subsidiaries of which conduct the day-to-day operations of the company's various business activities. The company's main business is electronic retailing conducted by Home Shopping Club, Inc. Home Shopping Network is based in St. Petersburg, FL.

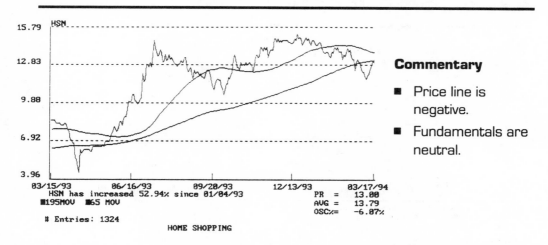

HSN has increased 52.94% since 01/04/93
■195MOV ■65 MOV
PR = 13.00
AVG = 13.79
OSC% = -6.07%

Entries: 1324

HOME SHOPPING

Commentary

■ Price line is negative.

■ Fundamentals are neutral.

YEAR	REVENUES	% CHANGE	NET INCOME	% CHANGE	RETURN ON EQUITY	% CHANGE
89	774.342	6.062	- 22.075	- 222.762	- 15.8	- 225.7
90	1008.272	30.210	32.464	NA	18.3	NA
91	1078.547	6.970	- 9.599	- 129.568	- 5.9	- 132.4
92	1097.787	1.784	37.405	NA	22.0	NA

HUGHES SUPPLY INCORPORATED

Symbol: HUG   Exchange: NYS

PRICE 3/4/94	RANGE	P-E RATIO	DIVIDEND	YIELD	BETA
24½	14 - 24½	21.12	0	0	0.5

LAST FOUR QUARTERS REPORTED

REVENUES	% CHANGE	NET INCOME	% CHANGE	RETURN ON EQUITY	% CHANGE
622.366	15.35	5.271	1154.2	5.834	NA

Corporate Summary

Hughes Supply, Inc. is a wholesale distributor of electric, plumbing, air conditioning, and heating parts to the construction industry and mechanical trades in the southeastern states. The company has shut down weak sales offices, consolidated its administrative functions, and installed computerized inventory replenishment and accounting systems. Hughes Supply is looking for acquisitions at this time.

HUG has not been marked.
■19SMOV ■65 MOV

Entries: 1329

HUGHES SUPPLY

PR = 26.75
AVG = 23.93
OSC%= 18.55%

Commentary

- Fundamentals are increasing favorably with a positive outlook.

- Price trend is positive.

YEAR	REVENUES	% CHANGE	NET INCOME	% CHANGE	RETURN ON EQUITY	% CHANGE
89	529.475	5.594	6.394	- 34.205	6.9	- 35.2
90	548.475	3.500	2.141	- 66.515	2.5	- 64.1
91	481.001	- 12.302	- 4.040	- 288.697	- 5.0	- 300.4
92	528.363	9.847	2.264	NA	2.7	NA

LURIA (L.) & SONS INCORPORATED

Symbol: LUR   Exchange: ASE

PRICE 3/4/94	RANGE	P-E RATIO	DIVIDEND	YIELD	BETA
13¾	10½ - 15	16.98	0	0	0.5

LAST FOUR QUARTERS REPORTED

REVENUES	% CHANGE	NET INCOME	% CHANGE	RETURN ON EQUITY	% CHANGE
240.253	9.64	4.303	127.79	5.31	114.63

Corporate Summary

Luria (L.) & Sons Inc. is the leading regional jewelry retailer in Florida, operating a chain of 50 stores. Luria's stores also offer china, crystal,
giftware, consumer electronics, and small appliances. Luria is a niche retailer with the majority of profits being jewelry-dominated. Luria was established in 1898 and is based in Miami Lakes, FL.

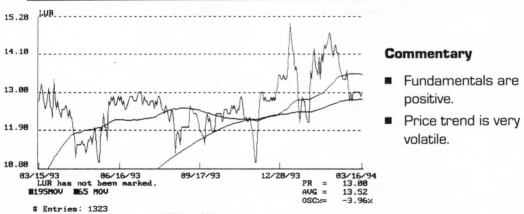

LUR has not been marked.
195MOV   65 MOV

PR = 13.00
AVG = 13.52
OSC% = -3.96%

Entries: 1323

LURIA & SON

Commentary

- Fundamentals are positive.
- Price trend is very volatile.

YEAR	REVENUES	% CHANGE	NET INCOME	% CHANGE	RETURN ON EQUITY	% CHANGE
89	221.017	2.377	3.048	- 38.844	4.0	- 42.1
90	213.756	- 3.285	1.082	- 64.501	1.4	- 64.9
91	207.581	- 2.889	1.179	8.965	1.5	7.2
92	235.567	13.482	3.407	188.974	4.2	176.4

OFFICE DEPOT INCORPORATED

Symbol: ODP   Exchange: NYS

PRICE 3/4/94	RANGE	P-E RATIO	DIVIDEND	YIELD	BETA
36$\frac{1}{2}$	19$\frac{7}{8}$ - 36$\frac{1}{2}$	54.48	0	0	1.6

LAST FOUR QUARTERS REPORTED

REVENUES	% CHANGE	NET INCOME	% CHANGE	RETURN ON EQUITY	% CHANGE
2579.493	48.85	63.417	67.81	11.91	10.45

Corporate Summary

Office Depot Incorporated operates the nation's largest chain of office products warehouse stores, with 228 stores in 29 states. The warehouse style stores offer approximately 5,100 brand name office products, including general office supplies, business machines, office furniture, and computer hardware and software.

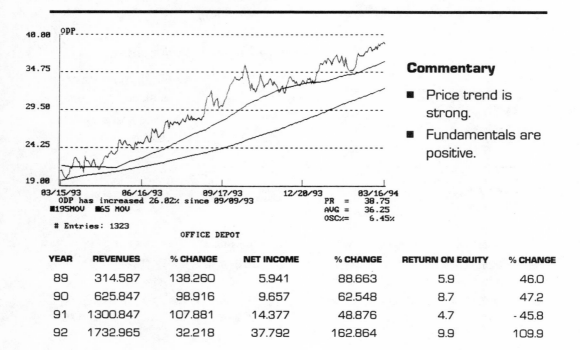

ODP has increased 26.82% since 09/09/93

PR = 38.75
AVG = 36.25
OSC% = 6.45%

■ 19 SMOV ■ 65 MOV

Entries: 1323

OFFICE DEPOT

Commentary

- Price trend is strong.
- Fundamentals are positive.

YEAR	REVENUES	% CHANGE	NET INCOME	% CHANGE	RETURN ON EQUITY	% CHANGE
89	314.587	138.260	5.941	88.663	5.9	46.0
90	625.847	98.916	9.657	62.548	8.7	47.2
91	1300.847	107.881	14.377	48.876	4.7	-45.8
92	1732.965	32.218	37.792	162.864	9.9	109.9

OUTBACK STEAKHOUSE INCORPORATED

Symbol: OSSI   Exchange: NMS

PRICE 3/4/94	RANGE	P-E RATIO	DIVIDEND	YIELD	BETA
$39\frac{1}{2}$	$26 - 39\frac{1}{2}$	46.4743	0	0	1.7

LAST FOUR QUARTERS

REVENUES	% CHANGE	NET INCOME	% CHANGE	RETURN ON EQUITY	% CHANGE
271.164	60	23.702	56.69	20.64	- 17.06

Corporate Summary

Outback Steakhouse Incorporated operates 199 restaurants spreading across the United States in 22 states. The restaurants serve dinner only and feature a limited menu of high quality, uniquely-seasoned steaks, prime rib, chops, chicken, fish, and pasta, all served with an Aussie theme.

OSSI has not been marked.
■195MOV ■65 MOV

PR = 28.38
AVG = 25.49
OSC%= 10.15%

\# Entries: 692

OUTBACK STEAKHOUSE INC.

Commentary

- Relatively new public company.
- Fundamentals are positive.
- Price of the stock has a positive trend in a weak market.

YEAR	REVENUES	% CHANGE	NET INCOME	% CHANGE	RETURN ON EQUITY	% CHANGE
89	NA	NA	NA	NA	NA	NA
90	22.713	NA	1.935	NA	61.6	NA
91	55.219	143.116	5.789	199.173	21.7	- 64.8
92	123.984	124.531	12.501	115.944	13.5	- 37.9

RAYMOND JAMES FINANCIAL INCORPORATED

Symbol: RJF   Exchange: NYS

PRICE 3/4/94	RANGE	P-E RATIO	DIVIDEND	YIELD	BETA
$17^5/_8$	$14^5/_8$ - $18^5/_8$	7.30	.08	0	1.3

LAST FOUR QUARTERS REPORTED

REVENUES	% CHANGE	NET INCOME	% CHANGE	RETURN ON EQUITY	% CHANGE
492.850	31.94	52.292	21.82	25.44	- 4.63

Corporate Summary

Raymond James Financial Incorporated is a Florida-based financial services holding company. The company is engaged in retail and institutional
brokerage, origination, and distribution of limited partnership interests, underwriting, market making and trading of securities, asset management,
and research and advisory services.

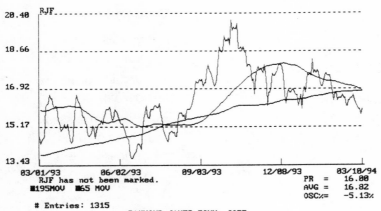

```
20.40   RJF
18.66
16.92
15.17
13.43
       03/01/93    06/02/93    09/03/93    12/08/93    03/10/94
             RJF has not been marked.              PR  =  16.00
       ■19SMOV  ■6S MOV                            AVG =  16.82
                                                   OSC%=  -5.13%
       # Entries: 1315
               RAYMOND JAMES FINN. CORP.
```

Commentary

■ Fundamentals
have been good,
but may be
slowing.

■ Price trend is
weakening and
crossing below its
moving average.

YEAR	REVENUES	% CHANGE	NET INCOME	% CHANGE	RETURN ON EQUITY	% CHANGE
89	226.366	33.240	12.428	125.758	17.4	87.7
90	256.681	13.392	17.947	44.408	18.5	6.8
91	286.047	11.441	26.735	48.966	21.9	18.0
92	361.133	26.250	41.022	53.439	25.5	16.4

RYDER SYSTEM INCORPORATED

Symbol: R   Exchange: NYS

PRICE 3/4/94	RANGE	P-E RATIO	DIVIDEND	YIELD	BETA
$26^7/_8$	$26^1/_2$ - $33^1/_8$	18.79	.15	.01	1.4

LAST FOUR QUARTERS REPORTED

REVENUES	% CHANGE	NET INCOME	% CHANGE	RETURN ON EQUITY	% CHANGE
4217.029	4.91	111.105	26.91	8.74	36.04

Corporate Summary

Ryder Systems Incorporated, through its subsidiaries, engages primarily in full service leasing and short-term rental of trucks. The company also offers dedicated logistics services, public transit management and student transportation, transportation by truck of automobiles, repair and overhaul of aircraft and helicopter turbine and turboprop engines, and the sale and leasing of aircraft parts to the worldwide aviation industry. Ryder was established in 1955 and is based in Miami, FL.

Commentary

- Slightly negative price.
- Fundamentals are positive.

RYDER SYSTEM INC.

YEAR	REVENUES	% CHANGE	NET INCOME	% CHANGE	RETURN ON EQUITY	% CHANGE
89	5073.425	0.872	52.189	-61.243	3.8	-58.4
90	5162.332	1.752	82.216	57.535	6.2	64.4
91	5061.098	-1.961	65.720	-20.064	5.1	-17.5
92	5191.519	2.577	117.926	79.437	8.6	68.0

STEIN MART INCORPORATED

Symbol: SMRT   Exchange: NMS

PRICE 3/4/94	RANGE	P-E RATIO	DIVIDEND	YIELD	BETA
17¼	15⅝ - 23½	26.54	0	0	NA

LAST FOUR QUARTERS REPORTED

REVENUES	% CHANGE	NET INCOME	% CHANGE	RETURN ON EQUITY	% CHANGE
323.369	27.13	15.451	6.33	27.51	- 22.87

Corporate Summary

Stein Mart Incorporated operates a 55-store retail chain offering fashion-able, current season, primarily branded merchandise comparable in quality and presentation to that of traditional department and fine spe-cialty stores at prices competitive with off-price retail chains. Stein Mart caters to fashion-conscious, value-oriented customers who would usually shop at department stores.

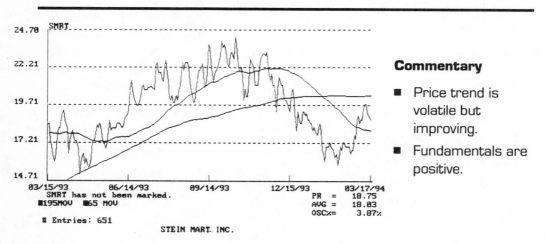

STEIN MART. INC.

Commentary

- Price trend is volatile but improving.

- Fundamentals are positive.

YEAR	REVENUES	% CHANGE	NET INCOME	% CHANGE	RETURN ON EQUITY	% CHANGE
89	NA	NA	NA	NA	NA	NA
90	NA	NA	NA	NA	NA	NA
91	225.389	NA	12.554	NA	39.8	NA
92	278.254	23.455	13.921	10.889	27.7	- 30.3

TECO ENERGY INCORPORATED

Symbol: TE   Exchange: NYS

PRICE 3/4/94	RANGE	P-E RATIO	DIVIDEND	YIELD	BETA
$20\frac{3}{4}$	$20\frac{3}{4}$ - $25\frac{1}{2}$	15.96	0.24	0.01	0.4

LAST FOUR QUARTERS

REVENUES	% CHANGE	NET INCOME	% CHANGE	RETURN ON EQUITY	% CHANGE
1283.911	8.52	150.259	0.83	14.81	- 6.30

Corporate Summary

TECO Energy Incorporated currently conducts no business and owns no operating assets. However, the company has five directly owned subsidiaries: Tampa Electric (utilities), TECO Diversified Incorporated (mainly energy), TECO Power Services Corp. (technology), TECO Investments (investments), and TECO Finance Inc. (financing for TECO). The majority of the company's revenues are generated from the utilities industry.

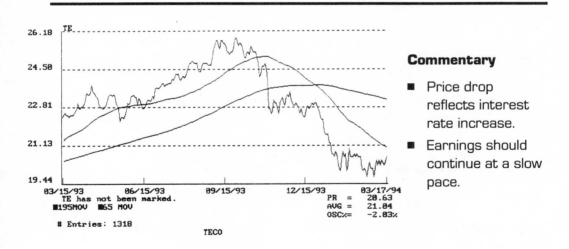

Commentary

- Price drop reflects interest rate increase.
- Earnings should continue at a slow pace.

YEAR	REVENUES	% CHANGE	NET INCOME	% CHANGE	RETURN ON EQUITY	% CHANGE
89	1060.022	2.519	138.131	9.556	15.7	3.3
90	1097.063	3.494	142.999	3.524	17.2	9.4
91	1154.073	5.197	148.868	4.104	16.7	- 3.0
92	1183.150	2.520	152.595	2.504	16.0	- 4.4

WAL-MART STORES

Symbol: WMT   Exchange: NYS

PRICE 3/4/94	RANGE	P-E RATIO	DIVIDEND	YIELD	BETA
$26\frac{1}{2}$	$24\frac{5}{8}$ - $32\frac{1}{2}$	27.46	.03	0	1.2

LAST FOUR QUARTERS REPORTED

REVENUES	% CHANGE	NET INCOME	% CHANGE	RETURN ON EQUITY	% CHANGE
64105.797	23.28	2214.852	19.88	22.26	- 2.97

Corporate Summary

Wal-Mart Stores Incorporated is the world's largest retailer. The company operates an expanding chain of modern discount retail stores in cities and towns across the United States. The company targets its retail units towards value-oriented consumers. Additionally, Wal-Mart operates chains of Sam's Wholesale Clubs in metropolitan areas.

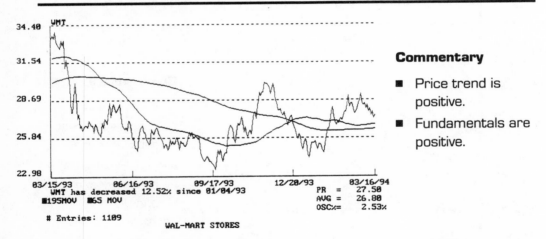

WMT has decreased 12.52% since 01/04/93
■195MOV ■6S MOV
PR = 27.50
AVG = 26.80
OSC%= 2.53%

Entries: 1109

WAL-MART STORES

Commentary

- Price trend is positive.
- Fundamentals are positive.

YEAR	REVENUES	% CHANGE	NET INCOME	% CHANGE	RETURN ON EQUITY	% CHANGE
89	25810.598	24.997	1075.900	28.508	27.1	- 2.5
90	32601.500	26.311	1291.024	19.995	24.1	- 11.3
91	43886.898	34.616	1608.476	24.589	23.0	- 4.4
92	55483.699	26.424	1994.794	24.018	22.77	- 1.0

Chapter 4

Florida Financial Institutions and Services

Financial institutions are a little like gambling casinos. Think about it. If the odds are always stacked in favor of the house, you're better off owning the casino than placing a bet.

I doubt the financial institutions would like the gambling analogy, and yet they operate under a similar principle. A lender stacks the cards so that the lender is always favored. If you can find a bank or savings and loan that is prudently run, it will make money and its shareholders will benefit.

Does this mean that you will always make money investing in banks and savings and loans? Of course not. It does mean that this industry is worth watching because financial institutions have a good chance of making money. When all of the economic factors are going their way, you can feel more comfortable knowing that the banking system of operation and the company product are both sound.

I have grouped several different kinds of businesses in this chapter under the heading of financial institutions. In addition to banks, you will find other kinds of mortgage lending companies, as well as stock brokerage companies and insurance companies. Each of these industries is related to the financial markets and the rise or fall of interest rates. Putting them together gives us the opportunity to get a big-picture view of the entire industry at the same time.

The Florida investor purist will face a small problem when studying the banks listed. Many of the banks in Florida are wholly owned subsidiaries of larger out-of-state holding companies. Since the Florida company is not publicly traded, we have listed the parent company.

Banks

An improving economy brings good news and bad to the banking industry. The good news is that credit quality is improving as the business customers of banks perform better. Most of the commercial real estate problem is behind them, and they have either sold or written off the bad loans.

The other side of the story is that an improving economy will also bring higher interest rates. A rise in rates reduces the bank's margin until they adjust, and ultimately affects profitability. For 1994, we see these rate increases to be small and offset by increases in loan demand.

On the longer-term view, there are new profit opportunities opening to banks as they expand their business into mutual funds, insurance and other financial services. These fee generating businesses are highly profitable add-ons to a bank's existing infrastructure.

Diversified Financial

The overall outlook for this industry is positive, but not spectacular. The interest rate increases in 1994 will slow some refinancing, but this should be offset by an increase in new mortgage loans as the economy improves and people start buying houses again.

Brokerage

The brokerage business has benefited from the flight out of CDs as investors scrambled for higher yields. This year may prove slower than 1993 since the big rush of new investors has taken place. Longer-term, this industry needs to be concerned about the growing trend to lower commissions and the new competition from banks entering the brokerage business.

Insurance

The near term outlook for the life insurance industry is neutral. A low interest rate environment keeps the return of fixed policies down and produces less interesting investment. As rates begin to rise, the fortunes of these companies may follow. The new tax increase leaves the insurance companies' annuity product one of the few safe tax shelters. Unfortunately, annuity returns are ultimately taxed at ordinary income rates which reduces the tax shelter benefit on shorter term investments.

Property and casualty insurers enter 1994 on a weak note following a poor showing in 1993. Although payouts for 1993 were improved over 1992, no one is sure what the total burden will be for the mid-west flooding or the California earthquake. A boom in this industry is not expected this year.

AMERICAN BANKERS INSURANCE GROUP

Symbol: ABIG   Exchange: NMS

PRICE 3/4/94	RANGE	P-E RATIO	DIVIDEND	YIELD	BETA
$26^3/_8$	$24 - 29^1/_8$	9.25	.17	.011	.4

LAST FOUR QUARTERS REPORTED

REVENUES	% CHANGE	NET INCOME	% CHANGE	RETURN ON EQUITY	% CHANGE
973.324	19.86	53.30	26.08	14.03	- 14.41

Corporate Summary

American Bankers Insurance Group, based in Miami, is a specialty insurance holding company. Through its major subsidiaries, the company markets credit life, credit property, unemployment, accident and health, homeowners, physical damage, livestock, individual, and group life products.

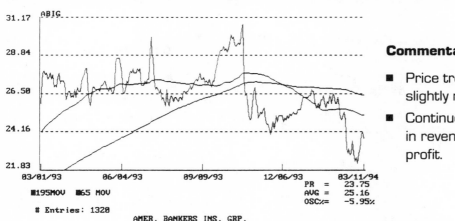

AMER. BANKERS INS. GRP.

PR = 23.75
AVG = 25.16
OSC%= -5.95%

■195MOV ■65 MOV

Entries: 1320

Commentary

- Price trend is slightly negative.
- Continued growth in revenues and profit.

YEAR	REVENUES	% CHANGE	NET INCOME	% CHANGE	RETURN ON EQUITY	% CHANGE
89	657.268	- 10.411	17.627	4.998	11.2	-5.1
90	745.551	13.432	27.782	57.610	15.6	39.9
91	768.389	3.063	37.385	34.566	17.3	10.6
92	812.078	5.686	42.275	13.080	15.7	- 8.9

AMERICAN HERITAGE LIFE INVESTMENT

Symbol: AHL   Exchange: NYS

PRICE 3/4/94	RANGE	P-E RATIO	DIVIDEND	YIELD	BETA
18¾	18¾ - 24½	11.79	0.15	.01	0

LAST FOUR QUARTERS REPORTED

REVENUES	% CHANGE	NET INCOME	% CHANGE	RETURN ON EQUITY	% CHANGE
291.788	7.27	19.715	16.68	10.72	- 6.13

Corporate Summary

American Heritage Life Investment is a service-oriented provider of life and health insurance products, fixed and variable annuities as well as related financial services. The company has special expertise in payroll deduction, Section 125 plans, and business life insurance. American Heritage is based in Jacksonville, FL and is licensed in 49 states.

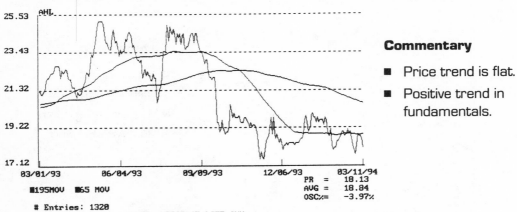

```
25.53   AHL
23.43
21.32
19.22
17.12
       03/01/93    06/04/93    09/09/93    12/06/93    03/11/94
                                              PR  =   18.13
   ■195MOV  ■65 MOV                           AVG =   18.84
                                              OSC%=   -3.97%
   # Entries: 1320
              AMER. HERITAGE LIFE INV.
```

Commentary

- Price trend is flat.
- Positive trend in fundamentals.

YEAR	REVENUES	% CHANGE	NET INCOME	% CHANGE	RETURN ON EQUITY	% CHANGE
89	201.629	- 12.675	11.6222	6.977	10.6	- 0.4
90	220.842	9.529	13.072	12.476	11.5	7.7
91	250.495	13.427	15.078	15.346	11.5	0.4
92	272.020	8.593	16.896	12.057	11.4	- 0.7

BARNETT BANK INCORPORATED

Symbol: BBI   Exchange: NYS

PRICE 3/4/94	RANGE	P-E RATIO	DIVIDEND	YIELD	BETA
42$\frac{1}{4}$	41$\frac{3}{8}$ - 47$\frac{3}{4}$	10.31	.360	.01	1.9

LAST FOUR QUARTERS REPORTED

REVENUES	% CHANGE	NET INCOME	% CHANGE	RETURN ON EQUITY	% CHANGE
3129.947	- 9.08	402.754	111.98	15.15	86.61

Corporate Summary

Barnett Bank Incorporated is a bank holding company operating 735 banking offices in Florida and Georgia. The company's banks, while providing traditional banking services, are complemented by non-banking affiliates. The affiliates provide support services and specialized financial services including trust, full-service brokerage, credit card, and mortgage banking.

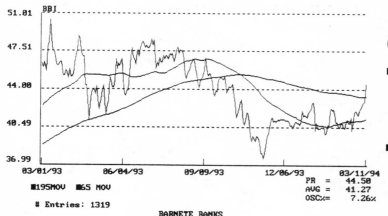

Commentary

- Fundamentals show profits to be increasing faster than revenues.
- Price line shows a potential break out.

YEAR	REVENUES	% CHANGE	NET INCOME	% CHANGE	RETURN ON EQUITY	% CHANGE
89	3037.580	19.320	256.514	13.389	15.2	- 1.9
90	3275.981	7.848	66.963	- 73.895	4.3	- 71.7
91	3273.989	- 0.061	113.540	69.556	6.5	50.1
92	3456.548	5.576	189.998	67.340	8.12	25.8

CITY NATIONAL CORPORATION

Symbol: CYN   Exchange: NYS

PRICE 3/4/94	RANGE	P-E RATIO	DIVIDEND	YIELD	BETA
$8\frac{1}{4}$	$6\frac{7}{8}$ - $10\frac{1}{2}$	NM	0	0	1.2

LAST FOUR QUARTERS REPORTED

REVENUES	% CHANGE	NET INCOME	% CHANGE	RETURN ON EQUITY	% CHANGE
202.431	- 35.37	- 14.034	NA	- 4.78	NA

Corporate Summary

City National Corporation is a multibank holding company with subsidiaries throughout the United States. Through the company's banks and their non-bank subsidiaries, the company provides a diversified list of general banking and non-banking services including mortgage services, credit cards, investment services, information services, as well as a limited number of insurance products.

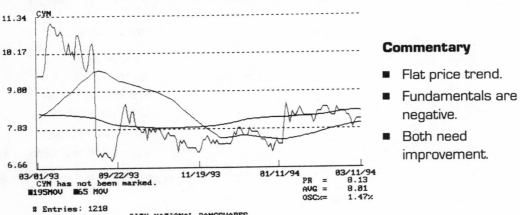

Commentary

- Flat price trend.
- Fundamentals are negative.
- Both need improvement.

CYN has not been marked.
195MOV   65 MOV

PR =	8.13
AVG =	8.01
OSC%=	1.47%

Entries: 1218

CITY NATIONAL BANCSHARES

YEAR	REVENUES	% CHANGE	NET INCOME	% CHANGE	RETURN ON EQUITY	% CHANGE
89	475.771	28.355	59.111	19.871	21.0	0.4
90	501.433	5.394	43.997	- 25.569	13.8	- 34.1
91	436.562	-12.937	- 21.220	- 148.231	- 7.4	- 153.4
92	280.043	- 35.853	- 60.152	NA	- 26.39	NA

CORPORATE MANAGEMENT GROUP INCORPORATED

Symbol: KORP   Exchange: OTC

PRICE 3/4/94	RANGE	P-E RATIO	DIVIDEND	YIELD	BETA
$3\frac{3}{4}$	$3\frac{1}{4}$ - $4\frac{1}{4}$	5.28	0	0	1.1

LAST FOUR QUARTERS REPORTED

REVENUES	% CHANGE	NET INCOME	% CHANGE	RETURN ON EQUITY	% CHANGE
45.719	29.48	2.839	1.25	33.93	- 42.04

Corporate Summary

Corporation Management Group Incorporated is an investment banking firm based in Boca Raton. The company engages in retail and institutional brokerage, underwriting, distribution, market making, and trading of securities, mutual fund distribution, and research services.

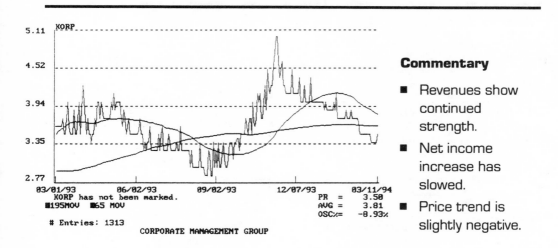

KORP

5.11
4.52
3.94
3.35
2.77

03/01/93   06/02/93   09/02/93   12/07/93   03/11/94
KORP has not been marked.
195MOV 65 MOV
Entries: 1313
CORPORATE MANAGEMENT GROUP

PR = 3.50
AVG = 3.81
OSC%= -8.93%

Commentary

- Revenues show continued strength.
- Net income increase has slowed.
- Price trend is slightly negative.

YEAR	REVENUES	% CHANGE	NET INCOME	% CHANGE	RETURN ON EQUITY	% CHANGE
89	7.492	65.569	0.183	79.412	19.4	168.0
90	7.55	0.841	- 0.616	- 436.612	- 86.4	- 535.3
91	28.929	282.912	2.321	NA	82.8	NA
92	39.723	37.312	3.135	35.071	53.7	- 35.2

EQUICREDIT CORPORATION

Symbol: EQCC   Exchange: NMS

PRICE 3/4/94	RANGE	P-E RATIO	DIVIDEND	YIELD	BETA
$23\frac{1}{8}$	19 - 24	10.23	0	0	NA

LAST FOUR QUARTERS REPORTED

REVENUES	% CHANGE	NET INCOME	% CHANGE	RETURN ON EQUITY	% CHANGE
75.908	14.03	21.245	15.86	21.46	NA

Corporate Summary

Equicredit Corporation is a nationwide mortgage company specializing in second mortgages for residential and commercial building as well as buying. The company does not sell mortgages for investments. Equicredit is based in Jacksonville, FL and has 84 branches nationwide.

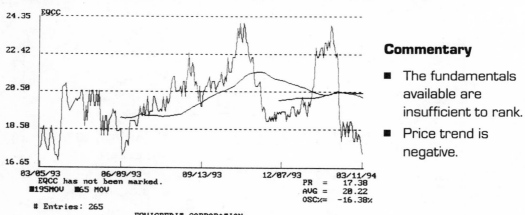

EQUICREDIT CORPORATION

EQCC has not been marked.
■19SMOV ■65 MOV

PR = 17.38
AVG = 28.22
OSC%= -16.38%

Entries: 265

Commentary

■ The fundamentals available are insufficient to rank.

■ Price trend is negative.

YEAR	REVENUES	% CHANGE	NET INCOME	% CHANGE	RETURN ON EQUITY	% CHANGE
89	NA	NA	NA	NA	NA	NA
90	NA	NA	NA	NA	NA	NA
91	NA	NA	NA	NA	NA	NA
92	66.570	NA	18.337	NA	54.5	NA

EQUIVEST FINANCE INCORPORATED

Symbol: EQVI   Exchange: OTC

PRICE 3/4/94	RANGE	P-E RATIO	DIVIDEND	YIELD	BETA
$4^3/_4$	$4^1/_8$ - 6	NM	0	0	0.1

LAST FOUR QUARTERS REPORTED

REVENUES	% CHANGE	NET INCOME	% CHANGE	RETURN ON EQUITY	% CHANGE
3.631	1.54	- 2.668	NA	- 83.27	NA

Corporate Summary

Equivest Finance Incorporated is licensed as a casualty and property insurance premium finance company. As a finance company, the company does not assume any of the risks of an insurance company. The company offers financing primarily to Florida purchasers of automobile insurance policies, including policies covering collision, comprehensive, and liability insurance, of generally up to 70 percent of insurance premiums.

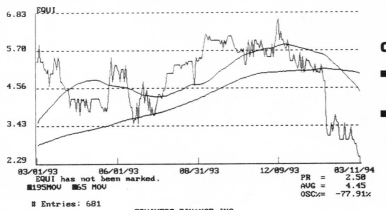

EQUIVEST FINANCE INC.

Commentary

- Fundamentals are negative.
- Price trend is negative.

YEAR	REVENUES	% CHANGE	NET INCOME	% CHANGE	RETURN ON EQUITY	% CHANGE
89	2.810	NA	0.220	NA	26.3	NA
90	3.707	31.922	0.310	40.903	27.8	5.7
91	3.709	0.054	0.094	- 69.677	5.8	- 79.1
92	3.657	- 1.402	- 0.315	- 435.106	- 29.0	- 598.8

FINANCIAL BENEFIT GROUP INCORPORATED

Symbol: FBIG   Exchange: OTC

PRICE 3/4/94	RANGE	P-E RATIO	DIVIDEND	YIELD	BETA
4½	1⅝ - 4½	2.62	0	0	- 0.3

LAST FOUR QUARTERS REPORTED

REVENUES	% CHANGE	NET INCOME	% CHANGE	RETURN ON EQUITY	% CHANGE
87.051	0.61	13.853	25.51	46.15	- 33.98

Corporate Summary

Financial Benefit Group Incorporated is a holding company specializing in
the annuity market through its subsidiaries. The company operates in
three distinct capacities: through the Financial Benefit Life Insurance Company (acting principally as a manufacturer of annuity products), through
Annuity International Marketing Corporation (designer, developer and distributor) and through The Insurance Mart, Inc. (wholesaler).

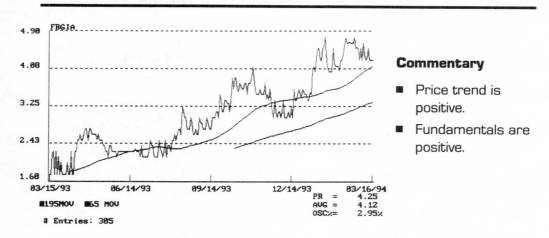

4.90 FBGIA

4.88

3.25

2.43

1.60

83/15/93   06/14/93   09/14/93   12/14/93   03/16/94

PR = 4.25
AVG = 4.12
OSC% = 2.95%

■195MOV ■65 MOV

Entries: 305

Commentary

- Price trend is
  positive.
- Fundamentals are
  positive.

YEAR	REVENUES	% CHANGE	NET INCOME	% CHANGE	RETURN ON EQUITY	% CHANGE
89	24.861	- 67.583	0.496	27.506	4.5	- 5127.4
90	41.060	65.158	- 6.924	- 1495.968	- 226.1	NA
91	73.954	80.112	6.129	NA	63.9	- 22.1
92	81.204	9.803	9.966	62.604	49.8	4.5

FIRST UNION CORPORATION

Symbol: FTU   Exchange: NYS

PRICE 3/4/94	RANGE	P-E RATIO	DIVIDEND	YIELD	BETA
43$\frac{1}{2}$	40$\frac{5}{8}$ - 48$\frac{1}{2}$	9.20	.40	.01	1.2

LAST FOUR QUARTERS REPORTED

REVENUES	% CHANGE	NET INCOME	% CHANGE	RETURN ON EQUITY	% CHANGE
5349.839	- 0.81	791.870	115.30	15.76	87.13

Corporate Summary

First Union Corporation, a multibank corporation, along with its subsidiaries, currently operates 942 banking branches throughout the Southeast. The company provides a wide range of commercial and consumer banking and trust services as well as other financial services including mortgage banking, home equity lending, consumer lending, leasing, securities brokerage services, and some insurance services.

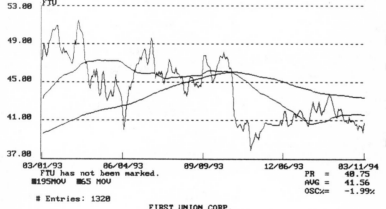

```
53.00  FTU
49.00
45.00
41.00
37.00
       03/01/93      06/04/93      09/09/93      12/06/93      03/11/94
       FTU has not been marked.                      PR  =  40.75
       ■19SMOV  ■65 MOV                              AVG =  41.56
                                                     OSCx=  -1.99x
       # Entries: 1320
                    FIRST UNION CORP.
```

Commentary

- Revenues have remained relatively flat, but profits are up.

- Price trend is neutral.

YEAR	REVENUES	% CHANGE	NET INCOME	% CHANGE	RETURN ON EQUITY	% CHANGE
89	3313.245	14.287	256.191	- 13.711	12.3	- 20.1
90	4068.705	22.801	271.808	6.096	10.7	- 13.0
91	4321.160	6.205	285.512	5.042	9.6	- 10.8
92	4354.503	0.772	484.562	69.717	12.75	33.1

INDEPENDENT INSURANCE GROUP

Symbol: INDHK   Exchange: NMS

PRICE 3/4/94	RANGE	P-E RATIO	DIVIDEND	YIELD	BETA
16¼	13⅞ - 17⅝	NM	0.06	0	0.6

LAST FOUR QUARTERS REPORTED

REVENUES	% CHANGE	NET INCOME	% CHANGE	RETURN ON EQUITY	% CHANGE
466.990	- 12.46	- 0.860	NA	- 0.27	NA

Corporate Summary

Independent Insurance Group, based in Jacksonville, is principally engaged in a variety of life insurance operations. The company also engages in property and casualty servicing operations. Independent Insurance Group currently conducts life insurance operations through a number of branches across the United States.

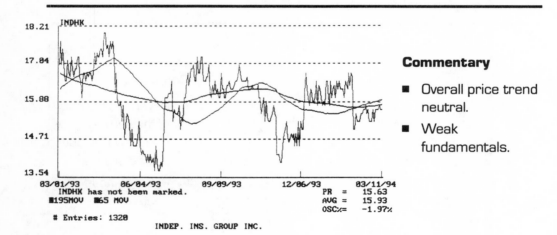

INDEP. INS. GROUP INC.

Commentary

- Overall price trend neutral.
- Weak fundamentals.

YEAR	REVENUES	% CHANGE	NET INCOME	% CHANGE	RETURN ON EQUITY	% CHANGE
89	517.009	3.317	29.306	11.366	8.9	1.9
90	559.566	8.231	31.027	5.873	9.1	2.4
91	569.612	1.795	28.642	- 7.687	7.8	- 14.3
92	533.466	- 6.346	- 16.994	- 159.332	- 5.0	- 163.9

JOHN ALDEN FINANCIAL CORPORATION

Symbol: JA   Exchange: NYS

PRICE 3/4/94	RANGE	P-E RATIO	DIVIDEND	YIELD	BETA
39¾	17⅞ - 39¾	12.08	0.08	0	NA

LAST FOUR QUARTERS REPORTED

REVENUES	% CHANGE	NET INCOME	% CHANGE	RETURN ON EQUITY	% CHANGE
1406.855	18.72	78.682	43.50	30.15	13.21

Corporate Summary

John Alden Financial Corporation, along with its subsidiaries, is a publicly held insurance company with operations in individual and group life/health insurance, property/casualty insurance, reinsurance, and other insurance-related areas. The company is based in Miami, FL.

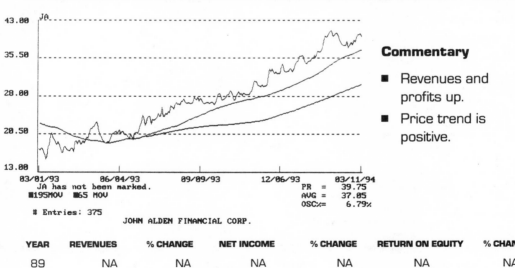

Commentary

- Revenues and profits up.
- Price trend is positive.

JA has not been marked.
■19SMOV ■65 MOV

PR = 39.75
AVG = 37.85
OSC% = 6.79%

Entries: 375

JOHN ALDEN FINANCIAL CORP.

YEAR	REVENUES	% CHANGE	NET INCOME	% CHANGE	RETURN ON EQUITY	% CHANGE
89	NA	NA	NA	NA	NA	NA
90	NA	NA	NA	NA	NA	NA
91	1338.916	NA	49.134	NA	67.1	NA
92	1185.063	- 11.491	57.856	17.751	29.1	- 56.6

LOAN AMERICA FINANCIAL CORPORATION

Symbol: LAFCB   Exchange: NMS

PRICE 3/4/94	RANGE	P-E RATIO	DIVIDEND	YIELD	BETA
$11^{3}/_4$	$9 - 12^{3}/_4$	7.25	0	0	- 0.7

LAST FOUR QUARTERS REPORTED

REVENUES	% CHANGE	NET INCOME	% CHANGE	RETURN ON EQUITY	% CHANGE
47.039	- 9.22	5.603	13.03	13.39	- 33.46

Corporate Summary

Loan American Financial Corporation is a wholesale mortgage company based in Miami, FL. Loan America specializes in residential first mortgages, and will work with some second mortgages. However, the company will not do any commercial lending. Loan America has 9 offices nationwide.

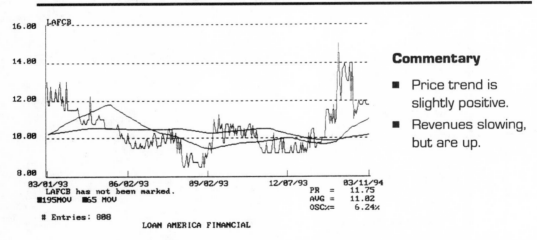

Commentary

- Price trend is slightly positive.
- Revenues slowing, but are up.

LOAN AMERICA FINANCIAL

YEAR	REVENUES	% CHANGE	NET INCOME	% CHANGE	RETURN ON EQUITY	% CHANGE
89	23.246	- 8.775	0.967	- 39.863	5.6	- 42.9
90	27.386	17.810	0.254	73.733	1.5	- 74.0
91	37.178	35.756	1.325	421.654	6.6	354.0
92	53.268	43.278	5.714	331.245	22.1	234.3

MOBILE AMERICA CORPORATION

Symbol: MAME   Exchange: OTC

PRICE 3/4/94	RANGE	P-E RATIO	DIVIDEND	YIELD	BETA
13$\frac{1}{2}$	12 - 17$\frac{1}{2}$	16.26	0.21	0.01	0.2

LAST FOUR QUARTERS REPORTED

REVENUES	% CHANGE	NET INCOME	% CHANGE	RETURN ON EQUITY	% CHANGE
44.636	15.35	5.230	- 27.89	22.07	NA

Corporate Summary

Mobile America Corporation, along with its subsidiaries, is a fully licensed insurance company based in Jacksonville, FL. The company is principally engaged in a variety of group and individual life insurance programs including life and health, property and casualty, reinsurance, as well as other insurance policies.

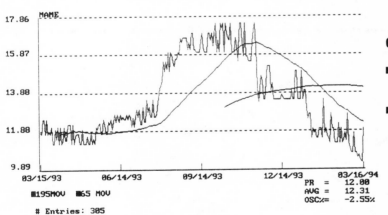

Commentary

- Price trend is negative.
- Fundamentals are positive but slowing.

YEAR	REVENUES	% CHANGE	NET INCOME	% CHANGE	RETURN ON EQUITY	% CHANGE
89	21.717	49.865	3.398	134.507	36.2	62.2
90	27.632	27.237	4.930	45.085	38.7	6.8
91	34.221	23.846	5.846	10.580	33.7	- 13.0
92	39.317	14.891	6.361	8.809	29.7	- 11.9

NATIONSBANK

Symbol: NB   Exchange: NYS

PRICE 3/4/94	RANGE	P-E RATIO	DIVIDEND	YIELD	BETA
$50\frac{3}{4}$	$46\frac{5}{8} - 54\frac{5}{8}$	10.15	.42	.01	1.8

LAST FOUR QUARTERS REPORTED

REVENUES	% CHANGE	NET INCOME	% CHANGE	RETURN ON EQUITY	% CHANGE
9765.00	- 6.89	1291.00	15.17	14.80	- 2.66

Corporate Summary

NationsBank is a bank holding company with its principal assets being the stock of its banking subsidiaries. Through the banks and its various non-banking subsidiaries, the company provides domestic banking and banking-related services. NationsBank provides a diverse range of financial services including general banking business, mortgage services, the issuance of credit cards, mergers/takeovers services, and some insurance services.

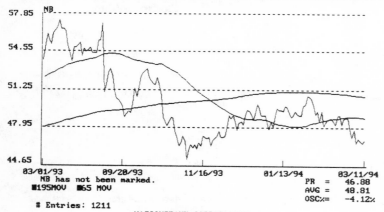

NATIONSBANK CORPORATION

NB has not been marked.
■195MOV ■65 MOV

PR = 46.88
AVG = 48.81
OSC% = -4.12%

Entries: 1211

Commentary

- Revenues are down, but profits are up.
- Price trend is neutral.

YEAR	REVENUES	% CHANGE	NET INCOME	% CHANGE	RETURN ON EQUITY	% CHANGE
89	6036.277	113.032	427.069	72.643	14.4	13.1
90	6682.257	10.702	345.699	- 19.053	11.7	- 19.1
91	11594.000	73.504	171.000	- 50.535	2.7	- 76.6
92	9942.000	- 14.249	1121.000	555.556	14.38	425.9

NORTHERN TRUST CORPORATION

Symbol: NTRS   Exchange: OTC

PRICE 3/4/94	RANGE	P-E RATIO	DIVIDEND	YIELD	BETA
43	38 - 49⅝	14.53	0.22	.01	1.1

LAST FOUR QUARTERS REPORTED

REVENUES	% CHANGE	NET INCOME	% CHANGE	RETURN ON EQUITY	% CHANGE
1246.899	1.13	161.500	13.17	17.08	- 4.03

Corporate Summary

Northern Trust Corporation is a multibank holding company with subsidiaries throughout the United States. The company provides financial services including fiduciary, general banking, investment consulting services for individuals as well as credit, operation, trust, and advisory services for corporations, institutions and organizations. Also, the company provides services in corporate banking, automated clearinghouse and leasing services.

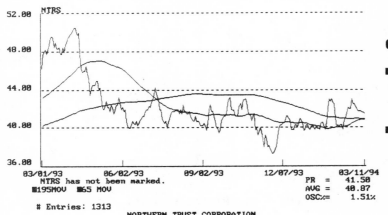

```
52.00   NTRS
48.00
44.00
40.00
36.00
        03/01/93      06/02/93      09/02/93      12/07/93      03/11/94
        NTRS has not been marked.                    PR  =  41.50
        ■195MOV  ■65 MOV                             AVG =  40.87
                                                     OSC%=   1.51%
        # Entries: 1313
                NORTHERN TRUST CORPORATION
```

Commentary

- Revenues are flat to negative, but profits are up.
- Price trend remains relatively flat.

YEAR	REVENUES	% CHANGE	NET INCOME	% CHANGE	RETURN ON EQUITY	% CHANGE
89	1229.800	22.600	105.800	3.624	19.9	- 20.1
90	1322.900	7.570	109.200	3.214	18.6	- 6.8
91	1260.200	- 4.740	121.400	11.172	17.3	- 6.6
92	1231.300	- 2.293	142.700	17.545	16.98	- 2.0

POE & BROWN INCORPORATED

Symbol: POBR   Exchange: MNS

PRICE 3/4/94	RANGE	P-E RATIO	DIVIDEND	YIELD	BETA
18¼	16½ - 20½	29.43	0.20	0.01	0.2

LAST FOUR QUARTERS REPORTED

REVENUES	% CHANGE	NET INCOME	% CHANGE	RETURN ON EQUITY	% CHANGE
84.672	9.47	5.243	2.84	21.10	- 35.56

Corporate Summary

Poe & Brown Incorporated, along with its subsidiaries, offers a number of different insurance products as well as financial planning and investment services. The majority of the company's revenues are generated through the sale of life/health and property/casualty insurance policies. The company is based in Daytona Beach, FL.

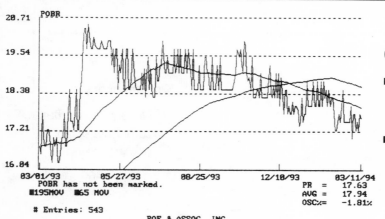

Commentary

- Net profits are negative on higher revenues.
- Price line negative and volatile.

POBR has not been marked.
■19SMOU ■6S MOU
PR = 17.63
AVG = 17.94
OSC% = -1.81%

Entries: 543

POE & ASSOC. INC.

YEAR	REVENUES	% CHANGE	NET INCOME	% CHANGE	RETURN ON EQUITY	% CHANGE
89	41.107	16.712	3.109	- 24.337	48.6	- 54.1
90	46.630	13.436	4.104	32.004	43.6	- 10.3
91	48.643	4.317	4.595	11.964	34.2	- 21.6
92	51.767	6.422	2.865	- 37.650	21.5	- 37.0

RAYMOND JAMES FINANCIAL INCORPORATED

Symbol: RJF   Exchange: NYS

PRICE 3/4/94	RANGE	P-E RATIO	DIVIDEND	YIELD	BETA
17⅝	14⅝ - 18⅝	7.30	.08	0	1.3

LAST FOUR QUARTERS REPORTED

REVENUES	% CHANGE	NET INCOME	% CHANGE	RETURN ON EQUITY	% CHANGE
492.850	31.94	52.292	21.82	25.44	- 4.63

Corporate Summary

Raymond James Financial Incorporated is a Florida-based financial services holding company. The company is engaged in retail and institutional brokerage, origination, and distribution of limited partnership interests, underwriting, market making and trading of securities, asset management, and research and advisory services.

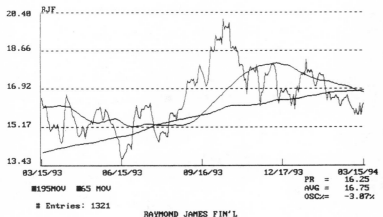

Entries: 1321

RAYMOND JAMES FIN'L

PR = 16.25
AVG = 16.75
OSC% = -3.87%

Commentary

- Fundamentals have been good, but may be slowing.

- Price trend is weakening and crossing below its moving average.

YEAR	REVENUES	% CHANGE	NET INCOME	% CHANGE	RETURN ON EQUITY	% CHANGE
89	226.366	33.240	12.428	125.758	17.4	87.7
90	256.681	13.392	17.947	44.408	18.5	6.8
91	286.047	11.441	26.735	48.966	21.9	18.0
92	361.133	26.250	41.022	53.439	25.5	16.4

SOLAR FINANCIAL SERVICES INCORPORATED

Symbol: SOFIE   Exchange: OTC

PRICE 3/4/94	RANGE	P-E RATIO	DIVIDEND	YIELD	BETA
NA	$3^7/_8$ - $4^7/_8$	NA	0	NA	NA

LAST FOUR QUARTERS REPORTED

REVENUES	% CHANGE	NET INCOME	% CHANGE	RETURN ON EQUITY	% CHANGE
19.739	29.82	1.326	64.93	21.79	- 8.16

Corporate Summary

Solar Financial Services Incorporated is based in Miami and consists of 3 car lot locations. Solar Financial sells and finances the sale of used cars, trucks, and vans through its three locations, all of which are centralized around Miami.

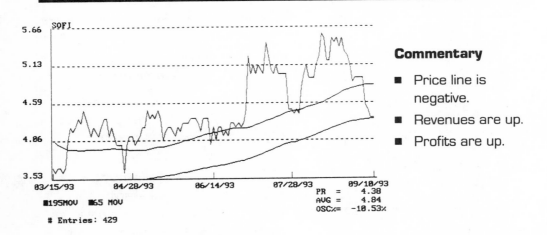

Commentary

- Price line is negative.
- Revenues are up.
- Profits are up.

PR   =   4.38
AVG =   4.84
OSC%= -10.53%

■195MOV ■65 MOV

Entries: 429

YEAR	REVENUES	% CHANGE	NET INCOME	% CHANGE	RETURN ON EQUITY	% CHANGE
89	NA	NA	NA	NA	NA	NA
90	NA	NA	NA	NA	NA	NA
91	2.275	NA	0.187	NA	7.7	NA
92	18.589	717.099	0.966	416.578	29.1	276.1

SOUTHERN SECURITY LIFE INSURANCE

Symbol: SSLIA   Exchange: OTC

PRICE 3/4/94	RANGE	P-E RATIO	DIVIDEND	YIELD	BETA
6 1/8	4 7/8 - 6 1/8	6.45	0	0	0

LAST FOUR QUARTERS REPORTED

REVENUES	% CHANGE	NET INCOME	% CHANGE	RETURN ON EQUITY	% CHANGE
12.578	14.06	1.755	201.03	14.81	158.11

Corporate Summary

Southern Security Life Insurance Company, along with its wholly owned subsidiaries, generates business in the areas of insurance and financial planning as well as investments. The company attributes the bulk of its yearly revenues to the area of insurance, which covers property and casualty as well as life and health insurance along with a host of other insurance products.

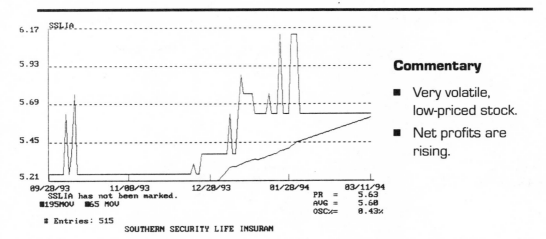

Commentary

- Very volatile, low-priced stock.
- Net profits are rising.

YEAR	REVENUES	% CHANGE	NET INCOME	% CHANGE	RETURN ON EQUITY	% CHANGE
89	7.277	17.903	0.526	80.756	5.8	70.4
90	8.732	19.995	0.294	- 44.106	3.2	- 45.8
91	10.388	18.956	0.255	- 13.265	2.6	- 16.5
92	12.767	22.901	1.770	594.118	15.6	490.9

SOUTHTRUST CORPORATION
Symbol: SOTR   Exchange: OTC

PRICE 3/4/94	RANGE	P-E RATIO	DIVIDEND	YIELD	BETA
19	$17\frac{1}{4}$ - $20\frac{5}{8}$	9.79	.15	.01	1.0

LAST FOUR QUARTERS REPORTED

REVENUES	% CHANGE	NET INCOME	% CHANGE	RETURN ON EQUITY	% CHANGE
1066.096	11.79	150.535	31.76	15.21	5.31

Corporate Summary
Southtrust Corporation, a multibank holding company, currently owns 40 banks and several bank-related affiliates throughout the Southeast. The company, through its subsidiaries, provides a number of different services including general banking services, investments, mortgage services and also a limited number of insurance products.

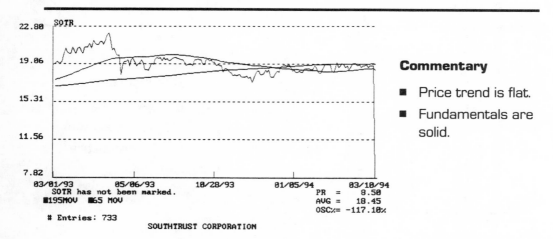

SOTR has not been marked.
195MOV 65 MOV
PR = 8.50
AVG = 18.45
OSC%= -117.18%
Entries: 733
SOUTHTRUST CORPORATION

Commentary
- Price trend is flat.
- Fundamentals are solid.

YEAR	REVENUES	% CHANGE	NET INCOME	% CHANGE	RETURN ON EQUITY	% CHANGE
89	763.310	21.861	72.775	7.674	14.4	- 5.3
90	867.745	13.682	69.708	- 4.214	12.7	- 11.6
91	932.606	7.475	90.006	29.119	13.6	7.2
92	964.763	3.448	114.246	26.932	13.28	- 2.3

SUNTRUST BANKS INCORPORATED

Symbol: STI   Exchange: NYS

PRICE 3/4/94	RANGE	P-E RATIO	DIVIDEND	YIELD	BETA
46$\frac{1}{8}$	43 - 47$\frac{1}{8}$	12.23	.32	.01	1.2

LAST FOUR QUARTERS REPORTED

REVENUES	% CHANGE	NET INCOME	% CHANGE	RETURN ON EQUITY	% CHANGE
3075.313	- 5.38	473.738	17.15	16.39	10.66

Corporate Summary

Suntrust Banks Incorporated, along with its subsidiaries, is a banking and financial services company with the focus of its business located in the Southeast. The primary businesses of the company include traditional deposit and credit services as well as trust and investment services. Additionally, Suntrust provides investment banking, mortgage banking, discount brokerage, credit-related insurance and data processing and information services.

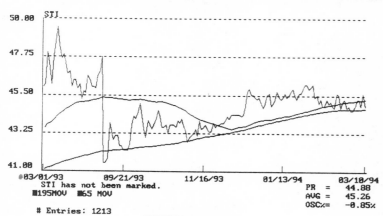

STI has not been marked.
■19SMOV ■65 MOV
Entries: 1213

PR = 44.88
AVG = 45.26
OSC%= -0.85%

SUNTRUST BANKS INC.

Commentary

■ Price trend is neutral.

■ Revenues are negative, profits up.

YEAR	REVENUES	% CHANGE	NET INCOME	% CHANGE	RETURN ON EQUITY	% CHANGE
89	3295.802	14.083	337.318	9.260	16.1	- 1.7
90	3408.488	3.419	350.370	3.869	15.2	- 5.9
91	3360.586	- 1.405	370.667	5.793	14.6	- 4.2
92	3110.294	- 7.448	413.321	11.507	15.29	5.0

Chapter 5

Florida Utility Companies

Utilities had a great run for almost two years, but in November of 1993, things changed. Stock prices began to fall and have continued through early 1994.

Two things are having a major impact on utility prices. One, the fear of interest rate increases which hurt capital intensive utility companies. Two, the announcement that debt ratings for the electric utilities would be lowered due to the increased competition they will be facing under the National Energy Policy Act.

In the past, I have recommended utilities as solid investments for conservative investors. Due to the recent events, I feel forced to remove the recommendation for now.

Interest rates are important to utility companies because they are capital intensive. There is a great deal of expense to building and operating plants. Like individuals, these companies are refinancing long-term debt at the lower rates and positioning themselves for stronger earnings and cash flow. The negative factor facing the industry will be a desire not to increase rates by regulatory utility commissions. This would result in holding down profits.

In October of 1992, the National Energy Policy Act became law. The goal Congress had when it passed the law was to create more competition for both the creation and sale of energy power at the wholesale level. The result of this Act may be the breakup of some of the services provided by existing companies. At this point, it is too soon to tell what the actual effects will be.

Utilities are a good investment for the more conservative investor. There is price fluctuation, but if you are looking for a good income producer that has long-term potential, the utilities are it. Where else can you invest in a government monopoly?

FLORIDA PROGRESS CORPORATION

Symbol: FPC   Exchange: NYS

PRICE	RANGE	P-E RATIO	DIVIDEND	YIELD	BETA
$31\frac{3}{8}$	$31\frac{3}{8}$ - $35\frac{5}{8}$	14.13	0.50	0.02	0.5

LAST FOUR QUARTERS REPORTED

REVENUES	% CHANGE	NET INCOME	% CHANGE	RETURN ON EQUITY	% CHANGE
2449.00	16.88	195.800	11.44	10.79	6.25

Corporate Summary

Florida Progress Corporation defines its principal business segments as
utility and diversified operations. The utility segment is composed of Florida Power, the company's largest subsidiary, and encompasses all regu-
lated public utility operations. The diversified operations include Electric
Fuels, Talquin, Progress Credit Corp., and Mid-Continent Life Insurance.

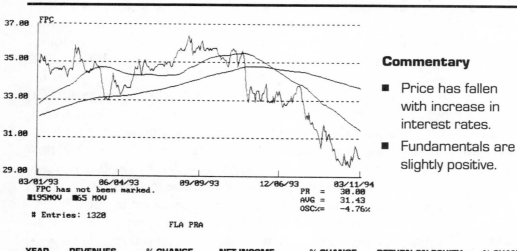

FPC has not been marked.
■19SMOV ■6S MOV

Entries: 1320

FLA PRA

PR = 30.00
AVG = 31.43
OSC%= -4.76%

Commentary

- Price has fallen
  with increase in
  interest rates.
- Fundamentals are
  slightly positive.

YEAR	REVENUES	% CHANGE	NET INCOME	% CHANGE	RETURN ON EQUITY	% CHANGE
89	2129.400	6.364	203.900	3.713	14.9	- 0.5
90	2010.800	- 5.570	196.600	- 3.580	13.8	- 7.1
91	2074.700	3.178	191.300	- 2.696	12.0	- 12.7
92	2095.300	0.993	192.400	.0575	11.1	- 8.1

FLORIDA PUBLIC UTILITIES COMPANY

Symbol: FPU   Exchange: ASE

PRICE	RANGE	P-E RATIO	DIVIDEND	YIELD	BETA
18¼	18¼ - 21⅝	16.74	0.28	0.02	0.4

LAST FOUR QUARTERS REPORTED

REVENUES	% CHANGE	NET INCOME	% CHANGE	RETURN ON EQUITY	% CHANGE
66.429	- 1.26	1.533	- 19.15	7.04	- 20.25

Corporate Summary

Florida Public Utilities Company is a public utility company based in West Palm Beach which provides utility services to West Palm Beach, Sanford, Deland, Marianna, and Fernandina Beach. The utility services provided include natural gas, propane gas, electricity, and water.

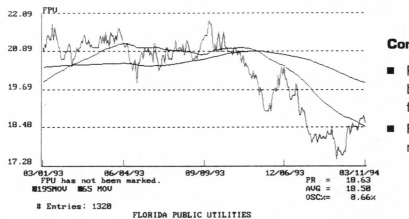

Commentary

- Price trend may be recovering from recent fall.
- Fundamentals are neutral.

```
FPU has not been marked.          PR  = 18.63
■195MOU  ■65 MOU                  AVG = 18.50
                                  OSCx=  0.66x
# Entries: 1320
```

FLORIDA PUBLIC UTILITIES

YEAR	REVENUES	% CHANGE	NET INCOME	% CHANGE	RETURN ON EQUITY	% CHANGE
89	57.640	6.506	1.311	9.615	9.2	3.1
90	59.826	3.810	1.076	- 17.925	7.5	- 19.1
91	62.887	5.099	1.597	48.420	10.5	41.2
92	67.049	6.618	1.843	15.404	8.61	- 18.6

FPL GROUP INCORPORATED

Symbol: FPL   Exchange: NYS

PRICE	RANGE	P-E RATIO	DIVIDEND	YIELD	BETA
$36^7/_8$	$36^7/_8$ - $39^1/_2$	16.03	0.62	0.2	0.6

LAST FOUR QUARTERS REPORTED

REVENUES	% CHANGE	NET INCOME	% CHANGE	RETURN ON EQUITY	% CHANGE
5347.293	2.96	428.749	- 8.18	10.43	- 15.28

Corporate Summary

FPL Group Incorporated is a holding company, whose largest principal sub-sidiary is Florida Power & Light Company (FPL), one of the largest investor-owned electric utilities in the nation. FPL provides electric service to more than 6 million people—about half the population of the State of Florida. FPL's service area covers almost the entire eastern seaboard of mainland Florida and the state's west coast south of Tampa.

Commentary

- Price trend may be starting a recovery.

- Fundamentals are neutral.

YEAR	REVENUES	% CHANGE	NET INCOME	% CHANGE	RETURN ON EQUITY	% CHANGE
89	6179.792	5.574	454.198	- 7.928	13.2	- 12.9
90	6289.035	1.768	- 347.405	- 176.488	- 11.0	- 183.5
91	5249.433	- 16.530	417.404	NA	12.4	NA
92	5193.324	- 1.069	510.850	22.387	13.3	7.0

SOUTHEASTERN PUBLIC SERVICE COMPANY

Symbol: SPV   Exchange: NBB

PRICE 3/4/94	RANGE	P-E RATIO	DIVIDEND	YIELD	BETA
$18\frac{3}{4}$	$13\frac{5}{8} - 23\frac{3}{4}$	NM	0	0	0.1

LAST FOUR QUARTERS REPORTED

REVENUES	% CHANGE	NET INCOME	% CHANGE	RETURN ON EQUITY	% CHANGE
NA	NA	- 0.663	- 107.89	- 0.62	- 108.13

Corporate Summary

Southeastern Public Service Company is a publicly traded utility company and a subsidiary of DWG Corporation, both of which are based in Miami Beach. The company provides services in the areas of natural gas, propane gas, electricity, and water, and mainly provides these services in South and Central Florida.

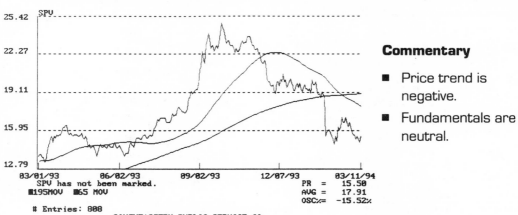

Commentary

- Price trend is negative.

- Fundamentals are neutral.

SOUTHEASTERN PUBLIC SERVICE CO

YEAR	REVENUES	% CHANGE	NET INCOME	% CHANGE	RETURN ON EQUITY	% CHANGE
89	219.417	3.743	5.460	NA	6.2	NA
90	217.315	- 0.958	- 3.654	- 166.923	- 4.3	- 169.7
91	229.573	5.641	6.107	NA	5.8	NA
92	233.234	1.595	7.030	15.114	6.5	13.0

TECO ENERGY INCORPORATED

Symbol: TE   Exchange: NYS

PRICE 3/4/94	RANGE	P-E RATIO	DIVIDEND	YIELD	BETA
$20\frac{3}{4}$	$20\frac{3}{4}$ - $25\frac{1}{2}$	15.96	0.24	0.01	0.4

LAST FOUR QUARTERS

REVENUES	% CHANGE	NET INCOME	% CHANGE	RETURN ON EQUITY	% CHANGE
1283.911	8.52	150.259	0.83	14.81	- 6.30

Corporate Summary

TECO Energy Incorporated currently conducts no business and owns no operating assets. However, the company has five directly owned subsidiaries: Tampa Electric (utilities), TECO Diversified Incorporated (mainly energy), TECO Power Services Corp. (technology), TECO Investments (investments), and TECO Finance Inc. (financing for TECO). The majority of the company's revenues are generated from the utilities industry.

Commentary

- Price drop reflects interest rate increase.
- Earnings should continue at a slow pace.

```
26.18  TE
24.50
22.81
21.13
19.44
03/01/93    06/02/93    09/03/93    12/07/93    03/11/94
        TE has not been marked.              PR  =  20.50
   195MOV   65 MOV                           AVG =  21.17
                                             OSC%=  -3.29%
   # Entries: 1314
            TECO ENERGY INC
```

YEAR	REVENUES	% CHANGE	NET INCOME	% CHANGE	RETURN ON EQUITY	% CHANGE
89	1060.022	2.519	138.131	9.556	15.7	3.3
90	1097.063	3.494	142.999	3.524	17.2	9.4
91	1154.073	5.197	148.868	4.104	16.7	- 3.0
92	1183.150	2.520	152.595	2.504	16.0	- 4.4

Chapter 6

Florida CDs and Money Markets

Among the most common investments made today are CDs (Certificate of Deposit) and money markets.

CDs are actual contractual agreements. You agree to leave your money with an institution for a certain length of time, and in return, the institution will agree to pay you a stated rate of interest.

CDs are a simple investment, and when purchased through an institution that is government insured, the principle is safe up to the insurance amount of $100,000 per account. This combination is also why CDs are so proliferate.

The problem for today's CD investors is the real rates of return. You must pay taxes on your income, and the return is also subject to inflation. Add these two factors, and you will have times that CDs produce a negative "real" rate of return.

For some people, the real rate doesn't matter. They have enough money to live on, and CD investing is simple. The government protection to their principal is their long-term protection, and that is enough.

To those CD diehards this chapter is dedicated.

The first thing to understand about CDs is that they are not all alike even though they may be called by the same name. A CD is a CD whether it is government insured or not. A CD is a CD whether it's interest compounds daily or annually. A CD is a CD whether it is variable or fixed. In other words, a CD may be a CD, but the yield you receive and the protection you have may be quite different.

To get government insured CDs you must invest with either a bank insured by the FDIC or a savings and loan insured by FSLIC. You must fall within the guidelines for total dollars protected, and you must make sure it is a **Certificate of Deposit** not a bank bond or some other bank certificate that would not be insured. If in doubt, speak to an officer of the bank. Better yet, get it in writing.

When you purchase your CD, inquire as to the method of compounding and what the CD's APR (Annual Percentage Rate) is. You are looking for the true value of your money after compounding. By getting the APR you can rate shop among various institutions and compare apples to apples.

Does it pay to shop for rates? The answer is an unqualified yes. The list at the end of the chapter is a totally random sampling of CD and money market yields that were available on the day we conducted a survey. We took a list of banks, called and asked their quoted price. What we proved is that you can improve your yield from $1/2$ - 1% simply by calling around. Shop for money yields just as carefully as you do your groceries.

New CDs

The banks have been faced with losing CD money as interest rates fall. To counter the trend, the banks are adding various bells and whistles to make the CD more modern and attractive. These so called "designer CDs" may have floating interest, early withdrawals, or jumbo yields. Just recognize them for the gimmicks they are and rate shop the way you normally should.

Cautions

Be very careful of investing in long term CDs when interest rates are low. As rates go up you will find yourself, "locked into" an inferior return or subject yourself to penalty for early withdrawal.

Another concern is automatic renewal. Most bank CDs are set up to notify you when a CD is coming due, and it will be automatically renewed if you don't notify the bank within a certain time period. I think this is like the old book club game where you automatically buy the book they send you if you don't tell them no. Negative options were outlawed in book clubs, and they should be with banks. Ask the bank to delete this from your agreement with them. They are counting on you being lazy but that's no excuse for an investor.

Money Markets

Money Market funds are another investment that has different meaning depending on where you shop.

Originally, money markets were started by brokerage companies. They offered a higher rate of interest for your short-term savings, and people flooded out of banks.

Mutual funds got in the act and created pools of funds. This pulled even more money out of the banking system.

Finally, the banks could stand the drain no more and they started their own money market accounts.

Suffice it to say, no two money market accounts are the same. Brokerage company accounts tend to pay more interest, but they are not insured by the government. The account also exposes you to telephone calls by the brokerage firm who really would like you to move into a commissionable product.

Bank money markets have government insurance protection but normally offer the lowest return. You pay for that insurance one way or the other. One advantage to bank money markets is that it helps you establish a better relationship with a bank. Obviously, if you want to borrow money they look more favorably on you if you have a large money market balance. Of course, if you have a large money market balance you probably don't need the loan anyway.

Mutual Fund Money Markets may offer a nice middle ground. They aren't government insured but their safety has been proven. Stick with those backed by higher quality instruments like Treasuries if you want safety.

The bottom line for money markets is the same as CDs. Make a list of what you're looking for and shop. Saving money by shopping is probably the best investment you can make.

How to Get a Higher Return on Your CDs

The list below is a good sampling of CD rates across Florida. We personally compiled this list exclusively to prove you could increase your yield by simply making a phone call. It doesn't take long looking at a chart like this to see that comparison shopping for CDs is as important as shopping for groceries. For example, First Union has a one year CD at 3.17%, but First Commercial was offering 3.70% for the same term. (See the chart below.) Is there any difference between the quality of the two? Of course not. You get over $\frac{1}{2}$% just for calling another bank. How about Qunicy State Bank's 3.75% one year CD? Do you have any more risk with a smaller bank? Not if your account is under $100,000 and they are FDIC insured.

The point I hope you get from this is that the banks bet you are lazy. You can fool them and almost always improve your yield by $\frac{1}{2}$% - 1% simply by calling. The spread can be better for longer periods. Save this list and make more money.

FLORIDA BANKS

NAME	PHONE	MONEY MARKET	1-YR. CD	5-YR. CD
Barnett Bank	904-791-7500	2.03%	3.30%	4.74%
First Union	904-361-2265	2.03%	3.17%	4.53%
Sun Bank	407-299-4786	2.03%	3.25%	5.00%
NationsBank	813-224-5805	1.73%	3.20%	4.40%
		2.37% over 50,000		
Republic Banking	305-441-7200	2.25%	3.25%	5.00%
Southtrust of Fla.	904-798-6864	2.10%	3.25%	4.40%
Capital Bancorp	305-536-1550	2.05%	3.20%	4.89%
Northern Trust Bank				
of Florida	305-372-1000	2.15%	3.25%	3.80% - 2 Yr.
			3.35%	3.90%
			over 100,000	over 100,000
City National	305-577-7400	2.25%	3.25%	5.00%
Intercontinental	305-377-6900	2.25%	3.25%	5.00%
Consolidated Bank	305-558-1000	1.12%	3.20%	5.00%

Capital City Bank	904-224-1171	2.00%	3.40%	4.10% - 4 Yr.
Ocean Bancshares	305-446-9330	2.05%	3.30%	5.00%
First National	407-287-4000	2.10%	3.49%	4.64%
Peoples/Lakeland	813-687-6690	2.40%	3.34%	4.64%
American Bank	904-398-5012	2.00%	3.60%	5.00%
United Bankshares	305-371-2300	2.25%	3.00%	4.50%
Brannen Banks	904-726-1221	2.17%	3.25%	3.85% - 3 Yr.
American Bank	407-452-5480	2.49%	3.15%	3.90% - 2½ Yr.
Bank at Ormond	904-441-1200	2.25%	3.25%	4.85%
Bank of Pahokee	407-924-5272	2.38%	2.96%	3.50% - 2 Yr.
Charlotte State	813-624-5400	2.40%	3.20%	4.70%
Community Bank of Homestead	305-245-2211	2.24%	3.36%	4.19%
Community Bank of the Islands	813-472-5575	2.25%	3.50%	5.10%
Eurobank	407-750-9999	2.35%	3.15%	N/A
Central Bank	813-932-1885	2.25%	3.30%	4.90%
First American	407-567-0552	2.35%	3.60%	5.05%
First Commercial	813-287-0500	2.30%	3.70%	4.92%
First Navy Bank	904-453-3411	2.75%	3.25%	3.50% - 18 Mo.
First State Bank	305-296-8535	2.03%	3.20%	5.02%
First Sterling Bank	407-239-7866	2.20%	3.50%	5.00%
Compass Bank	904-833-6339	2.65%	3.85%	4.85%
Mercantile Bank	813-263-4400	2.96%	3.50%	5.00%
Peoples State Bank	813-845-5775	2.35%	3.19%	4.45%
Perkins State Bank	904-528-3101	2.25%	3.25%	4.75%
Quincy State Bank	904-875-1000	2.27%	3.75%	4.25% - 3 Yrs.
South Fla. Bank	813-334-2020	2.25%	3.44%	4.93%
Suburban Bank	407-833-7373	2.45%	3.50%	5.00%
TIB Bank	305-451-0211	2.47%	3.15%	4.74%

SAVINGS AND LOANS

NAME	PHONE	MONEY MARKET	1-YR. CD	5-YR. CD
Madison S& L Assoc.	813-786-3888	2.23%	3.34%	4.45%
Peoples First Financial	904-769-5261	2.96%	3.68%	5.35%
American Savings of Florida	305-653-5353	2.32%	3.44%	4.88%
Citibank Federal Savings Bank	305-599-5555	2.22%	2.95%	4.40%
Fortune Savings Bank	813-538-2265	2.65%	3.07%	4.85%
Coral Gables Federal	305-447-4711	1.875%	3.125%	4.375%
BancFlorida Federal Savings	813-597-1611	2.27%	3.34%	4.88%
Bank Atlantic Federal Savings	305-760-5000	2.30%	2.75%	4.48%

Chase Federal Bank	305-670-7600	2.32%	3.34%	4.83%
Society First Federal	813-334-4106	2.50%	3.45%	5.00%
Home Savings Bank	305-925-3211	2.225%	3.44%	5.22%
Financial Federal of Dade County	305-264-8911	2.27%	3.34%	4.83%
Amsouth Bank	904-854-0177	2.50%	3.40%	5.10%
Harbor Federal Savings & Loan	407-461-2414	2.23%	3.34%	4.88%
Hollywood Federal Savings Bank	305-925-8111	2.276%	3.455%	4.716%

Chapter 7

Florida Municipal Bonds

Under the new tax rates which went into effect in 1993, some of you will be paying as much as 39% tax on the investment income you earn. To lessen the impact on your return, you should compare the after-tax yield of tax-free versus taxable investing. You should look to tax-free investments to see if you can earn more on an after tax comparison basis.

The table below will show you the comparative earnings of a $10,000 investment.

TAX FREE YIELD	EARNINGS	TAXABLE EQUIVALENT	EARNINGS	TAX PAID (39%)	EARNING AFTER TAX
4%	$400	6.56%	656	256	$400
5%	$500	8.2%	820	320	$500
6%	$600	9.84%	984	384	$600

From the chart you can quickly see that to earn the same after-tax yield as you would get on a municipal bond paying 5% you would need to earn 8.2% on an investment that produced taxable income. On a 6% bond, you would have to earn 9.84%.

The result of this analysis will show you the importance of always comparing investments. For instance, I think a high-grade municipal bond is comparable in safety to a CD if you use a moving average to tell you when to sell. (Some people might disagree, but they can write their own book.) Right now, a one year CD might pay you 3%–3$\frac{1}{2}$%. On the other hand, you could get a AAA rated Florida municipal bond paying 4% which would give you a 6.5% yield for anyone in the highest tax bracket. Even if you weren't in the highest bracket, you would still benefit.

For those of you who might still be concerned with safety, you could minimize that concern even more by buying a municipal bond fund. You now have a great selection of these funds to choose from, and I have listed them for you. There are both load and no-load options.

For those of you who might be interested in individual bonds, I have listed a sampling of the higher quality issues which were available at this writing. To update the list, you can call any brokerage firm and ask them what's currently available.

Looking at the individual bond table you will see ratings by Moody and Standard & Poors. Both services are acceptable authorities in the industry. The quantity is simply the total number of bonds available on that date. The coupon rate is the interest rate the bond bore when it was sold. The yield is the actual rate you would earn if you bought the bond today at the price quoted. The maturity date is the day the bond will be paid off. Naturally, you aren't required to hold the bond to maturity, but should you sell sooner, your yield would be subject to price fluctuations.

FLORIDA INDIVIDUAL MUNICIPAL BONDS
The information presented below are examples of the types of individual bonds available at any point in time. Information is obtained from reliable sources, however, *The Florida Investor* does not guarantee its accuracy. Prices, yields, and availability are subject to change.

MOODY/S&P	ISSUE	COUPON	YIELD	MATURITY
Aaa/AAA	Boynton Beach Pub Svc (MBIA)	6.10	2.90	11/01/95
Aaa/AAA	Collier Cnty Sch Brd CTFS (FSA)	3.40	3.55	02/15/96
Aaa/AAA	Polk Cnty Sch Brd CTFS (FSA)	4.20	3.85	01/01/97
Aaa/AAA	Polk Cnty Cap Impt (AMBAC)	6.40	4.05	12/01/98
Aaa/AAA	Pembroke Pines Pub Impt (AMBAC)	4.375	4.25	10/01/99
Aaa/AAA	Miami GO (MBIA)	6.35	4.50	05/01/01
Aaa/AAA	FL State Div Bd Fln Dept (MBIA)	4.50	4.60	07/01/02
Aaa/AAA	Oakland Park Utils Sys (AMBAC)	4.40	4.70	09/01/03
Aaa/AAA	Polk Cnty Cap Impt (FGIC)	4.50	4.80	12/01/04
Aaa/AAA	Dade Cnty Sch Dist (MBIA)	4.60	4.80	08/01/04
Aaa/AAA	Miami Springs Util Sys (AMBAC)	4.55	4.90	09/01/05
Aaa/AAA	Lake Worth Swr Rev (FSA)	4.70	5.00	10/01/06
Aaa/AAA	Escambia Cnty Rd Impt (FGIC)	5.00	5.10	01/01/07
Aaa/AAA	Alachua Cnty Sch Dist (FSA)	4.85	5.15	07/01/08
Aaa/AAA	Dania Sales Tax Rev (AMBAC)	5.00	5.50	10/01/09
Aaa/AAA	Melbourne Wtr & Swr (FGIC)	4.875	5.25	10/01/10
Aaa/AAA	Dade Cnty Sch Dist (MBIA)	5.00	5.30	08/01/11
Aa/AA	FL State Brd Ed Cap Outlay	5.10	5.30	06/01/12
Aaa/AAA	Osceola Cnty Transn (MBIA)	0.00	5.60	04/01/13
Aaa/AAA	St. Lucie Cnty Solid Waste (FGIC)	5.00	5.35	09/01/15
Aaa/AAA	Kissimmee Util Auth (FGIC)	5.25	5.50	10/01/18
Aaa/AAA	Reedy Creek Impt Dist (MBIA)	5.00	5.50	10/01/19
Aa/AA	FL State Brd Ed Cap Outlay	5.50	5.40	06/01/23

COLONIAL FLORIDA TAX-EXEMPT FUND CLASS 'A'

CUSIP #: 196096788   Phone: 800-225-2365
Minimum Investment: $1,000   SYMBOL CFLAX

NAV	SALES LOAD	YIELD	ASSETS	1 YEAR AVERAGE	5 YEAR AVERAGE
7.98	4.75	4.93	49 MIL	9.07	NA*

* Fund was established on 1 February 1993

Fund Summary

Colonial Florida Tax-Exempt Fund (Class A) seeks tax-free income. The fund usually invests at least 80% of its assets in debt obligations issues from the State of Florida and its political subdivisions as well as provinces of the United States such as Puerto Rico, U.S. Virgin Islands, and Guam. These obligations provide interest that is exempt from regular federal income tax and the alternative minimum tax. The fund intends to maintain an average maturity of 10 years or more.

BECAUSE OF THE NEWNESS OF THE FUND, NO GRAPH IS CURRENTLY AVAILABLE.

- AAA Bonds   63.0%
- AA Bonds   12.0 %
- A Bonds   17.0 %
- BBB Bonds   4.0 %
- NR/NA   4.0%

TOTAL RETURN	1993	1992	1991	1990
1Q	NA	NA	NA	NA
2Q	3.67	NA	NA	NA
3Q	3.42	NA	NA	NA
4Q	NA	NA	NA	NA

DREYFUSS PREMIER STATE MUNICIPAL BOND
FLORIDA—CLASS A

Symbol: PSFLX   Phone: 800-242-8671
Minimum Investment: $1,000

NAV	SALES LOAD	YIELD	ASSETS	1 YEAR AVERAGE	5 YEAR AVERAGE
14.81	4.50	5.02	304 MIL	5.94	10.51

Fund Summary

Premier State Municipal Bond Fund Florida Series—Class A seeks maximum current income, exempt from federal income taxes, without undue risk. The fund will invest at least 80% of its net assets in municipal obligations and at least 65% of its net assets in Florida municipal obligations. At least 70% of the fund's assets will be invested in securities rated BBB or better. It may invest without limitation in private-activity bonds subject to the alternative minimum tax.

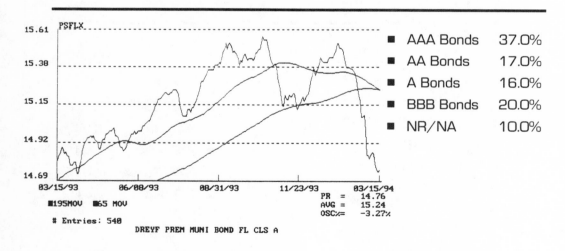

	AAA Bonds	37.0%
	AA Bonds	17.0%
	A Bonds	16.0%
	BBB Bonds	20.0%
	NR/NA	10.0%

DREYF PREM MUNI BOND FL CLS A

TOTAL RETURN	1993	1992	1991	1990
1Q	3.38	0.57	1.96	0.03
2Q	3.90	3.53	2.40	2.68
3Q	3.12	2.63	3.94	0.33
4Q	.99	2.03	3.55	4.17

EATON VANCE FLORIDA TAX-FREE

Symbol: EVFLX　　　　　Phone: 800-225-6265

Minimum Investment: $1,000

NAV	SALES LOAD	YIELD	ASSETS	1 YEAR AVERAGE	5 YEAR AVERAGE
10.94	6.00	5.44	840 MIL	12.90	10.50*

*Since inception in 1990

Fund Summary

Eaton Vance Florida Tax-Free Fund seeks tax-free current income. The fund normally invests at least 80% of its assets in debt obligations issued by or on behalf of the State of Florida and its political subdivisions, and the governments of Puerto Rico, U.S. Virgin Islands, and Guam. These obligations provide interest that is exempt from regular federal income and the alternative minimum tax. The fund intends to maintain an average maturity of 10 years or more.

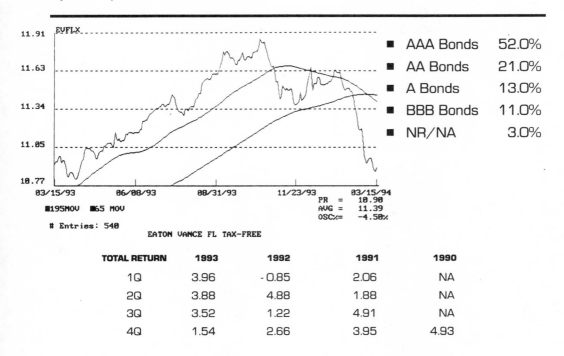

	AAA Bonds	52.0%
■	AA Bonds	21.0%
■	A Bonds	13.0%
■	BBB Bonds	11.0%
■	NR/NA	3.0%

TOTAL RETURN	1993	1992	1991	1990
1Q	3.96	-0.85	2.06	NA
2Q	3.88	4.88	1.88	NA
3Q	3.52	1.22	4.91	NA
4Q	1.54	2.66	3.95	4.93

EMERALD FLORIDA TAX-EXEMPT FUND

Symbol: EMFLX   Phone: 800-637-6336
Minimum Investment: $3,000

NAV	SALES LOAD	YIELD	ASSETS	1 YEAR AVERAGE	5 YEAR AVERAGE
10.93	4.50	4.79	156 MIL	5.75	10.48*

* Since inception on 08/01/91

Fund Summary

The primary investment objective of the Emerald Florida Tax-Exempt Fund
is to seek to provide high tax-free income and current liquidity. The potential for long-term capital appreciation is considered to be a secondary investment objective. In seeking to attain its objectives, the fund invests its
assets primarily in municipal obligations that are rated investment grade
or above. The Florida Tax-Exempt Fund will invest at least 80% of its net assets in securities, the interest on which is exempt from regular federal income tax.

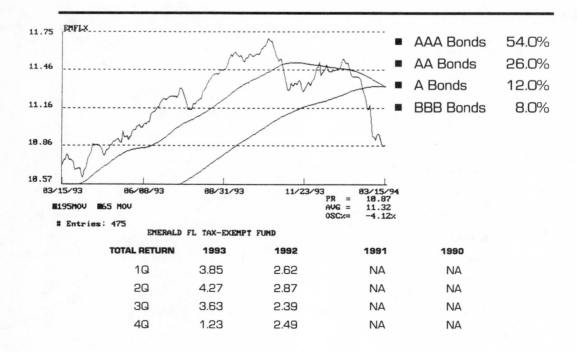

	AAA Bonds	54.0%
	AA Bonds	26.0%
	A Bonds	12.0%
	BBB Bonds	8.0%

PR = 10.87
AVG = 11.32
OSC% = -4.12%

#195MOV #65 MOV
Entries: 475

EMERALD FL TAX-EXEMPT FUND

TOTAL RETURN	1993	1992	1991	1990
1Q	3.85	2.62	NA	NA
2Q	4.27	2.87	NA	NA
3Q	3.63	2.39	NA	NA
4Q	1.23	2.49	NA	NA

FIDELITY SPARTAN FLORIDA MUNICIPAL INCOME FUND

Symbol: FFLIX   Phone: 800-544-8888

Minimum Investment: $10,000

NAV	SALES LOAD	YIELD	ASSETS	1 YEAR AVERAGE	5 YEAR AVERAGE
10.82	0.00	5.33	417 MIL	14.86	14.74*

*Since fund's inception in March 1992

Fund Summary

Spartan Florida Municipal Income Fund seeks the highest level of current income, exempt from federal income tax, available from municipal bonds judged by Fidelity management to be of investment-grade quality. The fund may also invest a portion of its assets in bonds rated below investment-grade quality. Under normal conditions, each fund will invest so that at least 80% of its income distributions are exempt from federal income tax.

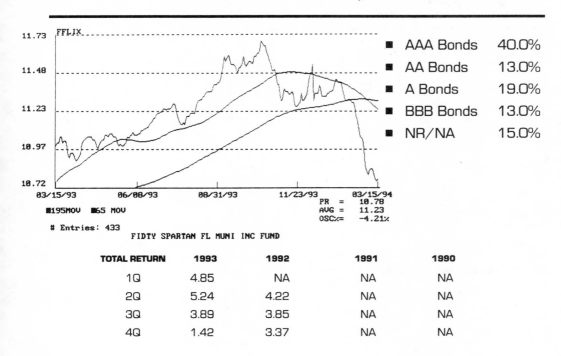

	AAA Bonds	40.0%
	AA Bonds	13.0%
	A Bonds	19.0%
	BBB Bonds	13.0%
	NR/NA	15.0%

```
PR  =  10.78
AVG =  11.23
OSC% = -4.21%
# Entries: 433
FIDTY SPARTAN FL MUNI INC FUND
```

TOTAL RETURN	1993	1992	1991	1990
1Q	4.85	NA	NA	NA
2Q	5.24	4.22	NA	NA
3Q	3.89	3.85	NA	NA
4Q	1.42	3.37	NA	NA

FLAGSHIP FLORIDA DOUBLE TAX-EXEMPT

Symbol: FLOTX   Phone: 800-227-4648

Minimum Investment: $3,000

NAV	SALES LOAD	YIELD	ASSETS	1 YEAR AVERAGE	5 YEAR AVERAGE
10.67	4.20	5.31	400 MIL	5.58	10.43

* Fund was established in June of 1990

Fund Summary

Flagship Florida Double Tax-Exempt seeks high current after-tax income
for its shareholders consistent with liquidity and preservation of capital.
The fund invests in investment-grade obligations, whose interest is exempt
from federal income tax and whose principal is exempt from Florida intangibles tax. Obligations issued by territories and possessions of the United
States (Puerto Rico, Guam, and the U.S. Virgin Islands) also qualify for investment. The average maturity of the portfolio is expected to range from
15 to 25 years.

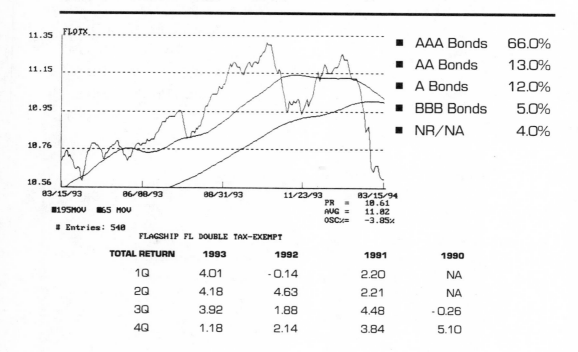

	AAA Bonds	66.0%
	AA Bonds	13.0%
	A Bonds	12.0%
	BBB Bonds	5.0%
	NR/NA	4.0%

PR = 10.61
AVG = 11.02
OSC% = -3.85%

Entries: 540

FLAGSHIP FL DOUBLE TAX-EXEMPT

TOTAL RETURN	1993	1992	1991	1990
1Q	4.01	-0.14	2.20	NA
2Q	4.18	4.63	2.21	NA
3Q	3.92	1.88	4.48	-0.26
4Q	1.18	2.14	3.84	5.10

FRANKLIN FLORIDA TAX-FREE INCOME

Symbol: FRFLX   Phone: 800-342-5236
Minimum Investment: $100

NAV	SALES LOAD	YIELD	ASSETS	1 YEAR AVERAGE	5 YEAR AVERAGE
11.61	4.00	5.68	1,300 MIL	6.84	9.42

Fund Summary

Franklin Florida Tax-Free seeks to maximize income exempt from federal income taxes and from personal income taxes of Florida. The fund will
attempt to invest 100% of its net assets, and will invest at least 80%, in
Florida municipal obligations exempt from the alternative minimum tax.
Only 20% of the fund's assets may be in other types of bonds or in other
states' obligations. The securities will be rated BBB or better, or, if un-
rated, deemed to be of comparable quality.

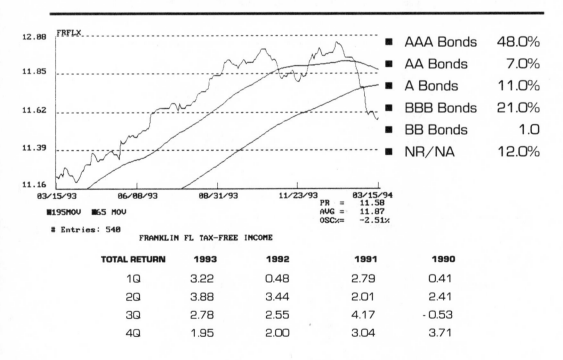

		AAA Bonds	48.0%
		AA Bonds	7.0%
		A Bonds	11.0%
		BBB Bonds	21.0%
		BB Bonds	1.0
		NR/NA	12.0%

PR = 11.58
AVG = 11.87
OSC% = -2.51%

Entries: 540

FRANKLIN FL TAX-FREE INCOME

TOTAL RETURN	1993	1992	1991	1990
1Q	3.22	0.48	2.79	0.41
2Q	3.88	3.44	2.01	2.41
3Q	2.78	2.55	4.17	-0.53
4Q	1.95	2.00	3.04	3.71

KEMPER FLORIDA TAX-FREE INCOME FUND

Symbol: KFLTX   Phone: 800-621-1048

Minimum Investment: $1,000

NAV	SALES LOAD	YIELD	ASSETS	1 YEAR AVERAGE	5 YEAR AVERAGE
10.25	4.50	4.98	137 MIL	8.40	10.32*

* Since inception on 25 April 1991

Fund Summary

The objective of the Kemper Florida Tax-Free Income Fund is to provide a high level of current income that is exempt from federal income taxes. The fund seeks to achieve its objective by investing primarily in a portfolio of obligations issued by the State of Florida, its political subdivisions, agencies, or instrumentalities and other securities that are exempt from the State of Florida's intangibles tax and whose interest is exempt from federal income taxes.

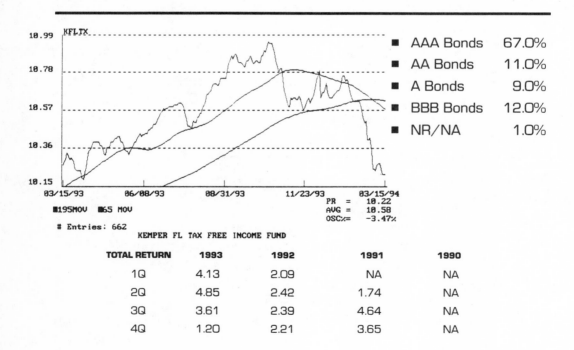

- AAA Bonds 67.0%
- AA Bonds 11.0%
- A Bonds 9.0%
- BBB Bonds 12.0%
- NR/NA 1.0%

KEMPER FL TAX FREE INCOME FUND

TOTAL RETURN	1993	1992	1991	1990
1Q	4.13	2.09	NA	NA
2Q	4.85	2.42	1.74	NA
3Q	3.61	2.39	4.64	NA
4Q	1.20	2.21	3.65	NA

KEYSTONE AMERICA FLORIDA TAX FREE FUND

Symbol: KAFLX Phone: 800-343-2898

Minimum Investment: $1,000

NAV	SALES LOAD	YIELD	ASSETS	1 YEAR AVERAGE	5 YEAR AVERAGE
10.66	4.75	5.36	48 MIL	12.24	11.31*

* Since inception in January 1991

Fund Summary

The Keystone America Florida Tax Free Fund's main objective is to earn the highest possible current income, exempt from federal income tax, while preserving capital. In addition, the fund seeks to ensure that its shares are exempt from the Florida intangible personal property tax. The fund offers shares in three different categories: Class A, Class B, and Class C.

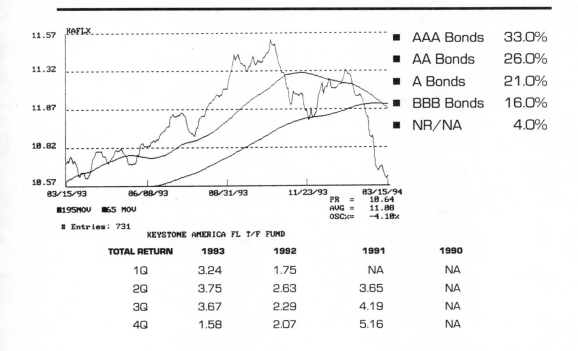

	AAA Bonds	33.0%
	AA Bonds	26.0%
	A Bonds	21.0%
	BBB Bonds	16.0%
	NR/NA	4.0%

PR = 10.64
AVG = 11.08
OSC%= -4.10%

Entries: 731

KEYSTONE AMERICA FL T/F FUND

TOTAL RETURN	1993	1992	1991	1990
1Q	3.24	1.75	NA	NA
2Q	3.75	2.63	3.65	NA
3Q	3.67	2.29	4.19	NA
4Q	1.58	2.07	5.16	NA

LORD ABBETT FLORIDA TAX-FREE FUND

Symbol: LAFLX   Phone: 800-426-1130

Minimum Investment: $1,000

NAV	SALES LOAD	YIELD	ASSETS	1 YEAR AVERAGE	5 YEAR AVERAGE
4.94	4.75	5.55	193 MIL	13.80	10.90*

* Since inception in September of 1991

Fund Summary

The Lord Abbett Florida Tax-Free Fund invests primarily in a portfolio of in-termediate-term (5-10 years) to long-term (over 10 years) municipal bonds, the interest on which is exempt from federal income tax in the opin-ion of bond counsel to the issuer. The interest on the municipal bonds in which the fund invests in is also exempt from state income tax.

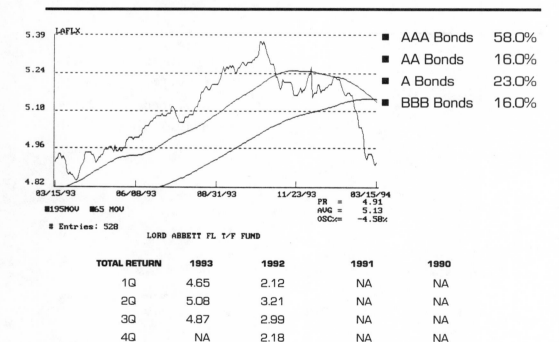

	AAA Bonds	58.0%
	AA Bonds	16.0%
	A Bonds	23.0%
	BBB Bonds	16.0%

PR = 4.91
AVG = 5.13
OSC% = -4.58%

Entries: 528

LORD ABBETT FL T/F FUND

TOTAL RETURN	1993	1992	1991	1990
1Q	4.65	2.12	NA	NA
2Q	5.08	3.21	NA	NA
3Q	4.87	2.99	NA	NA
4Q	NA	2.18	NA	NA

LORD ABBETT FLORIDA TAX-FREE FUND TRUST
(CLOSED-END FUND)

Symbol: FLLAX   Phone: 800-426-1130
Minimum Investment: $1,000

NAV	SALES LOAD	YIELD	ASSETS	1 YEAR AVERAGE	5 YEAR AVERAGE
4.74	BROKER FEE	5.32	1.6 MIL	NA*	NA*

* Fund was established in October of 1993

Fund Summary

The Lord Abbett Florida Tax-Free Trust invests primarily in a portfolio of in-
termediate-term (5-10 years) to long-term (10 years) municipal bonds,
the interest on which is exempt from federal income tax in the opinion of
bond counsel to the issuer. The interest on the municipal bonds in which
the trust invests is also exempt from state income tax.

BECAUSE OF THE
NEWNESS OF THE
FUND, NO GRAPH IS
CURRENTLY
AVAILABLE.

- AAA Bonds 71.0%
- AA Bonds 5.0%
- A Bonds 16.0%
- BBB Bonds 8.0%

TOTAL RETURN	1993	1992	1991	1990
1Q	NA	NA	NA	NA
2Q	NA	NA	NA	NA
3Q	NA	NA	NA	NA
4Q	NA	NA	NA	NA

MERRILL LYNCH FLORIDA MUNICIPAL BOND FUND CLASS 'A'

Symbol: MLFLX   Phone: 609-282-2800

Minimum Investment: $1,000

NAV	SALES LOAD	YIELD	ASSETS	1 YEAR AVERAGE	5 YEAR AVERAGE
10.12	4.00	4.72	320 MIL	8.18	9.14

* Since fund was established in 1991

Fund Summary

The Merrill Lynch Florida Municipal Bond Fund attempts to provide share-holders with as high a level of income exempt from federal income taxes as is consistent with prudent investment management. The fund also in-tends to provide shareholders with the opportunity to own shares, the value of which is exempt from Florida intangible personal property taxes. The fund seeks to achieve its objective by investing primarily in a portfolio of long-term obligations issued by or on behalf of the State of Florida.

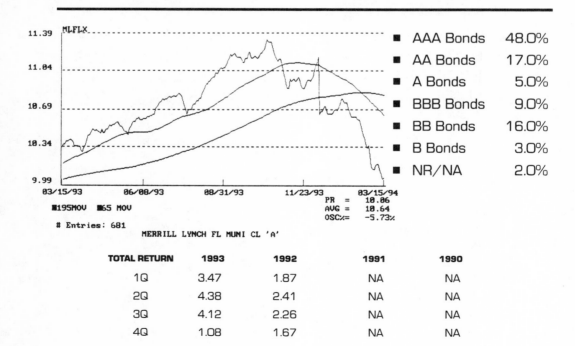

	AAA Bonds	48.0%
■	AA Bonds	17.0%
■	A Bonds	5.0%
■	BBB Bonds	9.0%
■	BB Bonds	16.0%
■	B Bonds	3.0%
■	NR/NA	2.0%

MERRILL LYNCH FL MUNI CL 'A'

TOTAL RETURN	1993	1992	1991	1990
1Q	3.47	1.87	NA	NA
2Q	4.38	2.41	NA	NA
3Q	4.12	2.26	NA	NA
4Q	1.08	1.67	NA	NA

NUVEEN FL INVESTMENT QUALITY MUNI FUND

(CLOSED-END FUND)

Symbol: NQF   Phone: 800-257-8787

Minimum Investment: $1,000

NAV	SALES LOAD	YIELD	ASSETS	1 YEAR AVERAGE	5 YEAR AVERAGE
15.59	BROKER FEE	6.37	364 MIL	15.17	NA*

* Fund was established in February of 1991

Fund Summary

The Nuveen Florida Investment Quality Muni Fund is registered under the Investment Company Act of 1940 as a closed-end, diversified management investment company. The fund's objectives are to produce current income exempt from regular federal income taxes, with a secondary objective of enhancement of portfolio value, relative to the municipal bond market, through investment of substantially all of the funds' assets in municipal bonds rated in the four highest ratings categories.

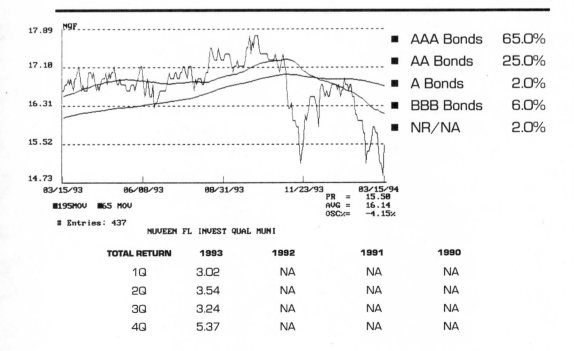

■ AAA Bonds	65.0%
■ AA Bonds	25.0%
■ A Bonds	2.0%
■ BBB Bonds	6.0%
■ NR/NA	2.0%

NUVEEN FL INVEST QUAL MUNI

TOTAL RETURN	1993	1992	1991	1990
1Q	3.02	NA	NA	NA
2Q	3.54	NA	NA	NA
3Q	3.24	NA	NA	NA
4Q	5.37	NA	NA	NA

NUVEEN FLORIDA QUALITY INCOME MUNICIPAL FUND

(CLOSED-END FUND)

Symbol: NUF   Phone: 800-257-8787
Minimum Investment: $1,000

NAV	SALES LOAD	YIELD	ASSETS	1 YEAR AVERAGE	5 YEAR AVERAGE
15.21	BROKER FEE	6.02	272 MIL	15.84	NA*

* Fund was established October of 1991

Fund Summary

The Nuveen Florida Quality Income Municipal Fund is registered under the Investment Company Act of 1940 as a closed-end, diversified management investment company. The fund's objectives are to produce current income exempt from regular federal income taxes, with a secondary objective of enhancement of portfolio value, relative to the municipal bond market, through investment of substantially all of the funds' assets in municipal bonds rated in the four highest ratings categories.

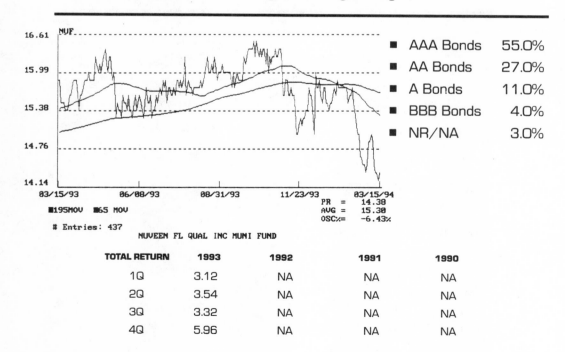

- AAA Bonds   55.0%
- AA Bonds   27.0%
- A Bonds   11.0%
- BBB Bonds   4.0%
- NR/NA   3.0%

```
PR  =   14.38
AVG =   15.30
OSC%=   -6.43%
```

NUVEEN FL QUAL INC MUNI FUND

TOTAL RETURN	1993	1992	1991	1990
1Q	3.12	NA	NA	NA
2Q	3.54	NA	NA	NA
3Q	3.32	NA	NA	NA
4Q	5.96	NA	NA	NA

NUVEEN FLORIDA TAX-FREE VALUE FUND

Symbol: NMFLX   Phone: 800-621-7227
Minimum Investment: $1,000

NAV	SALES LOAD	YIELD	ASSETS	1 YEAR AVERAGE	5 YEAR AVERAGE
11.03	4.75	4.67	41 MIL	11.45	NA*

* Fund was established in February of 1992

Fund Summary

Nuveen Florida Tax-Free Value Fund attempts to provide the investor with as high a level of current interest income exempt from both regular federal income tax and the Florida intangible personal property tax. Under ordinary circumstances, the fund will invest substantially all (at least 80%) of its net assets in Florida municipal obligations, and not more than 20% of its net assets in temporary investments.

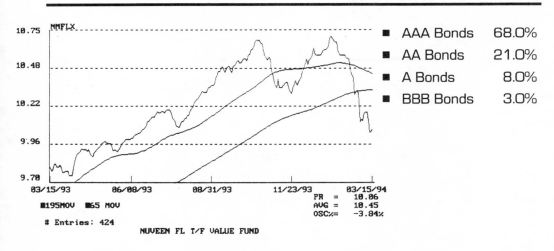

■ AAA Bonds 68.0%
■ AA Bonds 21.0%
■ A Bonds 8.0%
■ BBB Bonds 3.0%

NUVEEN FL T/F VALUE FUND

TOTAL RETURN	1993	1992	1991	1990
1Q	3.67	NA	NA	NA
2Q	4.12	NA	NA	NA
3Q	3.66	NA	NA	NA

NUVEEN INSURED FL PREMIUM INCOME MUNI FUND
(CLOSED-END FUND)

Symbol: NFL   Phone: 800-257-8787
Minimum Investment: $1,000

NAV	SALES LOAD	YIELD	ASSETS	1 YEAR AVERAGE	5 YEAR AVERAGE
13.85	BROKER FEE	5.70	202 MIL	13.87	NA*

* Fund was established in December of 1992

Fund Summary

The Nuveen Insured Florida Premium Income Municipal Fund is registered under the Investment Company Act of 1940 as a closed-end, diversified management investment company. The fund invests in municipal securities which are covered by insurance guaranteeing the timely payment of principal and interest, or backed by an escrow or trust account containing sufficient U.S. Government or U.S. Government agency securities to ensure the timely payment of principal and interest. Each insured municipal security is covered by original issue insurance, secondary market insurance, or portfolio insurance.

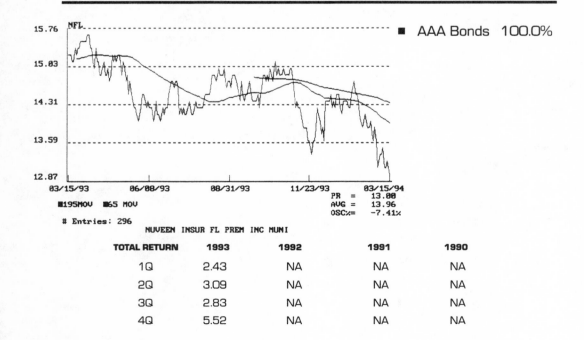

■ AAA Bonds 100.0%

PR = 13.00
AUG = 13.96
OSC% = -7.41%

■19SMOV ■6S MOV

Entries: 296

NUVEEN INSUR FL PREM INC MUNI

TOTAL RETURN	1993	1992	1991	1990
1Q	2.43	NA	NA	NA
2Q	3.09	NA	NA	NA
3Q	2.83	NA	NA	NA
4Q	5.52	NA	NA	NA

PUTNAM FLORIDA TAX EXEMPT INCOME FUND

Symbol: PTFLX   Phone: 800-225-1581
Minimum Investment: $500

NAV	SALES LOAD	YIELD	ASSETS	1 YEAR AVERAGE	5 YEAR AVERAGE
9.09	4.75	5.14	343 MIL	11.01	9.74*

* Since inception 23 August 1990

Fund Summary

Putnam Florida Tax Exempt Income Fund seeks as high a level of current income exempt from federal income tax as the fund's investment manager believes is consistent with preservation of capital. The fund invests primarily in a portfolio of tax-exempt securities of Florida issuers and other tax-exempt securities exempt from the Florida intangibles tax. The fund may also trade securities for short-term profit.

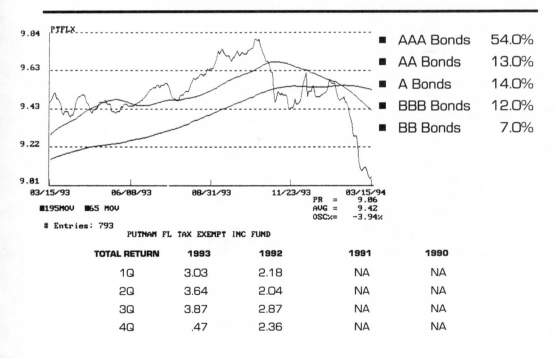

AAA Bonds	54.0%
AA Bonds	13.0%
A Bonds	14.0%
BBB Bonds	12.0%
BB Bonds	7.0%

PUTNAM FL TAX EXEMPT INC FUND

TOTAL RETURN	1993	1992	1991	1990
1Q	3.03	2.18	NA	NA
2Q	3.64	2.04	NA	NA
3Q	3.87	2.87	NA	NA
4Q	.47	2.36	NA	NA

95

T ROWE PRICE FLORIDA INSURED INTERMEDIATE BOND FUND

CUSIP #: 77957R-80-4

Phone: 800-638-5660

Minimum Investment: $2,500

SYMBOL FLTFX

NAV	SALES LOAD	YIELD	ASSETS	1 YEAR AVERAGE	5 YEAR AVERAGE
10.19	0.00	3.89	37 MIL	9.58	NA*

* Fund was established on 31 March 1993

Fund Summary

The T Rowe Price Florida Insured Intermediate Bond Fund will invest at least 80% of its net assets in Florida municipal insured securities. However, under certain circumstances, such as temporary decline in the issuance of Florida obligations, the fund may invest up to 20% of its assets in different areas such as United States provinces, like Puerto Rico and Guam. The fund is expected to maintain a dollar-weighted average maturity between 15 and 25 years.

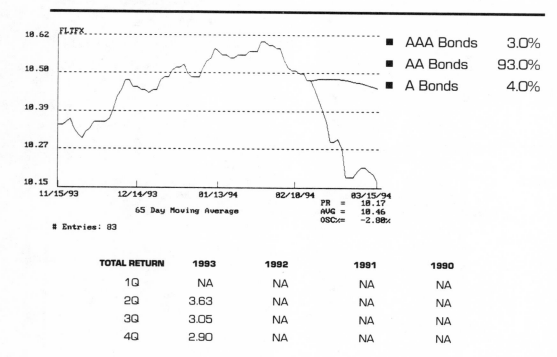

	AAA Bonds	3.0%
	AA Bonds	93.0%
	A Bonds	4.0%

65 Day Moving Average

PR = 10.17
AVG = 10.46
OSC%= -2.80%

Entries: 83

TOTAL RETURN	1993	1992	1991	1990
1Q	NA	NA	NA	NA
2Q	3.63	NA	NA	NA
3Q	3.05	NA	NA	NA
4Q	2.90	NA	NA	NA

VANGUARD FLORIDA INSURED TAX-FREE FUND

Symbol: VFLTX   Phone: 800-662-7447

Minimum Investment: $3,000

NAV	SALES LOAD	YIELD	ASSETS	1 YEAR AVERAGE	5 YEAR AVERAGE
10.55	0.00	5.14	302.4 MIL	13.42	NA*

*Since fund inception on 09/02/92

Fund Summary

The fund will invest at least 80% of its net assets in insured Florida municipal securities, exclusive of Florida AMT bonds. However, under certain
circumstances, such as temporary decline in the issuance of Florida obligations, the fund may invest up to 20% of its assets in different areas. The
fund is expected to maintain a dollar-weighted average maturity between
15 and 25 years.

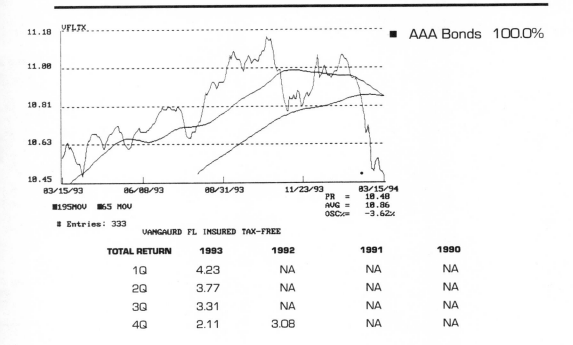

■ AAA Bonds 100.0%

VANGAURD FL INSURED TAX-FREE

TOTAL RETURN	1993	1992	1991	1990
1Q	4.23	NA	NA	NA
2Q	3.77	NA	NA	NA
3Q	3.31	NA	NA	NA
4Q	2.11	3.08	NA	NA

Chapter 8

Special Situations in Florida Real Estate

The allure of real estate has always been strong in Florida, not only for the millions of visitors who come to Florida each year but also for its natives. A fifth-generation Floridian, I was taught from early childhood the importance of "owning a few little rental properties," as my mother used to say. In fact, these rental properties are what today provide my mother—and my in-laws too, I might add—with comfortable retirements.

Real estate investing has many facets, most of which are covered extensively in hundreds of other books and at seminars around the country. I myself have, at one time or another, participated in everything from buying single-family homes to developing multi-million-dollar shopping centers and residential developments. What I have gained from all of this is an understanding of the role of real estate for most people. As usual, my mother was right. Everyone should own a little.

As with other commodities, there are two ways to buy real estate—retail and wholesale. It doesn't take a genius to figure out you're better off buying wholesale, but surprisingly, very few people go to the trouble of understanding the wholesale market. By the time you finish this chapter, you will know it better than 90 percent of the entire population in Florida.

Most people buy real estate because they fall in love with it. They become emotionally involved buyers and they pay too much for the property. Over the years that's worked out okay, because the appreciation of Florida real estate has forgiven their mistake. Since the real estate recession started in 1986, however, appreciation has been replaced by stability and even decreased prices in some areas. Consequently, it is more important than ever to become a wise buyer.

The wholesale real estate market is made up of a mixture of sellers, all coming under the broad heading of "motivated sellers." There are many reasons for a seller to find him- or herself in this category: the general economy, business failure, divorce, job transfer, death, and government regulations are all common examples. As an investor in real estate, you will want to learn about all of these categories of sellers and how to find them. That, of course, is what this chapter is all about.

HOW TO FIND MOTIVATED SELLERS

The unpleasant reality is that they are all over the place. Unpleasant, because what makes someone a motivated seller is problems. I just listed some of them. But stop: Before you chastise me for suggesting you take advantage of people with problems, let me stress that that is not what I am doing. On the contrary: By pointing out these situations, I will actually be delivering more potential buyers to these sellers, who may wind up getting more for their property than they otherwise would have.

Motivated sellers have a problem, and you are in the problem-solving business. They need to sell their property, and you are a buyer. True, you probably aren't offering what they would like to get for their property, but neither was anyone else, or it would have been sold by now. You are providing an extremely needed and valuable commodity—a sale.

Foreclosure

One of the first categories of motivated sellers is the owner who is being foreclosed, on or is about to be. Working this specialty involves dealing with the delinquent borrower, the lender, or both. Some investors who work foreclosed properties prefer to deal with the delinquent borrower before the property goes into foreclosure. They believe working early on in the foreclosure process gives them an edge because they can deal with the seller and potentially assume the loan with no cash or risk on their part. Sellers are frequently willing to forfeit their equity if they can get someone to take over their payments, because it enables them to avoid the stigma of foreclosure, the damage to their credit, and the potential liability for a deficiency judgment. In most cases, fear of the unknown is a strong motivator.

There are several ways to find sellers in these circumstances. One is to advertise. A quick glance in your newspaper under real estate financing will uncover people who are using this approach. They offer money to sellers who are in financial difficulty in return for a high interest return or first option to buy the property before it goes into foreclosure.

My own feeling is that dealing directly with sellers who have financial difficulties is a tough business for most investors. In order to be successful, you will have to become personally involved with the trials and tribulations of the seller, and very few of us have the temperament to do that. Those of you who do will have a field of opportunity, because so many investors avoid it.

A word of caution. Buying real estate prior to foreclosure is the epitome of "active" investing. You will not only need to be experienced in dealing with people and negotiating, you will need a superior understanding of real estate and its worth. In most cases, you will be buying the property "as is." Warranties from the seller, even if you can get them, will be of little value, since he will be financially unable to back them up.

You should also know that much of the profit made on foreclosures comes from fixing the property up after you buy it. You will need to know what it takes to get a property in marketable condition and how much you can afford to spend. The more of this work you can do yourself, the more profit you can expect.

None of this is said to discourage you in any way. I am simply pointing out the areas you should consider so that you don't find yourself simply transferring the property from one "don't wanter" (seller) to another (you).

Your next option is to contact lenders directly. You may wonder whether lenders will supply information on loans that are defaulted, but not foreclosed. Some will, some won't. Some won't tell you the name of the home-owner but will give him or her your name. If you have decided to work with the lender instead of the seller, you can take three positions. 1) Offer to buy out the lender's position (preferably at a discount) and foreclose yourself. 2) Work with the lender to find out the date of upcoming foreclosures and bid on the property at foreclosure. 3) Deal with lenders after the foreclosure sale has taken place but before the lender lists the property for sale.

All three of these approaches have advantages and disadvantages, depending on your time, resources, and desire to become emotionally involved. Nevertheless, it all starts with working with the lender and the specific departments they have established for problem real estate.

Once a person becomes delinquent on his or her real estate loan, the lender follows a set process to get the loan current. After a certain length of time (three or four months), the loan receives a classification as nonperforming; depending on the size of the bank, it then moves into a special department that deals with these kinds of loans. Contrary to popular belief, the last thing a lender wants to do is foreclose on a property and take the real estate. In fact, this looks very bad to the federal regulators who inspect lending institutions, and the lender gets "written up" for making a bad loan. Moreover, banks are only allowed to have a certain percentage of their assets in real estate. If they foreclose on too many properties and have too much real estate, they will also be "written up" by the bank examiners. Needless to say, if a bank gets written up too many times, people will begin to lose their jobs.

You should also remember that banks are in the lending business. If they have money tied up in real estate, they aren't earning interest or fees on new loans. At some point the lender's shareholders will become unhappy, and more people will lose their jobs. The point I'm trying to make is that banks, too, are motivated sellers. And they are among the easiest to deal with because they have absolutely zero personal involvement in the property.

Real Estate Owned (REO)

REO is the terminology lenders use for real estate they have taken back as collateral.

Depending on the size of the bank, they may have an entire department for REO's or they may have one officer who deals in that area.

The advantage to dealing with banks is that the lender has a great deal of flexibility. The lender can restructure the old loan on better terms, lower the interest rate, let you assume the loan, and even lower the purchase price. After all, they are now the seller and they have money tied up in the property, anyway.

The only real disadvantage of REOs is the bureaucracy you deal with. Most things have to be approved by a board, and this sometimes makes negotiations a moving target. You give up a negotiating point in exchange for something from the lender only to find that the board won't approve your great deal.

How do you find REO's? Almost every lender will have some. They will either be selling the properties themselves, or more than likely will place the property for sale with a broker.

Although you can quickly develop your own list, I'm starting you off with some initial names and phone numbers.

Each of these lenders has properties that they need and want to sell. If you are interested, call them and talk about the kinds of properties you are interested in. If you aren't ready yet, then do them the courtesy of waiting until you are.

Once you confirm the existence of the REO department, you will feel comfortable calling any bank. Remember, they are sellers. If you are a potentially interested buyer, they want to talk with you.

Citicorp Mortgage—For a complete list of properties they have available in the state, contact Carol S. Tanner, Assistant Vice-President, at 1-800-283-7918.

First Union National Bank—Has both commercial and residential properties taken back in foreclosure. For information about property in your area, contact William B. Ellisor, Vice-President, at 904-361-2265; or write P.O. Box 2080, Jacksonville, Florida 32231.

Barnett Bank—Contact Tony McConnell at 407-658-3605.

California Federal—For a list of Florida properties available, call Sheila Grand at 212-932-2177.

Veterans Administration—They publish a list of foreclosed properties every three weeks. Call 1-800-827-1000 for additional information.

Internal Revenue Service—1-800-829-1040. We also recommend you call your local IRS office and ask for the collections department.

Sun Bank REO Division—Call Betty Fowler at 407-237-4911.

Florida Department of Revenue—Periodic sales. Contact Betty at 1-800-352-3671.

This list is periodically updated by *The Florida Investor Newsletter*. To receive a free copy of the newsletter, write to J.W. Dicks Research Institute, Inc., 520 Crown Oak Centre Drive, Longwood, FL 32750. There is no charge for a copy of the current issue, but please include a self-addressed stamped envelope.

Probate and Estate Sales

When someone dies in Florida, his or her estate goes through a process known as probate. This is a judicial process handled by the state probate court.

At some point during the judicial process, it is likely that the judge will order the executor (the individual appointed to administer the estate) to arrange the sale of various assets, which will likely include real estate. Although not required, a growing trend is to conduct the sale at an estate auction. The auction method of sale is faster than a traditional sale, and the price received is competitive in comparison.

If the auction sale price of the property is comparable to that of a traditional sale, where do the bargains come from? From buying prior to the auction.

While the probate court will approve an auction sale, they will also approve what is called a negotiated sale. This takes place prior to the auction in direct negotiations between you and the auctioneer. Auctioneers are happy when this happens because they get their commission without having to go through the time, expense, and risk of auction.

Another method to use is to contact the probate court yourself. Let the judges, attorneys, and court employees know that you are a real estate buyer, and the relationships you establish may help you get contacted as soon as an auctioneer is appointed, or even sooner, in some cases.

Buying at probate sales can yield you discounts as high as 40 percent of value. Even if you aren't lucky to get that kind of bargain, you should certainly expect a 15-to-20-percent discount.

Your local probate court is listed in your phone book.

For a list of auctioneers who handle probate sales, please refer to chapter 12.

FDIC

FDIC stands for Federal Deposit Insurance Corporation. This is the government agency that insures you will get your money if a bank fails.

Unfortunately for the FDIC, in recent years a great many more banks have failed than expected, leaving the FDIC holding large amounts of unwanted real estate from the banks' portfolios.

While the FDIC has experimented with a few large auctions (see chapter 11 on auctions), most of its real estate is disposed of through local real estate brokers. For you as an investor, this can be both good news and bad, because now you must also deal with a variety of real estate brokers.

The FDIC has catalogs of real estate listings. To get one, contact the FDIC sales office in the area in which you are interested in buying property. Ask to speak with the liquidation division. When you get assistance, try to be as specific as you can about the kind of property you are looking for (residential, commercial, or vacant land) and the area you would like to buy in.

The catalog you receive will contain very brief information about the property, the broker to contact, and the listing price. Remember, this is the listed price of a foreclosed property—**do not pay it**. You should expect to negotiate on that price, and I think you should be aggressive. You may not actually buy the property at 30 to 40 percent off, but there's no harm in beginning with offers in that range. The government gets flexible depending on the state of the political winds, and sometimes they will blow in your favor.

If you can't find a local FDIC office in your city, start with the regional office: FDIC, Regional Director-Liquidations, Marquis One Building, Suite 1400, 245 Peachtree Center Avenue North, Atlanta, GA 30303. Phone 404-525-0308.

Fannie Mae

"Fannie Mae" is a nickname commonly given to the Federal National Mortgage Association. Once a government agency, it is now publicly owned, and its stock trades on the National Stock Exchange.

The role of Fannie Mae in today's marketplace is to buy loans from banks or other mortgage lenders that don't want to hold them in their own portfolios. Fannie Mae then either keeps the loan itself or, more than likely, packages it up and sells it to a group of investors with its personal guarantee of the loan.

Because Fannie Mae guarantees the performance of these loans, it often finds it necessary to foreclose on the property. The properties are mostly single-family and typically in the $125,000 to $150,000 price range. These properties tend to be nicer than some of the government-repossessed homes, because the lending requirements were more strict in the beginning.

To find out about properties available through Fannie Mae, start with its regional office in Atlanta: Federal National Mortgage Association, Southeast Region, 950 Pace Ferry Road, Suite 1800, Atlanta, GA 30326-1161. Phone 404-365-6000.

When you call the regional office, ask to speak with someone in the REO Department. Then ask for the names of real estate brokers in your area of interest who handle Fannie Mae homes. Almost all sales of Fanny Mae properties are handled by brokers. Contact the local real estate broker and ask him to send you a list of any of the Fannie Mae properties they currently have listed in your area.

Fannie Mae also provides a service for home buyers. You may call their office toll-free at 800-553-4636 and ask for a computer printout of Fannie Mae repossessed homes in your area. If you prefer, you can also write to them directly: Fannie Mae Properties, P.O. Box 13165, Baltimore, MD 20203.

Freddie Mac

"Freddie Mac" is the nickname given to the Federal Home Loan Mortgage Corporation. It is owned by banks and savings and loans. Its major purpose has been to provide financing to savings and loans, and as a result has wound up with some of their unwanted real estate.

Like Fannie Mae, it specializes in single-family homes, which it sells through local real estate brokers. To receive a list of brokers in your area, contact the regional office: Federal Home Loan Mortgage Corporation, Southeast Regional, 2839 Pace Ferry Road, Suite 700, Atlanta, GA 30339-3719. Phone 404-438-3800.

Department of Housing and Urban Development

The Department of Housing and Urban Development, commonly known as HUD, provides low-income housing through subsidized or special loan programs.

HUD always has a lot of property to sell—a seemingly never-ending supply, in fact. The reason is that it works with those at the lower-end of the economic spectrum, the kind of owner most likely to suffer problems as the economy changes. Good buys are available, although many will require some renovation, and you must be careful about your selection, because neighborhoods may be on the decline.

One of the most difficult aspects of dealing with HUD is its sealed bid program. To buy a HUD property, you must deal with a real estate broker that has filed with the department to handle their properties. This is not as easy as it sounds, because HUD tells telephone callers who ask for assistance that they don't recommend real estate brokers—meaning that out of the hundreds or thousands of licensed brokers in your area, you have to find the ones that deal with HUD. It's not easy, but it's not impossible either. Some advertise HUD properties; your local Board of Realtors may even maintain a list. If all else fails, you can write HUD and request a list of all brokers in your area that have completed form 9556, authorizing them to do business with HUD.

Once you find a broker, the broker will work with you to complete the normal bureaucratic form filing that allows you to bid. Although HUD has listed prices, you aren't required to bid the listed amount. If you get a good broker, they may also work with you in building your case with HUD as to why they should accept a lower price. Some areas actually get competitive bidding, and you don't have much of a chance unless you bid full price. In such cases you're better off using what's called an express bid and writing

"Full Price" on the outside of the envelope. This will help you if there is more than one full-price bid, since the first full-price bid received gets the property. But don't assume your area is that active in HUD bidding until you talk with several real estate brokers and become familiar with what's happening in your area. Remember, you are doing all of this to get good buys, so don't get caught up in the process.

HUD Regional Office, Richard Russell Federal Building, 75 Spring Street, Atlanta, GA 30303-3388. Phone 404-331-4739.

Florida HUD Offices, Suite 270 Langley Building, 3751 Maguire Blvd., Orlando, FL 32803-3032. Phone 407-648-6441. Tampa regional office, Timberlake Federal Building Annex, 501 E. Polk Street, Suite 700, Tampa, FL 33602-3945. Phone 813-228-2501.

Department of Veteran's Administration (VA)
One of the functions of the Veteran's Administration is to assist veterans in buying homes. They do this by guaranteeing lenders the repayment of a portion of a loan made to a veteran. Unfortunately, vets run into financial difficulty just like other Americans, and in order to protect its guarantee, VA has to foreclose on properties.

Although VA does not have as cumbersome a purchase process as HUD, you will still need to work through local real estate brokers who are familiar with the VA process.

To get a list of properties in your area, you can contact the Veterans Administration, 144 1st Avenue South, St. Petersburg, FL 33731. Phone 813-898-2121.

The VA has two listing categories: regular, or new, and special listings. The special listings are normally properties that have received price reductions because they haven't moved. VA tends to be much more agreeable about accepting lower offers on these properties than they are about those in the other category.

While good buys are available in VA properties, they tend to be in neighborhoods of a lower economic scale, and they are all sold "as is." Rarely will you find a VA property that doesn't need some work, given that people who are being foreclosed on tend to let the property go.

One advantage on VA property is financing. Money is available for owner occupants, even if you aren't a veteran.

Chapter 9

Florida Real Estate and Home-Building Companies

In the first chapter I discussed the difference between an active and a passive investor. We have just reviewed a very active form of investing — real estate. Because of the direct personal involvement it calls for, real estate won't appeal to everyone. Fortunately, there is a way to invest in real estate passively and that is through the stock of public real estate companies.

The Florida real estate companies were hurt in 1990 and 1991 by the industry-wide recession. They saw great improvement in 1993, and we see more to follow. The prices of some of the companies have already been adjusted for a lower interest rate environment and a better economy—although they still have a long way to go—and they offer profit potential.

For those companies that are primarily real estate holding companies, nothing helps more than lower interest rates. Refinancing properties can have tremendous effects on the bottom line. Higher cash flows are also especially attractive to investors desperate for higher income.

The long term for home builders has some negative implications that investors should keep in mind. Demographics are changing, with fewer household formations than during the baby boomer years. This may be somewhat mitigated by an insistence on modernization by the new generation. If tomorrow's buyers demand the conveniences that come with new homes, then home building will continue, but at the expense of older home sales. Either way there are fewer people entering the market, and that trend will ultimately have a negative impact on the home-building industry.

Building Material—Low interest rates have helped the housing market and the building materials industry along with it. In recent years the industry has suffered from the general economic downturn and an oversupply of inventory. We rank the industry slightly positive.

Construction and Engineering—The major plus for this industry has also been low interest rates. Companies that lean toward residential construction are leading those that emphasize commercial markets. It may still be some time before the commercial market returns.

Home-Building–Again, the favorable interest rate environment has been a key element in bringing this industry back. The only caution for a strong ranking of this industry is that many of its favorable factors have already been included in the current stock prices. Housing starts in December 1993 rose 6.2% from the previous month. This rise was the fourth consecutive monthly increase and the highest since February of 1990.

REITs–The Clinton tax bill may have a profound change on the potential value of real estate investment trusts, known as REITs. Formerly, pension funds were restricted in the amount they could invest in an REIT. Under the new law, the limit has been lifted. The potential investment dollars are tremendous. These large institutions are concerned over some of the lower yields they have been getting in other investments. The new law opens up new real estate options.

ALICO INCORPORATED

Symbol: ALCO   Exchange: NMS

PRICE 3/4/94	RANGE	P-E RATIO	DIVIDEND	YIELD	BETA
21½	18½ - 21½	50.00	0	0	0.8

LAST FOUR QUARTERS REPORTED

REVENUES	% CHANGE	NET INCOME	% CHANGE	RETURN ON EQUITY	% CHANGE
27.479	- 1.27	3.116	- 26.34	5.14	- 31.68

Corporate Summary

Alico Incorporated is generally recognized as an agribusiness company operating in Central and Southwest Florida. The company's primary asset is 171,162 acres of land located in Collier, Hendry, Lee, and Polk Counties. The company is involved in various operations and activities including citrus fruit production, cattle ranching, sugarcane production, forestry, and leasing for recreation and oil and gas exploration.

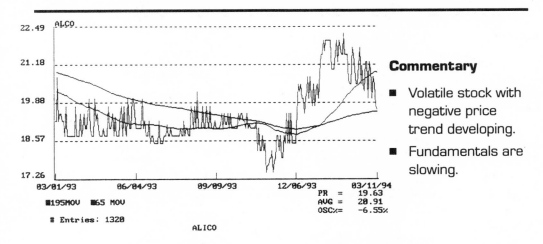

Commentary

■ Volatile stock with negative price trend developing.

■ Fundamentals are slowing.

PR   =   19.63
AVG =   20.91
OSC% =   -6.55%

■195MOV ■65 MOV

Entries: 1320

ALICO

YEAR	REVENUES	% CHANGE	NET INCOME	% CHANGE	RETURN ON EQUITY	% CHANGE
89	25.920	12.320	8.772	10.270	19.1	- 0.1
90	20.790	- 19.792	4.697	- 46.455	9.7	- 49.4
91	27.229	30.972	5.694	21.226	10.7	10.7
92	31.508	15.715	4.899	- 13.962	8.6	- 19.8

ATLANTIC GULF COMMUNITIES CORPORATION

Symbol: AGLF   Exchange: NMS

PRICE 3/4/94	RANGE	P-E RATIO	DIVIDEND	YIELD	BETA
11	$4\frac{3}{4}$ - 11	NM	0	0	NA

LAST FOUR QUARTERS REPORTED

REVENUES	% CHANGE	NET INCOME	% CHANGE	RETURN ON EQUITY	% CHANGE
76.400	21.85	- 13.90	NA	- 16.65	NA

Corporate Summary

Atlantic Gulf Communities Corporation is engaged primarily in real estate operations. The company's real estate operations include: the development and sale of improved and unimproved commercial, industrial, institutional, and agricultural land tracts; the development and sale of home sites, both to independent home builders and to individuals; and the construction and sale of single-family and multi-family housing.

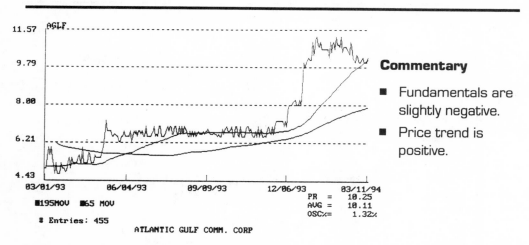

Commentary

■ Fundamentals are slightly negative.

■ Price trend is positive.

ATLANTIC GULF COMM. CORP

YEAR	REVENUES	% CHANGE	NET INCOME	% CHANGE	RETURN ON EQUITY	% CHANGE
89	NA	NA	NA	NA	NA	NA
90	148.100	NA	- 884.900	NA	101.4	NA
91	80.500	- 45.645	- 60.500	NA	6.6	- 93.5
92	72.500	- 9.938	- 20.100	NA	- 21.3	- 423.9

AVATAR HOLDINGS
Symbol: AZTR Exchange: NMS

PRICE 3/4/94	RANGE	P-E RATIO	DIVIDEND	YIELD	BETA
35	32¾ - 36½	54.69	0	0	0.6

LAST FOUR QUARTERS REPORTED

REVENUES	% CHANGE	NET INCOME	% CHANGE	RETURN ON EQUITY	% CHANGE
105.546	2.87	7.370	231.84	3.93	NA

Corporate Summary

Avatar Holdings Incorporated and its subsidiaries are engaged in two principal business activities: real estate and water, including wastewater utilities operations. Avatar's real estate activities include the acquisition, development, and sale of home sites mainly under deed and mortgage arrangements.

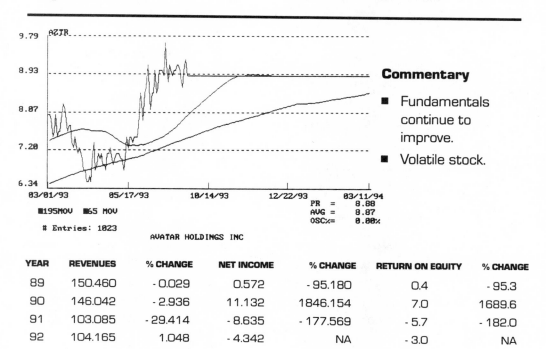

Commentary

- Fundamentals continue to improve.
- Volatile stock.

YEAR	REVENUES	% CHANGE	NET INCOME	% CHANGE	RETURN ON EQUITY	% CHANGE
89	150.460	-0.029	0.572	-95.180	0.4	-95.3
90	146.042	-2.936	11.132	1846.154	7.0	1689.6
91	103.085	-29.414	-8.635	-177.569	-5.7	-182.0
92	104.165	1.048	-4.342	NA	-3.0	NA

CCR INCORPORATED

Symbol: CCRC   Exchange: OTC

PRICE 3/4/94	RANGE	P-E RATIO	DIVIDEND	YIELD	BETA
1³⁄₄	1³⁄₄ - 8¹⁄₂	19.44	0	0	NA

LAST FOUR QUARTERS REPORTED

REVENUES	% CHANGE	NET INCOME	% CHANGE	RETURN ON EQUITY	% CHANGE
4.931	33.85	0.390	121.62	6.72	NA

Corporate Summary

CCR Incorporated is a publicly-owned holding company based in Ocala. The company, mainly through its subsidiaries, has substantial endeavors in the field of construction, trucking, and education. The company's main emphasis is in construction.

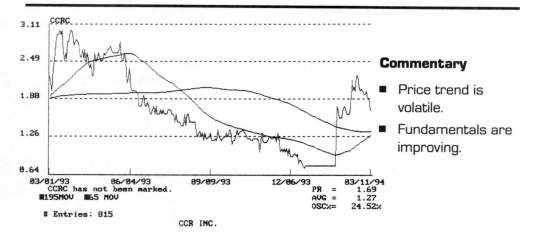

Commentary

- Price trend is volatile.
- Fundamentals are improving.

CCRC has not been marked.
■19SMOV ■65 MOV
PR = 1.69
AVG = 1.27
OSC% = 24.52%

Entries: 815

CCR INC.

YEAR	REVENUES	% CHANGE	NET INCOME	% CHANGE	RETURN ON EQUITY	% CHANGE
89	9.049	NA	- 0.545	NA	- 9.3	NA
90	8.196	- 9.426	0.287	NA	6.8	NA
91	5.056	- 38.311	- 0.435	- 251.568	- 11.3	- 266.8
92	2.999	- 40.684	- 2.312	NA	- 53.0	NA

COMMERCIAL NET LEASE REALTY

Symbol: NNN   Exchange: ASE

PRICE 3/4/94	RANGE	P-E RATIO	DIVIDEND	YIELD	BETA
14	11 $\frac{7}{8}$ - 14 $\frac{3}{8}$	14.74	.28	.02	0.1

LAST FOUR QUARTERS REPORTED

REVENUES	% CHANGE	NET INCOME	% CHANGE	RETURN ON EQUITY	% CHANGE
5.069	94.66	3.522	125.48	8.86	- 17.80

Corporate Summary

Commercial Net Lease (CNL) Realty is a real estate investment trust based in Orlando. The company syndicates real estate limited partnerships. The major focus of the investments are in the area of fast food restaurant acquisition. The company does invest in some retail properties as well as commercial properties.

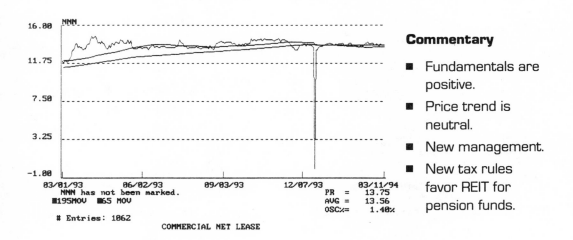

Commentary

- Fundamentals are positive.
- Price trend is neutral.
- New management.
- New tax rules favor REIT for pension funds.

YEAR	REVENUES	% CHANGE	NET INCOME	% CHANGE	RETURN ON EQUITY	% CHANGE
89	1.784	- 2.086	1.296	- 3.929	10.3	- 2.5
90	1.868	4.709	1.389	7.176	11.2	8.3
91	1.895	1.445	1.255	- 9.647	10.3	- 7.3
92	2.604	37.414	1.562	24.462	10.9	4.9

CONSOLIDATED TOMOKA LAND COMPANY

Symbol: CTO   Exchange: ASE

PRICE 3/4/94	RANGE	P-E RATIO	DIVIDEND	YIELD	BETA
15	$12\frac{1}{4}$ - $15\frac{1}{4}$	60.00	0	0.01	0.3

LAST FOUR QUARTERS REPORTED

REVENUES	% CHANGE	NET INCOME	% CHANGE	RETURN ON EQUITY	% CHANGE
36.478	- 9.31	1.529	261.47	6.18	244.76

Corporate Summary

Consolidated Tomoka Land Company is a real estate holding company in the residential and commercial markets. Consolidated also has subsidiary companies, their largest holdings being in the oil and mineral rights and citrus grove markets. The company is based in Daytona Beach, FL.

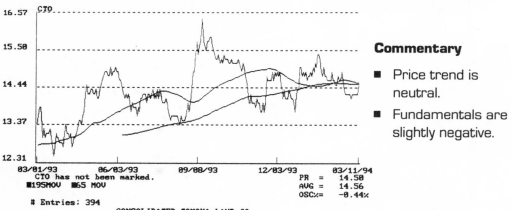

CTO has not been marked.
■195MOV ■65 MOV

PR = 14.58
AVG = 14.56
OSC%= -0.44%

\# Entries: 394

CONSOLIDATED TOMOKA LAND CO.

Commentary

- Price trend is neutral.
- Fundamentals are slightly negative.

YEAR	REVENUES	% CHANGE	NET INCOME	% CHANGE	RETURN ON EQUITY	% CHANGE
89	47.091	3.281	1.780	- 15.117	4.9	- 16.3
90	31.872	- 32.318	- 12.661	- 811.292	- 56.2	- 1250.3
91	46.701	46.527	2.004	NA	8.2	NA
92	40.951	- 12.312	2.510	25.250	9.0	9.7

114

CV REIT INCORPORATED

Symbol: CVI   Exchange: NYS

PRICE 3/4/94	RANGE	P-E RATIO	DIVIDEND	YIELD	BETA
$9\frac{1}{2}$	$8\frac{3}{8}$ - $10\frac{5}{8}$	7.36	0.25	0.03	0.1

LAST FOUR QUARTERS REPORTED

REVENUES	% CHANGE	NET INCOME	% CHANGE	RETURN ON EQUITY	% CHANGE
16.840	- 30.23	9.512	- 2.22	14.47	- 1.87

Corporate Summary

CV Reit Incorporated together with its subsidiaries, has operated as a real estate investment trust (REIT) since January 1, 1982. The company has invested in a portfolio of real estate interests consisting primarily of real estate mortgage notes. CV Reit is primarily invested in the citrus and resort industries, mostly through its wholly-owned subsidiaries.

Commentary

- Volatile stock.
- Favorable REIT environment.
- Price trend is positive.

```
CVI has not been marked.          PR  =  11.00
195MOV  65 MOV                    AVG =   9.92
                                  OSC%=   9.81%
# Entries: 1320
          CV REIT INC.
```

YEAR	REVENUES	% CHANGE	NET INCOME	% CHANGE	RETURN ON EQUITY	% CHANGE
89	30.800	10.557	7.368	- 41.616	8.8	- 39.1
90	23.008	- 25.299	- 15.481	- 310.111	- 24.8	- 382.8
91	19.530	- 15.116	2.881	NA	4.8	NA
92	24.135	23.579	9.728	237.661	14.7	209.5

DELTONA CORPORATION

Symbol: DLT   Exchange: NYS

PRICE 3/4/94	RANGE	P-E RATIO	DIVIDEND	YIELD	BETA
2	$1^7\!/\!8 - 3^5\!/\!8$	NM	0	0	2.4

LAST FOUR QUARTERS REPORTED

REVENUES	% CHANGE	NET INCOME	% CHANGE	RETURN ON EQUITY	% CHANGE
12.144	18.35	- 7.381	NA	NA	NA

Corporate Summary

Deltona Corporation is a real estate development company based in Miami. Deltona is the planner and developer of nine residential communities, extending from the Florida Panhandle to the state's Gulf Coast. The company's holdings currently encompass approximately 100,000 acres.

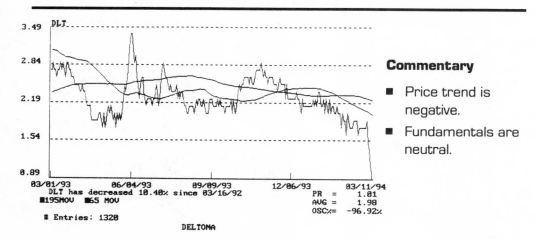

Commentary

- Price trend is negative.
- Fundamentals are neutral.

YEAR	REVENUES	% CHANGE	NET INCOME	% CHANGE	RETURN ON EQUITY	% CHANGE
89	68.379	- 21.025	0.528	- 75.868	1.8	- 78.9
90	29.033	- 57.541	- 17.008	- 3321.21	- 126.4	- 7307.8
91	10.784	- 62.856	- 26.629	NA	202.2	NA
92	11.769	9.134	- 6.808	NA	123.4	- 39.0

DEVCON INTERNATIONAL CORPORATION

Symbol: DEVC   Exchange: NMS

PRICE 3/4/94	RANGE	P-E RATIO	DIVIDEND	YIELD	BETA
$6\frac{5}{8}$	$5\frac{3}{4}$ - $9\frac{1}{8}$	NM	0	0	0.6

LAST FOUR QUARTERS REPORTED

REVENUES	% CHANGE	NET INCOME	% CHANGE	RETURN ON EQUITY	% CHANGE
59.186	- 21.52	- 9.425	NA	- 14.37	NA

Corporate Summary

Devcon International Corporation is a heavy construction company that is based in south Florida, but works strictly in the Caribbean. The duties of the company include earth moving, excavating, and dredging. The company's primary work is construction of airports, buildings, and roads.

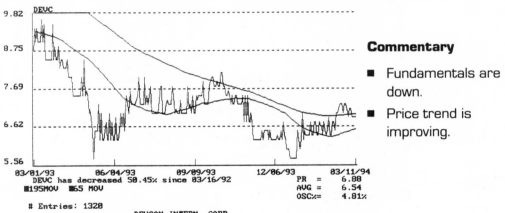

DEVC has decreased 50.45% since 03/16/92
195MOV 65 MOV
PR = 6.88
AVG = 6.54
OSC% = 4.81%

Entries: 1320

DEVCON INTERN. CORP.

Commentary

- Fundamentals are down.
- Price trend is improving.

YEAR	REVENUES	% CHANGE	NET INCOME	% CHANGE	RETURN ON EQUITY	% CHANGE
89	75.821	17.064	12.003	7.941	19.9	- 25.9
90	90.056	18.774	12.628	5.207	17.4	- 12.5
91	89.675	- 0.423	2.798	- 77.843	4.0	- 77.1
92	75.290	- 16.041	- 1.445	- 151.644	- 2.1	- 153.1

ENGLE HOMES INCORPORATED

Symbol: ENGL   Exchange: NMS

PRICE 3/4/94	RANGE	P-E RATIO	DIVIDEND	YIELD	BETA
$16\frac{1}{2}$	$10\frac{3}{4} - 16\frac{1}{2}$	15.00	.04	0	1.6

LAST FOUR QUARTERS REPORTED

REVENUES	% CHANGE	NET INCOME	% CHANGE	RETURN ON EQUITY	% CHANGE
155.480	54.03	7.26100	30.50	NA	NA

Corporate Summary

Engle Homes Incorporated is engaged principally in the development, construction, marketing, and sale of residential homes in Florida. The
company also engages in the development and sale of land to outside builders and develops recreational and community amenities on some of its
properties for the benefit of property owners.

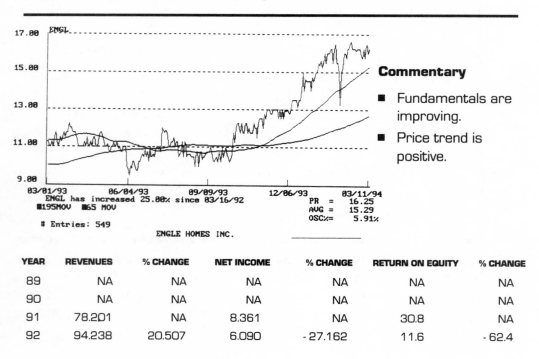

Commentary

- Fundamentals are improving.
- Price trend is positive.

ENGL has increased 25.00% since 03/16/92
■195MOV ■65 MOV
Entries: 549

PR = 16.25
AVG = 15.29
OSC%= 5.91%

ENGLE HOMES INC.

YEAR	REVENUES	% CHANGE	NET INCOME	% CHANGE	RETURN ON EQUITY	% CHANGE
89	NA	NA	NA	NA	NA	NA
90	NA	NA	NA	NA	NA	NA
91	78.201	NA	8.361	NA	30.8	NA
92	94.238	20.507	6.090	- 27.162	11.6	- 62.4

FLORIDA EAST COAST INDUSTRIES

Symbol: FLA   Exchange: NYS

PRICE 3/4/94	RANGE	P-E RATIO	DIVIDEND	YIELD	BETA
60¼	48 - 70	24.79	.10	0	0.6

LAST FOUR QUARTERS

REVENUES	% CHANGE	NET INCOME	% CHANGE	RETURN ON EQUITY	% CHANGE
180.997	3.33	21.830	- 37.02	4.23	- 39.42

Corporate Summary

Florida East Coast Industries Incorporated is the holding company for Florida East Coast Railway (operating division) and Grand Central Corp (the realty unit). Together, the two companies build industrial real estate and lease the properties to outside companies. Florida East Coast is based in Jacksonville, FL.

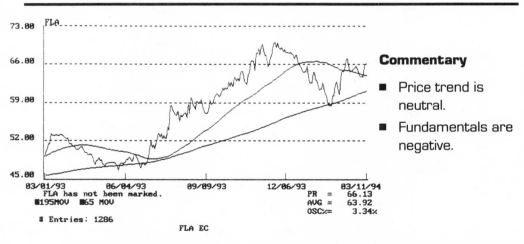

FLA has not been marked.
■195MOV ■65 MOV

PR =   66.13
AVG =   63.92
OSC%=   3.34%

Entries: 1286

FLA EC

Commentary

- Price trend is neutral.
- Fundamentals are negative.

YEAR	REVENUES	% CHANGE	NET INCOME	% CHANGE	RETURN ON EQUITY	% CHANGE
89	167.980	11.343	39.629	11.174	9.0	2.1
90	169.870	1.125	31.352	- 20.886	6.7	- 25.5
91	166.561	- 1.948	29.056	- 7.323	6.0	- 10.0
92	175.755	5.520	24.045	- 17.246	4.8	- 20.6

GOLDFIELD CORPORATION
Symbol: GV   Exchange: ASE

PRICE 3/4/94	RANGE	P-E RATIO	DIVIDEND	YIELD	BETA
⁵⁄₈	¹⁄₂ - ⁷⁄₈	NM	0	0	0.2

LAST FOUR QUARTERS REPORTED

REVENUES	% CHANGE	NET INCOME	% CHANGE	RETURN ON EQUITY	% CHANGE
12.073	- 13.99	- 0.043	- 100.70	- 0.24	- 100.70

Corporate Summary
Goldfield Corporation is the parent for companies in two major industries: electrical construction and precious metal mining. Goldfield's holdings include one company in the electrical construction field and three companies in precious metal mining. The company is based in Melbourne, FL.

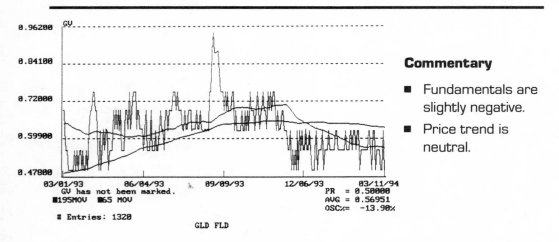

Commentary
- Fundamentals are slightly negative.
- Price trend is neutral.

GV has not been marked.
■195MOV ■65 MOV
# Entries: 1320
PR = 0.50000
AVG = 0.56951
OSC%= -13.90%
GLD FLD

YEAR	REVENUES	% CHANGE	NET INCOME	% CHANGE	RETURN ON EQUITY	% CHANGE
89	17.984	5.231	2.637	- 4.870	23.4	- 39.5
90	15.464	- 14.012	0.632	- 76.033	5.3	- 77.3
91	10.505	- 32.068	4.700	643.671	28.4	433.8
92	14.476	37.801	1.124	- 76.085	6.7	- 76.5

HOMEOWNERS GROUP INCORPORATED

Symbol: HOMG   Exchange: NMS

PRICE	RANGE	P-E RATIO	DIVIDEND	YIELD	BETA
4	$1^3/_4 - 6^1/_2$	7.02	0	0.01	1.0

LAST FOUR QUARTERS REPORTED

REVENUES	% CHANGE	NET INCOME	% CHANGE	RETURN ON EQUITY	% CHANGE
51.344	12.65	3.191	69.82	37.65	336.00

Corporate Summary

Homeowners Group Incorporated is a holding company which conducts its business through various operating subsidiaries. The majority of the business generated by the subsidiaries is in the real estate brokerage industry. Homeowners is based in Hollywood and has offices in 49 states.

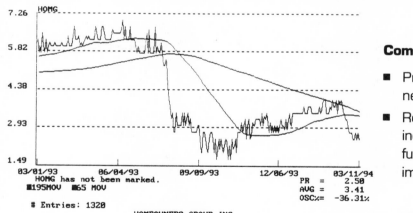

HOMEOWNERS GROUP INC.

Commentary

- Price trend is negative.
- Revenues and net income fundamentals are improving.

YEAR	REVENUES	% CHANGE	NET INCOME	% CHANGE	RETURN ON EQUITY	% CHANGE
89	40.650	29.735	4.735	42.620	23.4	9.1
90	48.276	18.760	4.695	- 0.845	22.4	- 4.5
91	42.241	- 12.501	0.275	- 94.143	1.3	- 94.2
92	43.190	2.247	1.879	583.273	8.6	560.2

HMG COURTLAND PROPERTIES

Symbol: HMG   Exchange: ASE

PRICE 3/4/94	RANGE	P-E RATIO	DIVIDEND	YIELD	BETA
$7\frac{5}{8}$	$5 - 7\frac{5}{8}$	76.25	0	0	0

LAST FOUR QUARTERS REPORTED

REVENUES	% CHANGE	NET INCOME	% CHANGE	RETURN ON EQUITY	% CHANGE
3.583	- 9.63	0.115	210.58	0.56	NA

Corporate Summary

HMG Courtland Properties is a real estate investment company based in Coconut Grove, FL. The company is syndicated as a real estate investment trust whose main focus is in the buying and selling of commercial real estate.

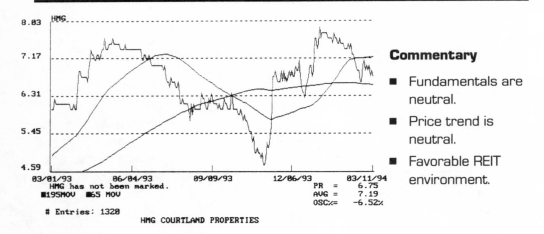

HMG COURTLAND PROPERTIES

Commentary

- Fundamentals are neutral.
- Price trend is neutral.
- Favorable REIT environment.

YEAR	REVENUES	% CHANGE	NET INCOME	% CHANGE	RETURN ON EQUITY	% CHANGE
89	4.472	- 9.198	- 1.220	- 115.635	- 5.5	- 117.0
90	4.018	- 10.152	- 0.622	NA	- 3.0	NA
91	3.442	- 14.335	- 0.869	NA	- 4.3	NA
92	3.676	6.798	0.546	NA	2.6	NA

HUGHES SUPPLY INCORPORATED

Symbol: HUG   Exchange: NYS

PRICE	RANGE	P-E RATIO	DIVIDEND	YIELD	BETA
24$\frac{1}{2}$	14 - 24$\frac{1}{2}$	21.12	0	0	0.5

LAST FOUR QUARTERS REPORTED

REVENUES	% CHANGE	NET INCOME	% CHANGE	RETURN ON EQUITY	% CHANGE
622.366	15.35	5.271	1154.2	5.834	NA

Corporate Summary

Hughes Supply, Inc. is a wholesale distributor of electric, plumbing, air conditioning, and heating parts to the construction industry and mechanical trades in the southeastern states. The company has shut down weak sales offices, consolidated its administrative functions, and installed computerized inventory replenishment and accounting systems. Hughes Supply is looking for acquisitions at this time.

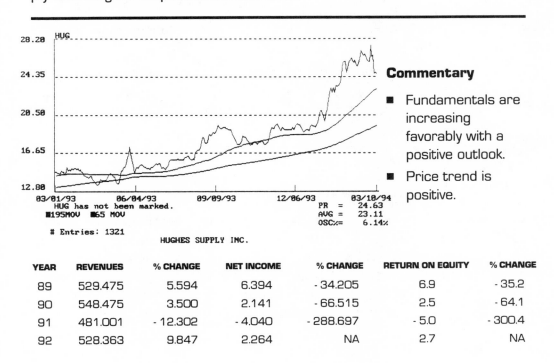

```
28.20   HUG
24.35
20.50
16.65
12.80
     83/01/93    06/04/93    09/09/93    12/06/93    03/10/94
     HUG has not been marked.           PR  =  24.63
     19SMOV   65 MOV                    AVG =  23.11
                                        OSC%=   6.14%
     # Entries: 1321
              HUGHES SUPPLY INC.
```

Commentary

- Fundamentals are increasing favorably with a positive outlook.
- Price trend is positive.

YEAR	REVENUES	% CHANGE	NET INCOME	% CHANGE	RETURN ON EQUITY	% CHANGE
89	529.475	5.594	6.394	- 34.205	6.9	- 35.2
90	548.475	3.500	2.141	- 66.515	2.5	- 64.1
91	481.001	- 12.302	- 4.040	- 288.697	- 5.0	- 300.4
92	528.363	9.847	2.264	NA	2.7	NA

KEITH GROUP COMPANIES INCORPORATED

Symbol: HKME   Exchange: OTC

PRICE 3/4/94	RANGE	P-E RATIO	DIVIDEND	YIELD	BETA
3/8	1/4 - 1 1/2	NM	0	0	0.6

LAST FOUR QUARTERS REPORTED

REVENUES	% CHANGE	NET INCOME	% CHANGE	RETURN ON EQUITY	% CHANGE
1.872	- 9.70	- 0.021	NA	- 0.21	NA

Corporate Summary

Keith Group Companies Incorporated plans, manufactures, and manages home trailer park communities throughout the state of Florida. Currently, the company manages around 150 trailer parks most of which are company owned. The company is based in Hallandale, FL.

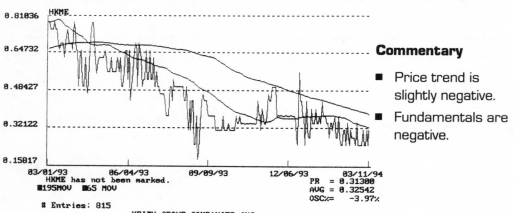

Commentary

- Price trend is slightly negative.
- Fundamentals are negative.

```
HKME
0.81036
0.64732
0.48427
0.32122
0.15817
        03/01/93      06/04/93       09/09/93      12/06/93      03/11/94
        HKME has not been marked.                  PR  = 0.31300
        ■195MOV  ■65 MOV                           AVG = 0.32542
                                                   OSC%=   -3.97%
        # Entries: 815
               KEITH GROUP COMPANIES INC.
```

YEAR	REVENUES	% CHANGE	NET INCOME	% CHANGE	RETURN ON EQUITY	% CHANGE
89	6.766	12.861	- 0.547	NA	- 36.7	NA
90	6.834	1.005	0.966	NA	34.2	NA
91	6.461	- 5.458	0.196	- 79.710	5.6	- 83.6
92	2.529	- 60.857	- 1.458	- 843.878	- 296.3	- 5390.3

KILLEARN PROPERTIES INCORPORATED

Symbol: KPI   Exchange: ASE

PRICE 3/4/94	RANGE	P-E RATIO	DIVIDEND	YIELD	BETA
$4^7/_8$	$2^3/_4$ - 5	37.50	0	0	0.6

LAST FOUR QUARTERS

REVENUES	% CHANGE	NET INCOME	% CHANGE	RETURN ON EQUITY	% CHANGE
16.392	- 8.78	0.194	10.86	1.10	8.98

Corporate Summary

Killearn Properties Incorporated plans and builds resident communities in the Southeast United States which provide the unique opportunity to live, work, and play in a single community. The company is based in Miami and has developed homesites and lifestyles for over 7,000 families.

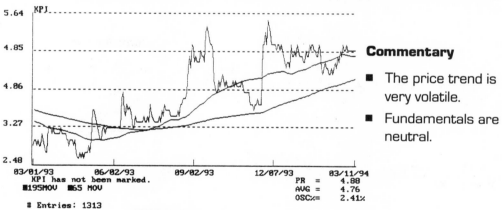

KILLEARN PROP. INC.

Commentary

- The price trend is very volatile.
- Fundamentals are neutral.

YEAR	REVENUES	% CHANGE	NET INCOME	% CHANGE	RETURN ON EQUITY	% CHANGE
89	17.759	27.855	2.207	77.269	15.7	49.5
90	19.778	.11.369	2.355	6.706	14.3	- 8.6
91	19.105	- 3.403	0.646	- 72.569	3.8	- 73.7
92	18.016	- 5.700	0.093	- 85.604	0.5	- 85.7

KOGER EQUITY INCORPORATED

Symbol: KE   Exchange: ASE

PRICE 3/4/94	RANGE	P-E RATIO	DIVIDEND	YIELD	BETA
7⅞	5½ - 9¼	65.63	0	0	0.3

LAST FOUR QUARTERS REPORTED

REVENUES	% CHANGE	NET INCOME	% CHANGE	RETURN ON EQUITY	% CHANGE
44.867	- 2.25	1.498	289.62	0.63	NA

Corporate Summary

Koger Equity Incorporated is a real estate investment trust. The company buys office centers and complexes, mainly from Koger Properties, and leases the space to outside businesses. Koger owns 126 office complexes throughout the Southeast.

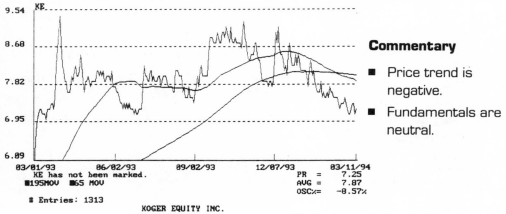

Commentary

- Price trend is negative.
- Fundamentals are neutral.

KE has not been marked.
■19SMOV ■6S MOV
PR = 7.25
AVG = 7.87
OSC%= -8.57%

Entries: 1313

KOGER EQUITY INC.

YEAR	REVENUES	% CHANGE	NET INCOME	% CHANGE	RETURN ON EQUITY	% CHANGE
89	30.472	NA	20.479	NA	7.7	NA
90	42.722	40.201	21.204	3.540	8.1	4.7
91	52.492	22.869	- 5.949	- 128.056	- 2.5	- 131.3
92	46.188	- 12.009	0.933	NA	0.4	NA

KOGER PROPERTIES

Symbol: KOG   Exchange: NYS

PRICE 3/4/94	RANGE	P-E RATIO	DIVIDEND	YIELD	BETA
NA	$^1/_{16}$ - $^1/_2$	NA	0	NA	NA

LAST FOUR QUARTERS REPORTED

REVENUES	% CHANGE	NET INCOME	% CHANGE	RETURN ON EQUITY	% CHANGE
59.402	- 11.58	- 16.155	NA	NA	NA

Corporate Summary

Koger Properties has developed and currently manages office parks for the Koger Equity real estate investment trust. Koger currently is managing 30 office parks in the Southeast United States. **The company is currently in Chapter 11 bankruptcy.**

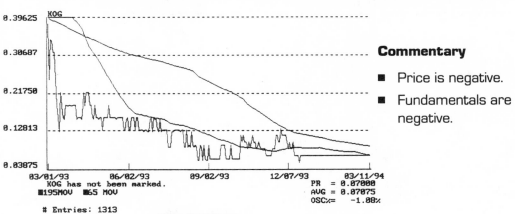

Commentary

■ Price is negative.

■ Fundamentals are negative.

KOGER PROPERTIES

YEAR	REVENUES	% CHANGE	NET INCOME	% CHANGE	RETURN ON EQUITY	% CHANGE
89	157.509	12.457	1.041	- 72.424	2.9	- 44.7
90	206.443	31.067	- 10.393	- 1098.367	45.0	1471.9
91	71.708	- 65.265	- 178.073	NA	102.5	128.0
92	61.056	- 14.855	- 33.326	NA	17.4	- 83.0

LENNAR CORPORATION

Symbol: LEN   Exchange: NYS

PRICE 3/4/94	RANGE	P-E RATIO	DIVIDEND	YIELD	BETA
35¼	28⅛ - 35¼	15.53	.03	0	1.3

LAST FOUR QUARTERS REPORTED

REVENUES	% CHANGE	NET INCOME	% CHANGE	RETURN ON EQUITY	% CHANGE
666.908	55.30	52.511	80.17	11.74	24.67

Corporate Summary

Lennar Corporation is a full-service real estate company primarily involved in home building, the development and management of commercial properties, and real estate-related financial services. Lennar is the largest home builder in Florida, has a major presence in Arizona, and has recently established home-building operations in Texas.

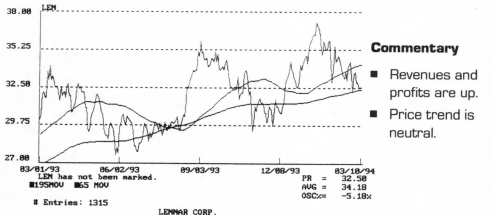

LEN has not been marked.
■195MOV ■65 MOV

PR = 32.50
AVG = 34.18
OSC%= -5.18%

Entries: 1315

LENNAR CORP.

Commentary

■ Revenues and profits are up.

■ Price trend is neutral.

YEAR	REVENUES	% CHANGE	NET INCOME	% CHANGE	RETURN ON EQUITY	% CHANGE
89	431.393	14.557	28.093	1.713	10.8	- 9.0
90	346.937	- 19.578	13.658	- 51.383	5.1	- 53.3
91	323.431	- 6.775	21.148	54.840	7.3	43.4
92	425.559	31.576	29.146	37.819	9.1	25.7

MAJOR REALTY CORPORATION

Symbol: MAJR   Exchange: OTC

PRICE 3/4/94	RANGE	P-E RATIO	DIVIDEND	YIELD	BETA
$1^{11}/_{16}$	$1^5/_8$ - $2^3/_8$	11.25	0	0	1.3

LAST FOUR QUARTERS REPORTED

REVENUES	% CHANGE	NET INCOME	% CHANGE	RETURN ON EQUITY	% CHANGE
55.503	1433.66	1.003	125.45	100.80	NA

Corporate Summary

Major Realty Corporation is based in Orlando and has been in the real estate business since 1969. Major Realty is in the business of buying and
selling commercial properties in the Orlando area. Overall, the majority of
the properties are sold for the purpose of having commercial buildings
constructed on them. However, some of the properties will have hotels
built on them.

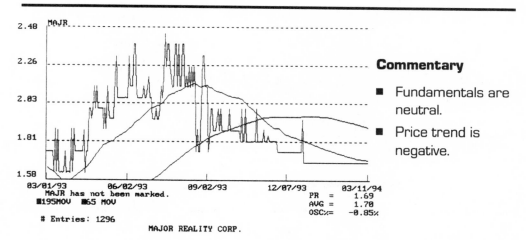

MAJOR REALITY CORP.

Commentary

- Fundamentals are neutral.
- Price trend is negative.

YEAR	REVENUES	% CHANGE	NET INCOME	% CHANGE	RETURN ON EQUITY	% CHANGE
89	34.670	679.276	2.091	NA	22.8	NA
90	2.150	- 93.799	- 5.036	- 340.842	- 122.1	- 634.8
91	1.545	- 28.140	- 3.177	NA	- 127.3	NA
92	4.723	205.696	- 3.671	NA	418.6	NA

MILESTONE PROPERTIES INCORPORATED

Symbol: MPI   Exchange: NYS

PRICE 3/4/94	RANGE	P-E RATIO	DIVIDEND	YIELD	BETA
$4\frac{3}{4}$	3 - 5	NM	0	0	- 0.2

LAST FOUR QUARTERS REPORTED

REVENUES	% CHANGE	NET INCOME	% CHANGE	RETURN ON EQUITY	% CHANGE
14.961	59.79	- 2.231	NA	- 5.34	NA

Corporate Summary

Milestone Properties Incorporated is a real estate management company based in Boca Raton, FL. The company buys and manages shopping centers throughout the state of Florida. The majority of the centers managed by Milestone are in the South Florida area.

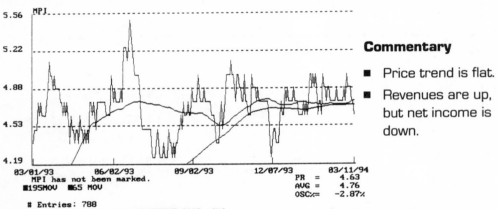

```
5.56  MPI
5.22
4.88
4.53
4.19
     03/01/93    06/02/93    09/02/93    12/07/93    03/11/94
        MPI has not been marked.              PR  =   4.63
     195MOV  65 MOV                           AVG =   4.76
                                              OSC%=  -2.87%
        # Entries: 788
              MILESTONE PROP. INC.
```

Commentary

- Price trend is flat.
- Revenues are up, but net income is down.

YEAR	REVENUES	% CHANGE	NET INCOME	% CHANGE	RETURN ON EQUITY	% CHANGE
89	NA	NA	NA	NA	NA	NA
90	NA	NA	NA	NA	NA	NA
91	7.712	NA	1.472	NA	3.0	NA
92	12.441	61.320	1.218	- 17.255	2.6	- 13.3

NOBILITY HOMES INCORPORATED

Symbol: NOBH   Exchange: OTC

PRICE 3/4/94	RANGE	P-E RATIO	DIVIDEND	YIELD	BETA
12⁷⁄₈	2½ - 12⁷⁄₈	12.76	0	0	1.4

LAST FOUR QUARTERS REPORTED

REVENUES	% CHANGE	NET INCOME	% CHANGE	RETURN ON EQUITY	% CHANGE
17.228	76.79	1.150	805.51	27.04	486.36

Corporate Summary

Nobility Homes Incorporated manufactures homes throughout the states of Florida and Georgia. The company builds two types of homes: single-wide and double-wide. In some cases, the houses manufactured will be used as offices for small companies. Nobility Homes has been in business for 25 years and is based in Ocala.

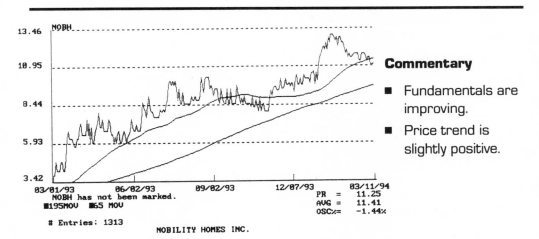

Commentary

- Fundamentals are improving.
- Price trend is slightly positive.

```
NOBH has not been marked.          PR  =   11.25
■195MOV  ■65 MOV                   AVG =   11.41
                                   OSC%=   -1.44%
# Entries: 1313
```

NOBILITY HOMES INC.

YEAR	REVENUES	% CHANGE	NET INCOME	% CHANGE	RETURN ON EQUITY	% CHANGE
89	11.843	8.423	0.459	NA	12.0	NA
90	10.942	- 7.608	0.475	3.486	11.0	- 8.3
91	9.655	- 11.762	- 1.412	- 397.263	- 49.3	- 594.4
92	9.745	0.932	0.127	NA	4.1	NA

ORIOLE HOMES CORPORATION CL A

Symbol: OHCA   Exchange: ASE

PRICE 3/4/94	RANGE	P-E RATIO	DIVIDEND	YIELD	BETA
12½	10¼ - 13	15.82	0.18	0	0.8

LAST FOUR QUARTERS REPORTED

REVENUES	% CHANGE	NET INCOME	% CHANGE	RETURN ON EQUITY	% CHANGE
106.096	10.40	3.640	- 27.94	4.80	- 28.64

Corporate Summary

Oriole Homes Corporation builds, and then sells, single-family homes, patio homes, townhouses, villas, duplexes, and low- and mid-rise condominiums in planned communities throughout South Florida. The company acts as the general contractor for the construction of its developments. The company headquarters is in Del Ray Beach and has been in business for thirty years.

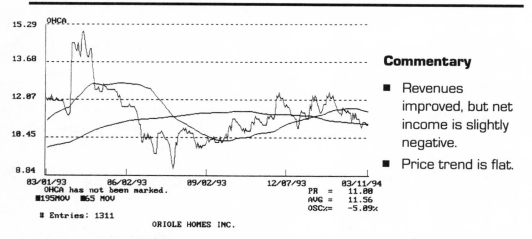

OHCA

| 15.29 |
| 13.68 |
| 12.07 |
| 10.45 |
| 8.84 |

83/01/93   06/02/93   09/02/93   12/07/93   03/11/94
OHCA has not been marked.   PR = 11.88
■195MOV ■65 MOV   AVG = 11.56
                                             OSC%= -5.89%
Entries: 1311

ORIOLE HOMES INC.

Commentary

- Revenues improved, but net income is slightly negative.
- Price trend is flat.

YEAR	REVENUES	% CHANGE	NET INCOME	% CHANGE	RETURN ON EQUITY	% CHANGE
89	103.382	- 14.239	7.542	- 24.821	13.0	- 30.3
90	93.395	- 9.660	4.837	- 35.866	8.0	- 38.2
91	79.165	- 15.236	5.177	7.029	8.0	0.1
92	96.103	21.396	5.051	- 2.434	6.6	- 18.5

Chapter 10

Florida Discount Mortgages

The Banker's Secret

Historically, one of the best ways to make money is to find someone successful and copy what they do. I think banks and savings and loans can safely be called successful. After all, they own all the high-rises in town! "Okay," you're going to say, "but what about the S&L bailout?" The fact is, that failure resulted from greed, not a problem with the fundamental business plan of a lender, which is to lend money.

If money lending is profitable (and it is), then it should follow that an investor who goes into that business will also do well. The investor's task in this case is the same as the bank's: to consider different lending possibilities and to weigh these considerations against the various risk factors attendant on each.

Traditionally, lenders have viewed home loans as among the most conservative types of loans. In the past this was due in large part to the fact that homes appreciated rapidly. A lender's loan-to-value ratio, after all, constantly improves as the value of the home increases. Yet even when the mid-eighties saw a nationwide change in real estate values, and appreciation was no longer automatic, home mortgages continued to be valued as a conservative investment. The lender simply changed his loan-to-value ratio to reflect the new reality. This should put into perspective the fundamental value of real estate loans as investments. Now let us look at how you, as an individual investor, can take advantage of this form of investment.

How to Make Money in Mortgages

Banks and savings and loan associations are considered primary lenders. If you need money, you normally go to one of these groups. If you are dealing in real estate, they will ask for a mortgage on the property as collateral.

There are times, however, when individuals also make loans secured by real estate. The most common example occurs when selling a house. A buyer interested in your property doesn't have quite enough money for a down payment, so in order to facilitate the sale taking place, you agree to loan him the small additional amount he needs. Being a prudent person, you ask for a mortgage on the property to secure the loan. This mortgage is recorded and is second to the first mortgage held by the bank. This kind of transaction goes on every day. The buyer is happy, the bank is happy, and for the most part, you are happy. I say "for the most part" because, although you did sell your house, you would rather have received all cash than loan the buyer money. After all, your kids are in college, you are buying a new house, the new house is going to need carpets and drapes and furniture—I'm sure you get the idea. You really didn't want to be a lender, but you are one.

Across town, another person just opened her bank statement and saw that her CD is coming due, and that she can renew for a whopping 3 percent. "There has got to be a better way," she says to herself. There is.

If our income-poor CD investor only knew about your predicament, she could solve both your problems. She could take her money out of her CD and give it to you in exchange for the mortgage you took as security. Just like that the investor would increase her return three to four times without substantially increasing her risk. She would be happy, and you would be overjoyed.

Buying at a Discount to Increase Your Yield
Sounds like a win-win situation for everyone, right? However, in reality, our investor would have overpaid for the mortgage she bought. Why? Because of an imbalance in motivation. While our theoretical investor would "like" a higher return, our seller (you) "really wants" cash. Because of the inequality in motivation, the mortgage investor can actually increase her return and still have a win-win situation. She can offer to buy the seller's mortgage at a "discount" instead of the full amount the seller is owed. Every dollar of discount she gets off the purchase price increases her yield, because the original buyer (borrower) will be paying her the full amount agreed to when the loan was placed.

The challenge in this transaction is to find the balance point. What is the lowest price the investor can pay for the mortgage that still "works" for the seller? If they can agree on that, a transaction will occur. This is the world of discount mortgage investing. It happens every day all over America and produces yields to investors as high as 25 to 30 percent. Normal transactions yield 11 to 15 percent.

You Have to Use Math
Still interested? Good. I'm going to put some numbers behind our illustration to give it more meaning and to help you see how a mortgage is actually discounted. One of the most difficult aspects of this entire transaction, and the number-one reason people don't invest in discount mortgages, is that you have to use math. Not complicated math. You're even allowed to use a calculator. But, nevertheless, it is still math.

Here's our example:

$180,000	Sale price
135,000	Loan—first mortgage (75 percent LTV)
45,000	Down payment required
35,000	Amount buyer has for down payment
10,000	Amount buyer needs from seller as a second mortgage

Terms for the second mortgage: a $10,000, seven-year-loan at 8 percent interest, fully amortized with payments of $155.86 per month.

In our illustration, the seller sold his property for $180,000. After the buyer got his bank financing, he was short $10,000. The seller agreed to loan him that amount and to take back a second mortgage to be paid off in seven years.

On the other side of town, our CD investor learns about this transaction from a realtor friend who sold the property and who knew that the seller would really have preferred cash. She likes the 8 percent much better than the 3 percent the CD gives her, but she also knows there is some additional risk. She likes the property as security and decides she would be happy if she could get 14 percent interest on her money.

Now, in order to solve our problem, we must use a financial calculator. I use a Hewlett Packard 12c simply out of habit. They cost around $75.00. Depending on your budget, other financial calculators are available for more or less money. The calculator is designed so that you can easily lay out the formula for our discount mortgage. The terms stay the same: monthly payments of $155.86 for seven years. The interest rate changes from 8 percent to 14 percent. Press the answer key for the amount, and the calculator tells you $8,316.96. This is the amount the investor would pay for the $10,000 mortgage to get a 14 percent yield on her money for the next seven years.

Will the seller accept the $8316.96 now, or would he prefer to wait and collect the full $10,000 at $155.86 a month? Naturally, it depends on his circumstances and motivations. If he doesn't need the money, he may wait. If he needs the $8,000 for a tax deficiency due on his house next week, what do you think he'll do?

Or perhaps the seller presents a counter-offer. "I won't take $8,316," he says, "but I will take $9,000." Our investor changes the number in her calculator, asking it to recompute the new interest rate, and gets back a figure of 11.37 percent. A lot better than a CD, she says to herself. Will she take it? Would you?

Welcome to the World of Discount Mortgage Investing
What we have just gone through is a simple but common transaction for buying discount mortgages. As you might guess, there is more. How much you learn about this kind of investing depends upon the amount of time you are

willing to spend. For example, you will learn that you can buy parts of a mortgage instead of the whole amount. You might buy just the first twelve payments, or the last twelve, or just the balloon payment. The variables are numerous. Each technique you learn is designed to help you create a transaction where mathematically you increase your yield to the level you seek. As I mentioned earlier, 25-to-30-percent yields are not out of the question.

Why would you do this? Why would you want to spend time learning something new? Let me show you. Let's assume you have a $50,000 portfolio and twenty years until retirement. If you earn 3-percent CD rates, you will have a nest egg of $91,037 at retirement. If, instead, you invest in discount mortgages and make 20 percent on your money, your nest egg would grow to $2,641,376 over the same time period. A big difference, don't you agree? Is it worth the time to learn something new?

How Do You Invest in Second Mortgages?

Your first decision will be whether to be an active or a passive investor in a mortgage investment program. If you are active, you will need to learn some of the basic lending laws and work with an attorney or title company. This approach is a little time-consuming in the beginning because of the learning curve involved. It isn't difficult; it's just that the information wasn't readily available to you before.

If you decide you aren't going to be active yourself, then you will deal with a broker who finds mortgages and sells (flips) them to you. The broker takes a spread for his efforts. The spread he makes is a negotiated one. In most cases the broker is dealing for himself, and he will try to sell (lay off) the mortgage to you for a price that will yield him the greatest return. You can also hire brokers for a set rate to find you a mortgage—also a negotiated point. Although mortgage brokers are licensed in the state of Florida (one of the few states where they are), they have had a tough reputation because of the mental association with loan sharking. That comparison is totally unwarranted and unfounded today. As with all other professions, you have good mortgage brokers and bad.

How Can You Find a Good Mortgage Broker?

Referrals are naturally the best way to find a broker, but they may not be forthcoming. The next best is to look in your own town. Take out the Yellow Pages and call every mortgage broker listed. Ask them whether they deal in discount mortgages and what kind of yield you can expect to make. From these conversations, narrow down your selection to three or four and ask them for client references. Call the state of Florida's Department of Professional Regulation at 1-800-342-7940 and confirm that the individual you have selected is licensed; find out whether there have been any complaints filed against him.

Finally, you might also check with the Better Business Bureau and your local Chamber of Commerce. Neither of these organizations will necessarily provide you with conclusive information, but they are worth checking out.

For those who are interested in taking the active role, I have a few recommendations. For a cassette on discount mortgage investing, call the J.W. Dicks Research Institute at 1-800-333-3700. The price of this cassette is $14.95.

Courses on buying discount mortgages are offered by: John Schaub, 1938 Ringling Blvd., Sarasota, FL 34263 (813-366-9024) and Laurence J. Pino, P.O. Box 2069, Orlando, FL 32802 (1-800-543-1211). I have known and/or have been in business with these individuals for some years and recommend them highly. John Schaub's course is a hands-on introductory course for beginners. Larry Pino's course is an intensive five-day seminar for people who want not only to buy mortgages for themselves but to sell to others. It's priced accordingly.

Chapter 11

Florida Tax Lien Certificates

I consider Florida tax lien certificates one the best investments in America. Weigh the pros and cons of purchasing tax certificates against those of traditional forms of investment that are available in the marketplace, I think it will be easy to see why I believe this is true. The problem with tax certificates as an investment vehicle is not that they aren't good but that they aren't well known (and most certificate investors think that's great). I have been an active investor in the Florida marketplace for well over twenty years, and it wasn't until two years ago that I actually purchased my first tax certificate. Why the secrecy? One reason may be the fact that no commissions are paid on the sale of the certificate; consequently you don't have a large group of brokers promoting their sales. Instead, promotion of the certificates is left to local county government, which has never been known for its terrific marketing abilities.

The result of this lack of promotion is that a great investment is being purchased only by the few investors who have taken the time to learn about tax lien certificate investing. This group of inside investors has gotten so jealous of their inside knowledge that when I took a camera crew from my local CBS affiliate station to film a tax lien auction in progress, I was booed by the group of people attending. They knew that once this information was let out to the general public, the competition would heat up for their precious tax lien certificates. (When you finish this chapter, if you decide you want a copy of the video, call my office at 1-800-333-3700. Tell them you bought this book, and you'll get a discount.)

What Are Tax Lien Certificates?
Tax lien certificate sales are conducted throughout the United States. The form the sale takes varies, as does the type of interest and rate of return. Florida is one of the most favorable states for tax certificate sales, from an investor's point of view. Each Florida county is mandated by the state to sell tax certificates on properties that have outstanding taxes by June 1 of every year. If it were not for the tax lien sales, the counties would have to bear the brunt of unpaid property taxes, and many would go without needed services. Tax lien sales ensure that the counties are paid all taxes due on the real property

within their jurisdiction in a timely fashion. In a nutshell, certificates on unpaid property taxes are auctioned to third parties at a tax certificate sale, advancing or loaning the money to the delinquent property owner. The county receives its taxes on time, the property owner gets temporary relief from paying taxes when he does not have the money to pay, and the third-party investor receives an above-average return on his investment. No wonder tax lien certificates are so successful: They truly create a win-win situation for all concerned.

Advantages of Tax Lien Certificates

Of course, as with any investment, there are advantages and disadvantages to tax lien certificates. Let's begin with advantages.

High return

The very first and most obvious advantage to investing in tax certificates is the return offered. In Florida the rate of return a certificate investor can receive on his investment begins at 18 percent, and because of early payoff of certain certificates, there are ways in which an investor can actually make substantially more than that. When you compare a typical risk-reward ratio, the return for investing in tax lien certificates is extremely high.

Low Risk

The reaction of most investors on hearing of this 18-percent annual return is: If it looks too good to be true, then it probably is. I absolutely agree with this statement in most circumstances, but after careful investigation, I believe I have determined that the risk involved with investing in tax lien certificates is in fact extremely low compared to other forms of investment that promise high returns. With tax lien certificate investing, not only is the rate of return guaranteed by the local government, an investor also receives security in the form of a lien against real estate. This security is given priority over all other liens, with the exception of some federal tax liens. That means that your tax lien certificate must be paid off ahead of even a first mortgage on the property. Compare that to the risk a typical lender is willing to accept when it loans money on real estate, and you'll find that tax lien certificates are actually much safer. Most lenders would feel that if they had an 80 percent loan-to-value ratio on a piece of residential real estate, they would have a relatively safe investment. If they actually had to foreclose on their property, they would likely be protected by an equity cushion of at least 20 percent. In the case of a tax lien sale, since the purchaser of the tax certificate would be paid off ahead of even a first mortgage holder, the former has the greater security.

Small Investment Amount

One of the traditional disadvantages of making good investments is that you need a lot of money to take advantage of specialized situations. That is not the case with tax lien certificates, many of which are sold for less than

$100. There are literally thousands of certificates available in every county for less than $1,000 and an equal or greater number for between $1,000 and $5,000. Buying the smaller certificates tends to be easier than buying the larger certificates, because the competition for the larger certificates is greater. Some certificates with values in the hundreds of thousands of dollars receive heated bidding at auction, with investors willing to accept a lower rate than 18 percent. These are the kinds of certificates that banks and other large institutions go after, because they can actually borrow the money from the Federal Reserve at 3 to 4 percent and bid down as low as 8 to 9 percent on a tax certificate. The bank still maintains an extremely safe spread of 5 to 6 percent on its investment. A nice return for a low risk on 100-percent borrowed money.

Upside Potential

It is rare to find a good income investment that also offers upside growth potential. Tax lien certificates have this potential, because you can ultimately force a sale of the property, creating the opportunity to buy it at auction, based on the amount you have paid on the tax lien certificate. At the auction, either your lien will be paid off with your stated amount of interest, or you may receive the property itself. Although you might doubt that people would let their properties go for the price of tax liens, it has happened, and during more difficult times such as recessionary periods, it occurs more frequently.

Ease of Investing

Investments with a good chance of high returns are frequently complicated. Specialized knowledge may be needed to make the investment or assess the risk factor. In the case of tax certificates, the investment is made quite simple by the local counties that conduct the auction. Remember, it is to their advantage to have many people participating in the sale so that the certificates are all sold. The counties are consequently very helpful with information on how to purchase tax lien certificates, and the process they establish is quite simple.

No Management Headaches

One of the biggest problems with many traditional forms of investment is the management headaches that arise once the investment is actually made. This is particularly true of real estate purchases: Not only does the investor need money, he or she has to be willing to accept the responsibility of ongoing management. Those who invest in stocks or mutual funds must commit to a certain amount of research, or blindly accept the whims of the overall market. A tax lien certificate, on the other hand, is simply a payment of money, with the collection process handled by the local county authorities. The only management required is keeping track of the number of certificates you have and the length of time you hold them. Only if you actually bought properties at auction would you be accepting the additional management responsibilities that would go along with all real estate.

Disadvantages of Tax Certificates

Liquidity

This is perhaps the single largest disadvantage of tax lien certificates. Unlike stocks, bonds, or money markets, an investor cannot simply cash in his tax lien certificates when convenient. He or she must wait until the owner of the property elects to pay off the certificate, or, after the minimum waiting period of two years, go through the process of asking the county to sell the property at auction. In either event, liquidity is controlled by factors other than the investor's immediate desire. Even this most obvious disadvantage, however, can be greatly minimized through diversifying your tax lien certificates, staggering their purchase dates so that you will always have certificates available to cash out. This approach is very similar to the one used by investors when they stagger the maturity dates of their CDs. Some counties also have investor lists available, should a tax lien purchaser need to liquidate. Investors on these lists may sometimes ask for an additional discount, hoping for a higher yield, but in other cases they may be very well satisfied with your 18 percent interest.

A third method of liquidity is knowing other people who buy the certificates. Once you own them, you are always willing to buy others.

Risk

I would be remiss if I did not mention the potential risks of tax certificate ownership. Although I think these risks are minimal, you should certainly know what they are. Some people worry, for instance, about the problems that may arise if the owner of the property on which you own a tax lien certificate goes into bankruptcy. If the court should determine that whatever assets the debtor has must go to other creditors rather than to pay off your tax lien certificate, they argue, you would lose your investment. I do not think, however, that this is likely to happen. While a judge could certainly take such a position, it would be most unusual. A tax lien certificate holder is a secured creditor, and in the bankruptcy process, particularly in Florida, secured creditors' liens are paid first out of the sale proceeds of the property they secure. The real risk, in my view, is the normal risk of tax lien investing. Is there adequate security in the real estate itself to pay your certificate?

Of course, in the event of bankruptcy being filed, you do face the likelihood of protracted delays. The process can take as long as a year or two during which time your investment could not be liquidated. The chance of any individual not recouping his original investment, plus some interest, is very slim, however, although the bankruptcy judge is free to lower your interest rate if he feels it is in the best interest of the other creditors.

The second risk in purchasing tax lien certificates is the environmental hazard risk—i.e., the chance that you might end up purchasing a certificate on real estate with hazardous waste problems. This is another one of those fears that is brought up by large tax lien certificate investors in order to scare off their competition. I say this for two reasons. First, although hazardous waste certainly exists as a risk, it is one you can easily minimize by limiting your investments to residential real estate. Second, Congress has passed various laws protecting lien holders who hold property where hazardous wastes are found. These actions were taken specifically on behalf of banks, but these lien protection laws should also protect tax lien certificate holders. At the present time, however, the law has not been tested for this application.

The third kind of risk, alluded to earlier, is that the security may be less than what was expected. An example of this has occurred when tax lien certificates were purchased on property that had a mobile home on it. After a couple of years had passed, the owner of the property removed the mobile home, leaving the tax certificate holder with a vacant plot of land worth less than his certificate. Again, a very conservative investor could eliminate this possibility by purchasing certificates based on neighborhoods or areas that didn't contain mobile homes.

How to Get Started
The state of Florida is divided into sixty-five counties, all of which have tax lien sales on property for unpaid taxes. According to the state law, these sales must be conducted by June 1 of every calendar year. The counties hold their sales at different times, and you should call each county in which you are interested in buying certificates to find out the specific date it plans to hold its auction and where. (See the tax collector chart at the end of this chapter for phone numbers. Most counties will not set their dates until mid-April.) The times and places of the tax lien certificate auctions will be announced in the local newspaper, but it would certainly be better for you to know this in advance.

Things to Think About
The first thing you should remember is that you are going to an auction. That means it will be easy to get caught up in the excitement and thrill of the actual bidding process. Some people have bid down the price of the tax lien certificates to returns less than they were willing to accept before they attended the auction. The way to handle all of this, of course, is to have a plan of attack ahead of time—to make a decision in your own mind about how much you want to invest in tax lien certificates, and then not to buy any more than that amount. Decide in advance the lowest rate of interest you would be willing to accept, and then, when you are actually bidding, stop if the rate drops below that amount. Are there neighborhoods you would prefer to bid on? This

143

should be considered in order to ensure that you at least buy properties with adequate security.

Are you willing to invest in vacant land? Some tax lien purchasers are not. Their reasoning is that if they buy certificates on property with improvements on it, they can probably use the property to generate income if they ultimately end up buying it. Buying vacant land can carry additional problems. Zoning is one: You may not be able to get the zoning to use the property for something worthwhile. Then there's flooding. The property may be in a flood plane and not fit for building on, making its actual value much lower than that of the certificate. Finally there's the risk of environmental problems. Vacant property is far more likely to have hidden environmental problems than property that already has improvements on it.

How the Auction Works

The auction process for tax lien certificates is really very simple. As with most things you are unfamiliar with, however, you'll probably need to go through the process once before you become accustomed to it.

When you arrive at the auction facility, the first thing you will need to do is check in with the official and put up a deposit. The amount of the deposit is predetermined; call the office ahead of time to find out what it is. In most cases the official will accept personal checks, but cash or a certified check is sometimes required, so it pays to ask in advance. Each person who places a deposit receives a bidding number. This number is on a card, which you will hold up during the auction in order to place your bid. If you would like to receive two numbers in order to have a better chance of having your number called out, you can put up two deposits, but since only one number is allowed per person, you would have to bring someone along to help you during the auction. This is frequently done by large institutions such as banks, who bring several people to the auction so they can get a larger number of certificates.

At the beginning of the auction, the auctioneer sits at the front of the room and calls out from the prepublished list of available tax certificates a certain tax number. Anyone interested in purchasing that tax lien certificate then raises his or her card and the auctioneer calls out one of the card numbers. On most certificates, everyone in the room raises their card, indicating their willingness to buy the certificate. The auctioneer randomly selects a bidder who is awarded that particular certificate. Once a number is called, other people in the room have the option of actually bidding a lower interest rate. For instance, say the opening number is called, and the person who holds that number will earn 18 percent interest on his tax certificate unless someone bids the certificate down. If another person is willing to accept a lower rate, 17 percent for example, she will call out that amount. Now others may join the bidding process, and the price (interest rate to be paid) may be driven down. If the original investor, the one whose number that was called would like to participate, then he must bid along with the others for the lowest interest rate. This happens very quickly, and you must remain alert, or you will be left out.

Once you are awarded a successful bid, you must now settle with the staff and arrange payment for the entire balance. In most cases, the tax collector's office will bill you for the balance within the next few days, and you then have forty-eight hours in which to pay that amount or forfeit your original deposit.

During the auction process, one of the ways to minimize the risk on your investment is to base your bid on the assessed value of the property. If the assessed value of the property is very low compared to other values in the neighborhood, you may consider this as a potential problem and elect not to bid on those properties. It is very common for the assessed value of the property to be stated on the forms you receive about all the properties that will be available. This assessed value, which is assigned by the county property appraiser, is equivalent to an appraisal and can give you an idea as to the real value of the property you are bidding on. A bad piece of property, such as a small strip of land that is not usable because of its size, will have a low assessed value compared to other property in the area. You can mentally eliminate this from your purchase list. Another way of potentially reducing your risk is to get to know the tax assessor's staff on an individual or informal basis. The staff will be able to tell you whether any of the properties going up at auction are less desirable or have unusual restrictions on them. In many counties the staff actually goes through the list of properties ahead of time and withdraws from the auction those that are not suitable for building. Speaking with the staff before the auction will enable you to determine whether this is a policy of the county in which you have decided to buy tax certificates.

Getting to know the staff also helps you learn of additional certificates that may become available after the auction. Sometimes people bid on properties and then, for some reason or another, don't follow through with their bid. These become no-sale certificates. No-sale certificates can be purchased directly from the county after the auction by contacting the local tax collector's office. Some counties also provide a list of individuals who need to sell certificates because their circumstances have changed. Although they do not provide a formal marketplace, as a courtesy to both buyers and sellers they will frequently make known different parties' interests. Some investors buy certificates in this after-market and ask for an additional discount above the 18 percent interest. Since the certificates aren't sold at auction you also have more opportunity to check out the underlying value of the property you desire.

There are other possibilities for buying tax certificates in post-auction sales. The Resolution Trust Corporation, RTC, as well as some of the failed thrifts, have tax certificates in their portfolios and have sold them directly to private investors. This provides liquidity to both the RTC and to individual thrifts and has been a boom to investors, who have negotiated direct purchases. In some cases the additional discounts they have been able to negotiate have been substantial. Moreover, buying directly from the RTC or these failed institutions may give the purchaser not only the higher rate of interest on the certificate but also the chance to purchase the property at auction. See chapter 12 for more about the RTC.

Transfer of a tax certificate to another party is an extremely simple process. Each county maintains a registration of each individual who owns a tax certificate, and the certificate can be transferred simply by endorsing over the actual certificate to another individual and by paying a two-dollar registration fee with the county. It is extremely important to pay the county registration fee; failure to do so means that the county considers the original owner of the certificate the true owner and will make any payments due to that individual.

How to Redeem Your Certificate

Once you own a certificate it may be redeemed in several ways, the most common of which is for the property owner to pay the county the amount of taxes owed plus interest, whereupon the county sends you a check in the mail. Many certificates don't even last a full year as an investment. The property owners have simply neglected to pay their taxes, and once they realize a certificate has been sold, they pay it off. In this case you receive a minimum stated interest of 5 percent of the face value of the certificate. From a calculation standpoint and a true rate of return, this could mean a real windfall, since the minimum amount of interest you can earn on a tax certificate is 5 percent of the value you paid. Last year, several people I knew purchased certificates that were redeemed the day after the sale. While this was somewhat frustrating from a long-term standpoint, it was a windfall from a return standpoint, since they immediately received 5 percent of the full face value of their purchase price, even after only one day of investment. Their true rate of return in that particular case was astronomical.

Tax certificates are good for a total of seven years. During that period of time, the property owner can pay you off at any time as long as he pays you the full amount plus interest. After two years you may ask the county to sell the property. After the sale, you will either have your tax certificate paid off or receive a tax deed. If you elect not to ask the county to sell the property, then you may continue to hold the certificate for up to the seven-year period. If anyone should own a certificate past seven years, it actually becomes worthless. (This is not a very bright thing to have happen to you.)

What Happens at a Tax Sale?

If, after two years, you do elect to have the property sold by the county at a tax sale, the process you go through is simply one of notifying the county that you would like to have your tax certificate redeemed. They will send you an application that must be completed, and you must pay all other taxes owing on the property, including any additional certificates sold on that property plus interest and penalties after yours was purchased. You will also be required to pay for a title search of the property to show any other liens and encumbrances, because these people must also be notified that a tax sale is about to take place.

Once the tax collector's office accepts your application, they deliver it to the circuit court and request that a tax sale be scheduled. A tax sale cannot occur sooner than thirty days following its acceptance by the circuit court. The sale is advertised by the circuit court during the four consecutive weeks prior to its scheduled date, and in addition, each of the parties who showed up in the title search as having a potential interest in the property must be notified by mail that the sale is about to occur.

All tax sales are actually conducted at auction. The opening bid against the property is the amount you paid with your original application for the tax sale. If there are no other bidders, you will be the automatic winner of the property and will receive a tax deed. If someone else bids a higher bid than your application amount, then the only way you could actually win the property is by contesting and bidding against the property at a higher price. This of course is the protection that other lienholders, such as mortgage holders, have of keeping the property from being taken away from them and foreclosed out. At the end of the sale, the winning bid must pay the tax collector's office the full amount of the payment plus any interest or penalties accrued within twenty-four hours. At that time the winning bid at the tax auction will receive a tax deed conveying full ownership of the property to that individual.

Without beating a good thing to death, you should by now have a thorough understanding of the value of tax lien certificates and why I think they are worthwhile. Although I believe that Florida has all of the good tax certificates you could ever want, you might also consider other states for your investment portfolio. The type and manner of sale varies; states have different advantages. Michigan, for example, pays as much as 50 percent on its certificates. Other states conduct outright property sales instead of paying interest. These states should be explored by those who are active real estate investors.

TAX COLLECTOR OFFICES

For the dates of county tax lien sales, call the appropriate office listed below. Only ask for the person listed if you have difficulty getting the information you need. Some counties will add you to their mailings for advance notice. Be sure to ask.

COUNTY	CONTACT/PHONE	COUNTY	CONTACT/PHONE
Alachua	Von Fraser, 904-374-5236	Lake	Sarah, 904-343-9622
Baker	Pat Cruz, 904-259-6880	Lee	Girtha, 813-339-6000
Bay	Ms. Callipo, 904-784-4090	Leon	Hanna, 904-488-4381
Bradford	Ms. Pierce, 904-964-6280	Levy	Don, 904-486-5100
Brevard	Nellie, 407-255-4453	Liberty	Linda, 904-643-2442
Broward	Ms. Smith, 305-468-3424	Madison	Brenda, 904-973-6136
Calhoun	Doris, 904-674-5338	Manatee	Susan, 813-748-8000
Charlotte	Lisa, 813-743-1356	Marion	Mr. Olson, 904-368-8200
Citrus	Ms. Mort, 904-637-9486	Martin	Lynn, 407-288-5749
Clay	Jean, 904-269-6329	Monroe	Ms. Pazo, 305-294-8403
Collier	Ms. Wells, 813-774-8171	Nassau	Julie, 904-261-5566
Columbia	Ronnie, 904-758-1131	Okaloosa	Donna, 904-689-5712
Dade	Barbara, 305-375-1790	Okeechobee	Ms. Shairey, 813-763-3084
DeSoto	Retha, 813-993-4861	Orange	Tina, 407-836-2700
Dixie	Linda, 904-498-1213	Osceola	Lori, 407-847-1525
Duval	Ms. Guy, 904-630-2000	Palm Beach	Alfea, 407-355-2264
Escambia	Linda, 904-438-6500	Pasco	Dottie, 904-521-4360
Flagler	Melissa, 904-437-7422	Pinellas	Dan, 813-464-3561
Franklin	Tresann, 904-653-9323	Polk	Terry, 813-534-4700
Gadsden	904-627-7255	Putnam	Mary, 904-329-0272
Gilchrist	Ms. Bruce, 904-463-2495	Santa Rosa	Carol, 904-623-0135
Glades	Gayle, 813-946-0626	Sarasota	Linda, 813-951-5600
Gulfnell	904-229-6652	Seminole	Joy, 407-321-1130
Hamilton	Norma, 904-792-1284	St. Johns	Pam, 904-823-2250
Hardee	April, 813-773-9144	St. Lucie	Sharon, 407-489-3565
Hendry	Debbie, 813-675-5339	Sumter	Janet, 904-793-0260
Hernando	Brenda, 904-754-4180	Suwanee	Jerry, 904-362-2816
Highlands	Mr. Collier, 813-382-5239	Taylor	Bonnie, 904-584-2859
Hillsborough	Elisa, 813-272-7260	Union	Lisa, 904-496-3331
Holmes	Fay, 904-547-1116	Volusia	Carolyn, 904-736-5939
Indian River	Bill, 407-567-8180	Wakulia	Elma, 904-926-3371
Jackson	Mary, 904-482-9653	Walton	Janet, 904 892 8121
Jefferson	Mrs. Walker, 904-997-5551	Washington	Mary, 904-638-6276
LaFayette	Marilyn, 904-294-1961		

Chapter 12

Florida Auctions

Buying real estate at auction is not a new idea, but it is a new trend. More auctions are taking place in Florida than ever before, which in itself creates more opportunities for the buyer who can master the process. Although most of this chapter concerns buying real estate at auction, there are also tremendous opportunities to buy cars, boats, jewelry, and equipment. Some people don't really consider these auctions investing. I think any time you make or save money, you're investing.

There are really three opportunities to buy real estate during the auction process:

1. Before the auction. Buying direct from the seller or through a negotiated bid managed by the auctioneer.

2. At the auction.

3. After the auction.

    a. Negotiating with a seller who did not receive the minimum bid required by the auctioneer.

    b. Negotiating with a buyer who may have purchased a great deal but is interested in flipping the property out to you for a quick profit, perhaps even before he closes.

Auctions can be both exciting and scary, especially for the novice. The fear, however, is unjustified. Buying at auction is simply another method of buying; like most techniques, it can be mastered through a little legwork.

To learn the auction process requires attendance. You can read all you want, but until you go to a few, you won't really know what's going on. At the end of this chapter, you will find a list of auctioneers. To our knowledge there is no other list like this available anywhere. Call or write the auctioneers in the area of the state where you have an interest in buying and ask them to put your name on their mailing list. Getting your name on their lists will ensure that you receive advance notice of all their auctions. This is very important, since watching for ads in the newspaper is a hit-or-miss proposition, and it won't give you enough advance time to deal directly should you desire to do so. You probably won't be buying anything on your first couple of trips, but it is better to have advance warning just in case.

If you really get serious about buying real estate at auctions, you will ultimately want to meet all of the auctioneers in your area and let them know the kind of things you are interested in buying. Although you'll find a lot of good deals at auctions, an equal number of good deals probably never reach the auction block. You want to become a part of the inner circle that hears about these properties, and establishing personal relationships is the only way to make that happen.

Foreclosure Sales

This is the first kind of auction most people think of. A lender has foreclosed on someone for nonpayment of a mortgage. In order to meet the statutory requirement of foreclosure, the lender is required to have a public sale of the property. You may be shocked to hear this, but almost no one attends these sales. In the vast majority of cases, the lender is the only person in attendance. The lender bids the amount of the unpaid loan, and since no one else is bidding, they are awarded the property. If you have cash or immediate access to cash, these sales can present great opportunities simply because of the weak attendance. The lender will bid their loan amount, and by bidding even one dollar more, you can win the property.

Unfortunately, that may not mean you got the best deal. Sometimes you are better off dealing directly with the lender after the sale. Since lenders generally don't want to be long-term property owners, they are likely to assist you with financing once they own the property. The lender may also be happy to negotiate a lower purchase price if you can either pay cash or get financing from another source.

Tax Sales

In the previous chapter, we discussed the benefits of buying tax lien certificates at auction. Another opportunity related to the tax assessor's office is presented when a certificate holder requests a sale of the property for the unpaid taxes. In this situation, you as the investor are now looking to buy the property at auction and redeem the tax certificates along with any unpaid liens on the property. This will be done at the tax sale itself.

Before the local tax assessor's office holds a tax sale, it is required by law to advertise the sale in the local newspaper as well as notify any existing lien holders that it is about to take place. If you read the newspaper every day and check the legal section, you will be aware of these sales as they come about. Unfortunately, if you are like the rest of normal Americans, you won't be reading all the legal notices in the paper every day. Consequently, the best way to find out about tax sales, is to call the tax assessor's office periodically and ask whether anything is being scheduled over the next month. You will find the tax assessor's office to be a friendly group of people: Afterall, they are there to collect money on behalf of the county, and tax auctions are certainly a method of doing that .

Each county has its own procedures and group of auctioneers to conduct the sales. A printed list of requirements will explain the method of bidding and whether or not a deposit is required prior to placing a bid at auction. Once you know these basics, you're ready. Tax auctions don't last very long because there are rarely many bidders. Normally the tax certificate holder will place the initial bid, followed by any institutional lender bidding the amount of their underlying debt. The owner may place a bid, but it is rare that anyone else would be there to enter into a bidding contest should you desire to try and win the property.

Should you decide to enter the world of tax sale auctions, where the property is actually conveyed, you may want to take the time to inspect the properties available for sale, and perhaps even hire an outside appraiser. In most cases an outside appraiser will not be necessary, since you will know the assessed value of the property—a form of comparative appraisal based on property valuations throughout the county. Remember, though, actually buying the property is different from buying a tax certificate. When you buy the property, you take it "as is." Real estate ownership is active investing, and you need to keep that in mind.

Bankruptcy Sales

Bankruptcy filings have increased dramatically over the past few years. The recession is the primary reason for this, but another factor is the growing but mistaken belief that bankruptcy is an easy out to being overburdened with debt. Whatever the reasons, the fact is that record numbers of individuals and corporations residing in the state of Florida are finding themselves in the local bankruptcy court.

In all bankruptcy filings, the debtor lists all of his or her assets and liabilities, and the court appoints a trustee to administer bankruptcy proceedings. The trustee's responsibility is to apportion the debtor's assets among his or her various creditors in accordance with the priorities that have been laid out by state statute. Any remaining assets after the creditors have been paid off are distributed to the debtor.

Real estate is an asset frequently held by people who find themselves in debt difficulties. In most cases the real estate is encumbered by one or two mortgages against the property, and also by some amount of equity, which belongs to the owner. That equity, of course, is a target the trustee can attach in order to distribute to creditors, and the only way the trustee will be able to distribute this equity is to convert it into cash by selling the property. Thus, the role of the trustee is to sell the property at auction and attempt to get the highest bid, one that would both satisfy existing lien holders and generate as much cash as possible for creditors. The trustee contacts bankruptcy auctioneers, who specialize in selling off these kinds of properties; the auctioneer, in turn, may hold an auction centered on one bankruptcy, or more commonly will group the property with several others in order to create more excitement. Grouping properties allows the auctioneer to spend more money advertising and promoting the auction, which in turn attracts more potential buyers to the auction itself.

At the end of this chapter is a list of auctioneers who specialize in real estate auctions. When you are ready to buy real estate, please feel free to contact them and get on their mailing lists of buyers who may be interested in purchasing at auction. I do suggest you respect auctioneers as businessmen and not place your name on their mailing lists unless you are truly interested in purchasing property. Maintaining auction lists and doing mailings are expensive for these professionals as well as for the sellers of the property.

Another avenue for participating in bankruptcy auctions is to deal directly with bankruptcy trustees, who in some cases are able to deal with negotiated sales of property that never make it to auction. Trustees are also frequently aware of property belonging to companies or individuals entering the bankruptcy process who have property available for sale prior to actually declaring bankruptcy. These companies and individuals will be interested in selling property in order to generate cash and avoid actually declaring bankruptcy. Such situations are ideal for negotiating sales with the trustee prior to an auction. To find bankruptcy trustees in your area, simply contact the local bankruptcy court and ask them for a list of trustees, along with their addresses and telephone numbers.

Another method is to look in the Yellow Pages of your local telephone directory under the listing "attorneys." You will find that certain attorneys have designated themselves specialists in the field of bankruptcy. Such professionals often become trustees for bankruptcies; they almost certainly work with clients who may be headed in that direction and are selling property in order to try and avoid bankruptcy. Add the names of these attorneys to your rolodex: They represent an additional source of motivated sellers.

Resolution Trust Corporation

In the summer of 1989 Congress created the largest real estate seller that ever existed—the Resolution Trust Corporation (RTC). If you haven't heard of the RTC, then you haven't been involved in real estate. The RTC has been appointed by Congress to head the Savings and Loan Association bailout, which has already cost the public hundreds of millions of dollars and may go higher. In addition to the vast sums of money being spent on the bailout, the RTC has also created long-term problems with the real estate industry by "dumping" properties into the marketplace at prices frequently far below what the actual costs of building and construction would be. Individual purchasers of these properties have certainly achieved a windfall, but it will be some time before the real estate industry overcomes the effects of the reduced sale prices, which have set the market for appraisals and commercial lending. The price affect of the RTC's actions are one reason that many commercial lenders today will not loan money on real estate projects, effectually drying up any new development. Of course, the positive aspect of all this is the probability that the existing properties will eventually increase in value as they become rented up. The demand for rental space increases existing rental rates for property and will ultimately cause a demand for new properties. Until that time, investors must realize that their goal in buying property is to buy as low as possible with the intention of holding the property for some time. Meanwhile they will need to keep it in good condition to maintain maximum cash flow until the market returns to normal. The investor who is able to maintain staying power could become extremely wealthy if he takes advantage of the current "bargain-basement" prices that exist through these government sales.

The RTC has a big promotions department because they have a big job. Phone them toll-free at 1-800-431-0600 to receive some educational information that will help you get started dealing with this huge government bureaucracy. You can also write to the RTC at the following address: RTC National Sales Center, Suite 710, 1133 21st Street NW, Washington, DC. In addition to their general information package, you may also want to find out about their special sales events, which occur periodically in Florida. These are promotional affairs in which different assets, including both real estate and personal property, are packaged and auctioned off to the highest bidder. You can receive information about these special sales events by calling 1-800-348-1484. There's a third number you can call to find out about specific assets the RTC has available for sale within the geographic area you are interested in. In some cases the RTC will charge you for this information, depending on the number of properties that you are interested in, but the fee is a very small one—typically less than five dollars. This information service can be reached at 1-800-RTC-3006.

The RTC also offers financing on the properties they sell. Expect down payments of 3 percent of the sales price, along the guidelines set in their specific mandates. Much of this is negotiable, including the closing costs, which may actually be paid by the RTC. For further information on their financing, the toll-free number is 1-800-533-8951.

There are basically two kinds of property sold at RTC auction: General and Affordable. General means that the property is available to anyone whether or not it is owner occupied. Affordable means that the buyer must occupy the property personally.

To bid at an auction, a cashier's check will be required as a deposit. The deposit of $1,000 if you are bidding in the general category and $500 if you are bidding in the affordable category. Once you have entered your deposit, you will receive a bidder's card, which you will hold up during the auction. Should you be awarded a property during the auction, your cashier's check will be applied to the deposit against the property, and the balance can be paid by personal check. It is important to note that none of the sales are conditioned upon financing. Should you be unable to secure financing on the property you have bid on, you will forfeit your deposit.

Immediately after you are awarded a property at auction, you will be asked to sign a confirmation form. You will also execute a purchase and sale agreement on the property. This can be a scary experience for people who have not gone through this process before. To overcome this feeling, attend an auction without bidding. Request the officials to let you review some of the documents you would have to sign if you purchased property.

Although great bargains can be found at RTC auctions, even better bargains can be found by dealing with the conservators and trustees who handle the assets of a failed thrift prior to the property's actually being sold at auction. This process can take anywhere from a couple of months to up to twenty-four months, meaning there is a lot of time for working on purchasing property prior to the auction. To get information on savings and loans in this stage of the government process, be on the lookout for newspaper stories about failed thrifts that are being taken over by the RTC. Follow up any story by calling the savings and loan itself and asking the name of the conservator who is handling their affairs; or contact the RTC directly. Once a conservator has been appointed, negotiations can be entered into for any of the assets of the failed S & L.

Needless to say, tremendous bargains are available through the RTC although you will have to weed through a lot of properties to find them. The program has been in existence for some four years now, and yet properties can still be purchased for as much as 60 percent below the value of what it would take to reproduce them today. There is no question that in the future this will be known as the second great government land rush giveaway.

Following is a list of Florida auctioneers and any specialty they may designate. Select one in your area and call them about upcoming auctions they have scheduled and how you can get involved.

AUCTIONEERS IN THE STATE OF FLORIDA

NAME	ADDRESS	TELEPHONE	SPECIALTY
Hometown Realty of FL	1002 NW 23rd Ave., Gainesville, FL 32609	904-373-4490	VA Repossessions
Coburns Service & Auction	7545 N Palm Oak Dr., Hernando, FL 34442	800-326-0159	Will auction all types
Al-Mack Sales & Auction	P.O. Box 1521, Newberry, FL 32669	904-472-4842	Real estate
Fishers Auction Service	2032 Hibiscus Dr., Edgewater, FL 32141	904-428-4125	All types

Colyer & Sons	P.O. Box 765, Lk. Panasoffkee, FL	904-793-6584	Commercial & Residential
Wilkinson Auction	24329 S.R. 46, Sorrento, FL 32776	904-383-2282	All types
Rhema Realty, Inc.	791 NE 5th St., Crystal River, FL 34429	904-795-7357	All types
Gill Auctions, Inc.	115 Courthouse Square, Inverness, FL 34450	904-726-6610	All types
Florida Auction Service	5305 S. Pine Avenue, Ocala, FL 34480	904-732-6991	All types
Chuck's Auction & Co.	1031 NE Pine Isl. Rd., Ft. Myers, FL 33903	813-772-1111	All types
Cliff Schuler - Auctioneer	422 Julia St., Titusville, FL 32796	407-267-8563	All types
Hudson & Marshall	1197 US Hwy. 1, Rockledge, FL 32955	407-631-6959	Commercial
Moody's Auction	2455 Pluckebaum Rd., Cocoa, FL 32926	407-631-7668	All types
Tom Laws Auctioneering	4005 Alan Sheperd Ave., Cocoa, FL 32926	407-636-1834	All types
Rainbow Auction Service	20643 Pennsylvania Ave., Dunnellon, FL 34431	904-489-4110	All types
National Auction Co.	1325 S Congress Ave., Boynton Bch, FL 33426	407-364-7004 800-659-7004	Government Properties
Lafayete Auction Galleries	141 NW 20th St., Boca Raton, FL 33431	407-393-0012	All types
Stampler Auctions	2835 Hollywood Blvd., Hollywood, FL 33020	800-330-2437	All types
Hough Auction	1408 NE Capital Cr., Tallahassee, FL 32308	904-656-2696	All types
Auction Col. of Neal Van De Ree	205 E. Base Ave., Venice, FL 34285	813-488-1500	All types
Dietch & Co.	6302 Manatee Ave., Bradenton, FL 34209	813-798-9966	All types/Large co.
El Con Realty	4400 El Conquistador, Bradenton, FL 34210	813-753-6789	FDIC/FTC Properties
Bill Roye Auctioneers	501 Goodlette Rd., Naples, FL 33940	813-262-2437	All types
Hughes Realty & Auction	4852 Palm Beach Blvd., Ft. Myers, FL 33905	813-693-1774	All types
Williams Marketing	634 Green St., Gainesville, FL 30501	800-955-8881	All types
Phillip Pollack & Co.	3000 Dundee Rd., Northbrook, IL 60062	800-238-2588	Commercial Property
E G & G Dynatrend	1173 NW 159th Dr., Miami, FL 33169	305-621-5136	U.S. Customs Confiscations
Regenhold Auction Consultants, Inc.	611 S. Myrtle Ave., Clearwater, FL 34616	813-461-1666	All types
Prudential Florida Realty Auction Division	2101 W. Commercial Blvd., Ft. Lauderdale, FL 33309	800-327-5227	All types
Sheldon Good & Co.	1300 S.E. 17th St., Suite 216, Ft. Lauderdale, FL 33316	305-767-6006	All types
Brancon, Inc.	2959 Mercury Rd., Jacksonville, FL 32207	904-730-2911	All types
First Coast Auction & Realty	5562-2 Timuquana Rd., Jacksonville, FL 32210	904-772-0110	Mostly county surplus and other government property
Florida Auctioneer Academy	1212 E. Colonial Dr., Orlando, FL 32803	800-422-9155	All types
Kerr's Auction Service	8383 Ramona Blvd. W., Jacksonville, FL 32201	904-786-2617	All types
Continental Realty & Auction Services, Inc.	3107 Spring Glenn Rd., Suite 208, Jacksonville, FL 32207	904-398-6455	All types
Coast to Coast Auctions	235 S. Maitland Ave., Maitland, FL 32714	407-339-4333	All types
Martin Higgenbothem CAI	1666 Williamsburg Sq., Lakeland, FL 33803	813-644-6681	All types
Regal Auction Company	4510 S. Florida Ave., Lakeland, FL 33803	813-644-9600	Residential & Commercial
Auctions Unlimited	605 Marcum Rd., Lakeland, FL 33809	813-682-7447	Mostly residential
Dave Newman Auctioneers	13540 N. Florida Ave., Tampa, FL 33613	800-348-5894	All types
Kincaid Auction	3224 US Hwy. 92 E., Lakeland, FL 33801	813-666-1977	Residentials & Commercials
Phil Riner Auctions	1010 Lake Elbert Dr. S., Winter Haven, FL 33880	813-299-6031	All types

Campbell Auctioneers	1047 Bayshore Dr., Englewood, FL 34223	813-475-7166	All types
Landis Auction, Inc.	6323 14th St. W., Bradenton, FL 34207	813-755-2441	All types
Latham Auctioneers, Inc.	409 Hillcrest Dr., Bradenton, FL 34209	813-747-5380	Nationwide government auctions of large properties
Venice Auction	601 Spur St., Venice, FL 34292	813-485-4964	All types
Louis Boyleston Realty & Auctions, Inc.	114 W. Wright St., Pensacola, FL 32501	904-434-0377	All types
Deep Creek Auction	1145 Capricorn Blvd., Port Charlotte, FL 33980	813-743-6743	All types
Richard M. Williams Realty & Auction	1556 S. Hwy. 97, Cantonment, FL 32533	904-968-1744	All types
Best Realty & Auction Company	2100 Construction Blvd., Sarasota, FL 34231	813-922-2021	All types
Ron Rennick Auctions, Inc.	15 Royal Palm Blvd., Vero Beach, Fl 32960	800-330-5015	All types
Tavares Auction & Retail Outlet	28206 County Road 561, Tavares, FL 32778	904-742-2120	All types
ERA Tom Grizzard, Inc.	1330 W. Citizens Blvd., Suite 301, Leesburg, FL 34748	904-787-6966	All types
Auction Realty	114 Gardiner Ct., Daytona Beach, FL 32114	904-252-5778	All types
Mecca Properties Auctioneers	175 Standish Drive, Ormond Beach, FL 32176	800-423-7687	All types
Bob Vagi Auctioneers	2140 SW 114th Ave., Davie, FL 33325	305-472-7653	All types
Kennedy-Wilson, Inc.	521 S. Andrews Ave., Suite 15, Ft. Lauderdale, FL 33301	305-525-6610	All types
Auction World USA, Inc.	111 Monticello, Monroeville, PA 15146 (main office)	800-262-3050	All types
Kelley Waltman	852 Anastacia Blvd., St. Augustine, FL 32085	904-824-6075	Government & County Surplus
Helton Delmas	3704 S. US Hwy. 1, Fort Pierce, FL	407-468-1054	All types
Cynthia Logan, Inc.	17940-G Toledo Blade Blvd., Port Charlotte, FL 33948	813-255-1503	All types
Eagle Auction Co.	901 S. Federal Hwy., Suite 102, Ft. Lauderdale, FL 33316	305-525-0003	All types
Roger Jacobson, Inc.	2128 N. US Hwy. 1, Ft. Pierce, FL 34946	407-466-1930	All types

* MOST AUCTION COMPANIES' NUMBER OF EMPLOYEES WILL INCREASE TWO TO THREE TIMES ON AUCTION DAY BECAUSE OF TEMPORARY HELP (DEPENDING ON AUCTION SIZE).

Chapter 13

Florida Restaurant Companies

Ever since the first McDonalds made it big, many have had a secret longing to own a restaurant franchise. The only problem with that dream is that it requires you to be in the restaurant business. Investing in restaurant stocks may be the answer that scratches the proverbial itch. By buying the stock of a public company, you can have some of the satisfaction, most of the profit (or loss), and none of the headaches.

Florida is an attractive state for restaurant companies. Large population, higher income, good weather, and a decent economy are all factors that work in its favor.

Restaurants tend to be the good news/bad news industry of today's economy. Positives are lower interest rate costs and the fact that the economy is slowly improving. Negatives are additional labor cost concerns arising from health care reform.

Lower-priced, value-added menus are the definite trend in the restaurant industry. Chains that adapt to this kind of pricing are doing much better than the high-priced restaurants that exist on low-volume, big-ticket meals.

Demographics are beginning to work in favor of mid-scale restaurants as families and older Americans move away from eating at home. This older group of restaurant-goers will gravitate more toward sit-down, family-style operations. Fast-food restaurants realize they will need to expand their options as the younger population dwindles, comparatively.

Of all the industries examined in this book, restaurants show the greatest variation in success, largely because of the diversity among the alternatives. You can use this knowledge to find individual restaurant stock that will do well even when the general stock market is not.

Restaurant companies may be the perfect example of "backyard" investing. If you like a place, your kids like it, and your mother-in-law agrees, it stands to reason there is a profit potential somewhere.

BAYPORT RESTAURANT GROUP

Symbol: PORTD   Exchange: NMS

PRICE 3/4/94	RANGE	P-E RATIO	DIVIDEND	YIELD	BETA
$4\frac{1}{2}$	$4\frac{1}{2}$ - $7\frac{1}{8}$	28.13	0	0	0.8

LAST FOUR QUARTERS REPORTED

REVENUES	% CHANGE	NET INCOME	% CHANGE	RETURN ON EQUITY	% CHANGE
23.713	10.63	1.078	168.75	5.40	NA

Corporate Summary

Bayport Restaurant Group operates two businesses: (1) a restaurant business in which it presently owns and operates six full-service and three drive-through take-out type seafood restaurants; and (2) a seafood processing operation. The company's restaurants offer a full compliment of prepared seafood items and a limited number of non-seafood items.

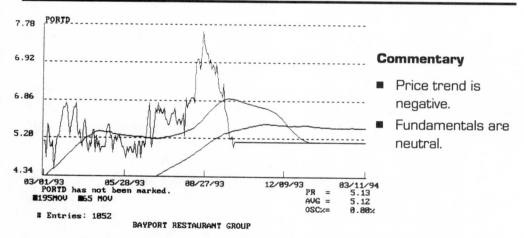

Commentary

- Price trend is negative.
- Fundamentals are neutral.

PORTD has not been marked.
■19SMOV ■65 MOV

PR = 5.13
AUG = 5.12
OSC%= 0.00%

Entries: 1852

BAYPORT RESTAURANT GROUP

YEAR	REVENUES	% CHANGE	NET INCOME	% CHANGE	RETURN ON EQUITY	% CHANGE
89	18.131	24.475	-0.466	-445.185	-9.6	-477.1
90	24.384	34.488	-0.046	NA	-1.1	NA
91	22.987	-5.729	-2.328	NA	-124.8	NA
92	20.100	-12.559	0.479	NA	12.1	NA

BENIHANA NATIONAL CORPORATION

Symbol: BNHN   Exchange: NMS

PRICE 3/4/94	RANGE	P-E RATIO	DIVIDEND	YIELD	BETA
3	$2^1\!/_{16}$ - $4^1\!/_8$	17.65	0	0	1.4

LAST FOUR QUARTERS REPORTED

REVENUES	% CHANGE	NET INCOME	% CHANGE	RETURN ON EQUITY	% CHANGE
40.455	8.11	0.950	26.50	7.34	17.19

Corporate Summary

Benihana National Corporation owns and operates 21 "Benihana" restaurants, five of which are located in Florida. The Benihana restaurants feature the teppanyaki style of Japanese cooking in which the food is prepared on a grill which forms a part of the table at which it is served. Most of the company's Benihana restaurants are open for both lunch and dinner.

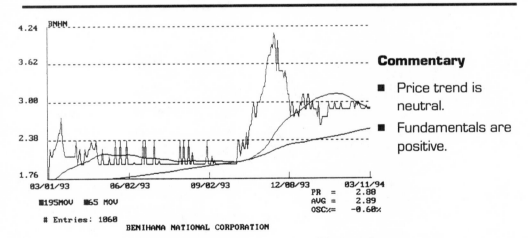

Commentary

■ Price trend is neutral.

■ Fundamentals are positive.

BENIHANA NATIONAL CORPORATION

YEAR	REVENUES	% CHANGE	NET INCOME	% CHANGE	RETURN ON EQUITY	% CHANGE
89	39.080	11.766	1.141	- 28.058	11.1	- 37.3
90	37.756	- 3.388	0.171	- 85.013	1.6	- 85.5
91	37.100	- 1.737	0.656	283.626	5.6	250.2
92	38.708	4.334	0.890	35.671	7.1	26.0

CHECKERS DRIVE-IN RESTAURANTS

Symbol: CHKR   Exchange: NMS

PRICE 3/4/94	RANGE	P-E RATIO	DIVIDEND	YIELD	BETA
11³⁄₈	10⁷⁄₈ - 15 ³⁄₁₆	36.34	0	0	0.6

LAST FOUR QUARTERS REPORTED

REVENUES	% CHANGE	NET INCOME	% CHANGE	RETURN ON EQUITY	% CHANGE
162.624	89.23	15.050	47.55	14.18	4.34

Corporate Summary

Checkers Drive-In Restaurants develops, produces, owns, operates, and franchises "double drive-thru" quick-service hamburger restaurants under the name "Checkers." The restaurants are designed around a distinctive 1950s diner and art deco theme that permits service of more than one automobile simultaneously from opposite sides of the restaurant.

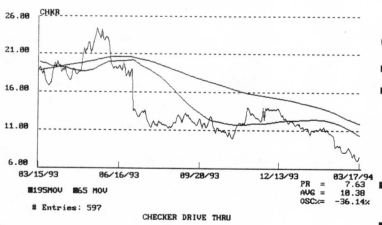

CHECKER DRIVE THRU

Commentary

■ Young company.

■ Good growth record, but much of revenue is due to franchise sales, not food.

■ Revenues are up and profits are up.

■ Volatile stock.

YEAR	REVENUES	% CHANGE	NET INCOME	% CHANGE	RETURN ON EQUITY	% CHANGE
89	NA	NA	NA	NA	NA	NA
90	22.925	NA	1.213	NA	106.1	NA
91	42.151	83.865	3.680	203.380	11.5	- 89.1
92	88.577	110.142	10.693	190.571	13.6	18.3

CLUCKER'S WOOD ROASTED CHICKEN

Symbol: CLUK   Exchange: OTC

PRICE 3/4/94	RANGE	P-E RATIO	DIVIDEND	YIELD	BETA
9½	6 $7/16$ - 11 $1/8$	NM	0	0	NA

LAST FOUR QUARTERS REPORTED

REVENUES	% CHANGE	NET INCOME	% CHANGE	RETURN ON EQUITY	% CHANGE
4.016	66.78	- 1.478	NA	- 62.28	NA

Corporate Summary

Clucker's Wood Roasted Chicken owns, operates, and franchises under
the name of "Cluckers," quick-service restaurants featuring marinated oak-
roasted rotisserie chicken. The company's operating philosophy is to provide higher quality, healthful, quick-service food rather than that
traditionally associated with the fast-food industry.

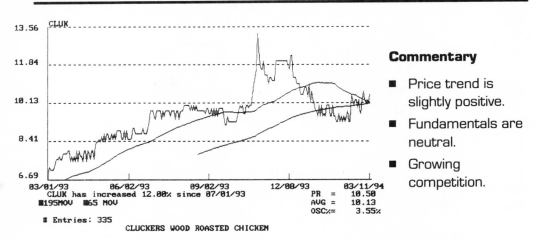

CLUK has increased 12.00% since 07/01/93
■195MOV ■65 MOV
PR = 10.50
AVG = 10.13
OSC%= 3.55%
Entries: 335

CLUCKERS WOOD ROASTED CHICKEN

Commentary

- Price trend is slightly positive.
- Fundamentals are neutral.
- Growing competition.

YEAR	REVENUES	% CHANGE	NET INCOME	% CHANGE	RETURN ON EQUITY	% CHANGE
89	NA	NA	NA	NA	NA	NA
90	NA	NA	NA	NA	NA	NA
91	1.833	NA	- 0.010	NA	- 10.2	NA
92	3.241	76.814	- 0.715	NA	- 22.0	NA

FAMILY STEAK HOUSES OF FLORIDA INCORPORATED

Symbol: RYFL   Exchange: NMS

PRICE 3/4/94	RANGE	P-E RATIO	DIVIDEND	YIELD	BETA
11/16	1/2 - 1	NM	0	0	0.9

LAST FOUR QUARTERS REPORTED

REVENUES	% CHANGE	NET INCOME	% CHANGE	RETURN ON EQUITY	% CHANGE
48.979	- 1.54	- 0.377	- 277.00	- 2.78	- 280.26

Corporate Summary

Family Steak Houses of Florida Incorporated is the exclusive franchisee of Ryan's Family Steak House restaurants in the state of Florida. A Ryan's restaurant is a family-oriented restaurant serving high-quality, reasonably-priced food in a casual atmosphere with cafeteria-style entry and some assistance with service. Ryan's restaurants serve lunch and dinner seven days a week and offer a variety of char broiled entrees.

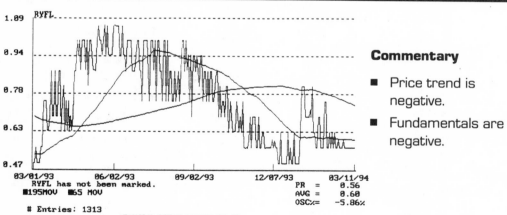

Commentary

- Price trend is negative.

- Fundamentals are negative.

RYFL has not been marked.
■195MOV ■65 MOV

PR = 0.56
AVG = 0.60
OSC%= -5.86%

Entries: 1313

FAMILY STEAK HOUSE OF FL

YEAR	REVENUES	% CHANGE	NET INCOME	% CHANGE	RETURN ON EQUITY	% CHANGE
89	45.772	35.697	1.057	- 31.050	8.3	- 37.1
90	48.116	5.121	0.091	- 91.391	0.7	- 91.5
91	48.518	0.835	0.376	313.187	2.8	300.0
92	49.694	2.424	0.291	- 22.606	2.1	- 25.0

LINIUM TECHNOLOGY INCORPORATED

Symbol: LINM   Exchange: OTC

PRICE 3/4/94	RANGE	P-E RATIO	DIVIDEND	YIELD	BETA
$\frac{1}{2}$	$\frac{1}{2} - 3\frac{3}{8}$	NM	0	0	NA

LAST FOUR QUARTERS REPORTED

REVENUES	% CHANGE	NET INCOME	% CHANGE	RETURN ON EQUITY	% CHANGE
6.578	8.46	- 1.559	NA	- 49.18	NA

Corporate Summary

Linium Technology is the holding company for a seafood restaurant chain by the name of "Cami's A Seafood Place." Cami's is a family-style, low-price restaurant which prides itself on quality service. Linium Technology is based in Miami and currently has three Cami's open in the Miami and South Miami areas.

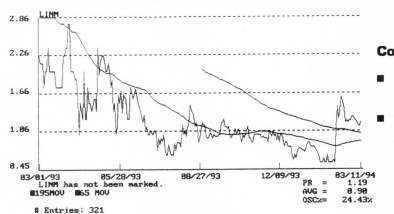

LINIUM TECHNOLOGY INC.

Commentary

- Price trend is neutral.
- Fundamentals are negative.

YEAR	REVENUES	% CHANGE	NET INCOME	% CHANGE	RETURN ON EQUITY	% CHANGE
89	.317	NA	- .354	NA	183.4	NA
90	.16	- 49.527	- .378	NA	106.5	- 41.9
91	2.805	1653.125	- .428	NA	- 79.9	- 175
92	6.49	131.373	- .583	NA	- 13.8	NA

MIAMI SUBS CORPORATION

Symbol: SUBS   Exchange: NMS

PRICE 3/4/94	RANGE	P-E RATIO	DIVIDEND	YIELD	BETA
4^{1}/16	2^{13}/16 - 4^{1}/16	03.10	0	0	1.2

LAST FOUR QUARTERS REPORTED

REVENUES	% CHANGE	NET INCOME	% CHANGE	RETURN ON EQUITY	% CHANGE
26.209	81.79	0.650	199.39	4.32	NA

Corporate Summary

Miami Subs Corp. operates and franchises quick-service restaurants across the United States, with one outlet in Cancun, Mexico. Miami Subs restaurants offer a moderately priced menu featuring food that is cooked to order. In addition, most of the restaurants offer beer, wine, and champagne.

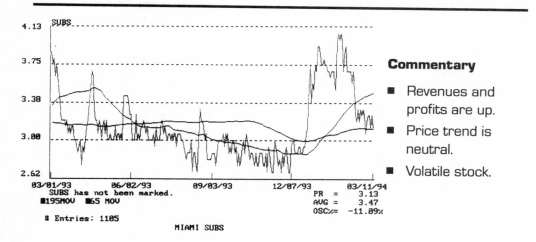

Commentary

- Revenues and profits are up.
- Price trend is neutral.
- Volatile stock.

YEAR	REVENUES	% CHANGE	NET INCOME	% CHANGE	RETURN ON EQUITY	% CHANGE
89	15.812	- 9.579	- 1.982	NA	- 173.3	NA
90	13.576	- 14.141	- .754	NA	- 189.9	NA
91	3.877	- 71.422	.006	NA	.7	NA
92	8.655	123.240	- .932	- 15633	- 6.5	- 975.9

OUTBACK STEAKHOUSE INCORPORATED

Symbol: OSSI   Exchange: NMS

PRICE 3/4/94	RANGE	P-E RATIO	DIVIDEND	YIELD	BETA
39½	26 - 39½	46.47	0	0	1.7

LAST FOUR QUARTERS REPORTED

REVENUES	% CHANGE	NET INCOME	% CHANGE	RETURN ON EQUITY	% CHANGE
271.164	60.00	23.702	56.69	20.64	- 17.06

Corporate Summary

Outback Steakhouse Incorporated operates 119 restaurants spreading across the United States in 22 states. The restaurants serve dinner only and feature a limited menu of high quality, uniquely seasoned steaks, prime rib, chops, ribs, chicken, fish and pasta, all served with an Aussie theme. Furthermore, the restaurants serve a unique assortment of appetizers.

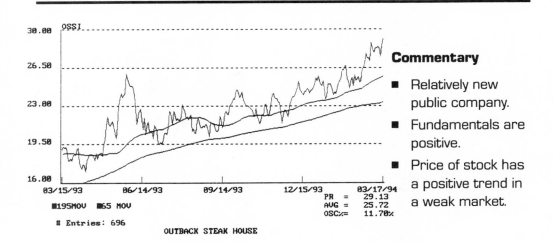

Commentary

- Relatively new public company.
- Fundamentals are positive.
- Price of stock has a positive trend in a weak market.

YEAR	REVENUES	% CHANGE	NET INCOME	% CHANGE	RETURN ON EQUITY	% CHANGE
89	NA	NA	NA	NA	NA	NA
90	22.713	NA	1.935	NA	61.6	NA
91	55.219	143.116	5.789	199.173	21.7	- 64.8
92	123.984	124.531	12.501	115.944	13.5	- 37.9

STACEY'S BUFFET INCORPORATED

Symbol: SBUF   Exchange: NMS

PRICE	RANGE	P-E RATIO	DIVIDEND	YIELD	BETA
3.69	3.88 - 2.00	NM	0	0	1.7

LAST FOUR QUARTERS REPORTED

REVENUES	% CHANGE	NET INCOME	% CHANGE	RETURN ON EQUITY	% CHANGE
37.038	- 26.17	- 10.091	NA	- 70.19	NA

Corporate Summary

Stacey's Buffet Incorporated owns and operates a line of restaurants throughout the state of Florida. The company's restaurants, operating under the name Stacey's Buffet, offer a broad selection of American and ethnic menu items as complete meals in a self-service, fixed-price buffet format. Stacey's currently operates thirty-four restaurants.

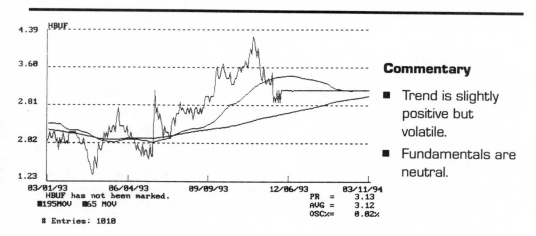

HBUF has not been marked.
■195MOV ■65 MOV

PR = 3.13
AVG = 3.12
OSC%= 0.02%

Entries: 1010

Commentary

■ Trend is slightly positive but volatile.

■ Fundamentals are neutral.

YEAR	REVENUES	% CHANGE	NET INCOME	% CHANGE	RETURN ON EQUITY	% CHANGE
89	22.891	122.135	1.268	122.067	8.7	11.6
90	41.119	79.630	1.149	- 9.385	4.5	- 48.2
91	49.447	20.253	- 0.856	- 174.50	- 3.4	- 176.2
92	48.933	- 1.039	- 9.760	NA	- 63.8	NA

TPI ENTERPRISES INCORPORATED

Symbol: TPIE   Exchange: NMS

PRICE 3/4/94	RANGE	P-E RATIO	DIVIDEND	YIELD	BETA
$9\frac{3}{8}$	$8\frac{5}{8}$ - $11\frac{7}{8}$	NM	0	0	0.8

LAST FOUR QUARTERS REPORTED

REVENUES	% CHANGE	NET INCOME	% CHANGE	RETURN ON EQUITY	% CHANGE
286.401	5.08	0.101	103.58	0.09	NA

Corporate Summary

TPI Enterprises Incorporated owns, operates, and franchises 199 Shoneys restaurants and 71 Captain D's fast-food restaurants, predominantly
throughout the southeastern United States. Shoneys serves a variety of
American food via buffet as well as table service, while Captain D's serves
mostly seafood. TPI Enterprises is the largest franchise owner for Shoneys in the United States.

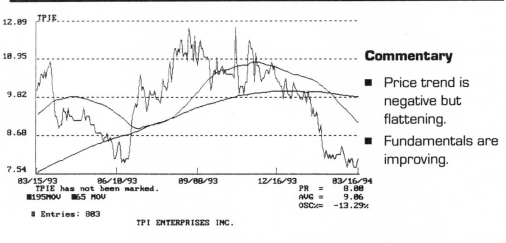

Commentary

- Price trend is negative but flattening.

- Fundamentals are improving.

TPIE has not been marked.
■195MOV ■65 MOV
PR = 8.00
AVG = 9.06
OSC%= -13.29%

Entries: 803

TPI ENTERPRISES INC.

YEAR	REVENUES	% CHANGE	NET INCOME	% CHANGE	RETURN ON EQUITY	% CHANGE
89	350.066	121.142	- 9.020	- 941.418	- 8.1	- 1035.3
90	397.194	13.463	1.528	NA	1.4	NA
91	262.612	- 33.88	- 12.053	- 888.809	- 12.4	- 995.6
92	279.430	6.404	0.662	NA	0.8	NA

Chapter 14

Florida Health Care Companies

The health care industry lived in a state of confusion for much of 1993 because of the looming changes that will be brought on by health care reform. Contrarian investors will have a field day picking over the companies that have good balance sheets but were sucked down by the price decline of the entire industry.

My near-term projections for the industry are neutral. Although I believe it has taken most of its lumps, until the health reform shake up is more defined, actual direction and timing will remain uncertain. Once we have a clear picture of what reform will ultimately mean, we expect to see some companies experiencing tremendous gains. This is one industry that deserves close watching because it has been beaten down more than it should have been.

Drugs

It appears that health care reform will not mean price controls on drugs. That does not mean major buying groups aren't doing everything they can to negotiate lower prices and increase the use of generic drugs. Stock prices seem to be firming as investors perceive that the worst is over.

Health Care Management

In the long run, HMOs will probably emerge as winners under the new health care plan. Over 37 million Americans are without health insurance, and HMOs have proven the best at providing affordable care. Other service providers and companies in diagnostic services are less certain where they stand. Prices at the start of 1994 were on the upswing after having been beaten down.

Medical Supplies

The country's demographics and aging population will begin to work in favor of this industry. Additionally, technology is yielding new methods of disease detection and prevention. The result is a steady flow of new product.

BELMAC CORPORATION

Symbol: BLM   Exchange: ASE

PRICE 3/4/94	RANGE	P-E RATIO	DIVIDEND	YIELD	BETA
$2\frac{1}{4}$	$1\frac{3}{4}$ - $5\frac{3}{8}$	NM	0	0	1.0

LAST FOUR QUARTERS REPORTED

REVENUES	% CHANGE	NET INCOME	% CHANGE	RETURN ON EQUITY	% CHANGE
18.725	116.77	- 11.456	NA	- 175.09	NA

Corporate Summary

Belmac Corporation is an international pharmaceutical company based in Tampa, FL, engaged in the research, development, marketing, and distribution of pharmaceutical products. The company also has chemical and pharmaceutical operations in France and Spain. Belmac is currently developing a portfolio of five pharmaceutical products, with a primary focus in anti-infectives.

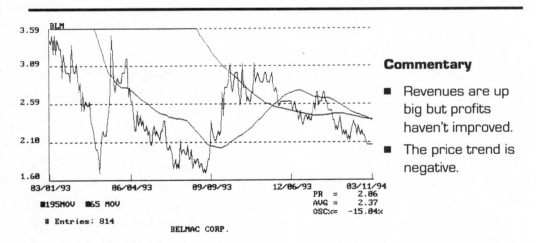

BELMAC CORP.

Commentary

- Revenues are up big but profits haven't improved.
- The price trend is negative.

YEAR	REVENUES	% CHANGE	NET INCOME	% CHANGE	RETURN ON EQUITY	% CHANGE
89	0.001	- 96.429	- 2.479	NA	- 657.6	NA
90	0.021	200.000	- 2.492	NA	- 140.6	NA
91	0.000	- 100.000	- 2.476	NA	- 111.0	NA
92	13.138	NC	- 10.811	NA	- 62.3	NA

COLUMBIA LABORATORIES INCORPORATED

Symbol: COB   Exchange: ASE

PRICE 3/4/94	RANGE	P-E RATIO	DIVIDEND	YIELD	BETA
5¾	4¹⁄₁₆ - 6	NM	0	0	1.9

LAST FOUR QUARTERS REPORTED

REVENUES	% CHANGE	NET INCOME	% CHANGE	RETURN ON EQUITY	% CHANGE
8.235	- 16.23	- 9.797	NA	- 250.31	NA

Corporate Summary

Columbia Laboratories Incorporated develops, on a worldwide basis, women's prescription and over-the-counter products which utilize the company's patented bioadhesive delivery technology. Formulated products using this system consist principally of a polymer, a polycarbophil, and an active ingredient.

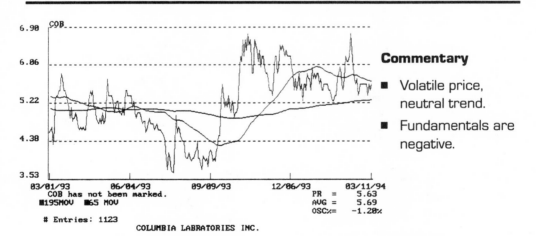

Commentary

- Volatile price, neutral trend.
- Fundamentals are negative.

COLUMBIA LABRATORIES INC.

YEAR	REVENUES	% CHANGE	NET INCOME	% CHANGE	RETURN ON EQUITY	% CHANGE
89	5.801	217.341	- 5.101	NA	- 51.1	NA
90	12.139	109.257	- 16.548	NA	413.3	NA
91	10.675	- 12.060	- 14.548	NA	2020.6	388.9
92	9.173	- 14.070	- 8.536	NA	122.1	- 94.0

CORDIS CORPORATION

Symbol: CORD   Exchange: NMS

PRICE 3/4/94	RANGE	P-E RATIO	DIVIDEND	YIELD	BETA
51³/₄	22⁷/₈ - 51³/₄	23.10	0	0	1.2

LAST FOUR QUARTERS REPORTED

REVENUES	% CHANGE	NET INCOME	% CHANGE	RETURN ON EQUITY	% CHANGE
275.518	13.84	32.588	21.95	18.97	- 6.84

Corporate Summary

Cordis Corporation designs and manufactures angiographic devices, neuroscience systems, and other specialized medical products. The company's main source of revenue is derived from the manufacturing and sale of angiographic devices, a market that Cordis dominates. The company is based in Miami Lakes, FL.

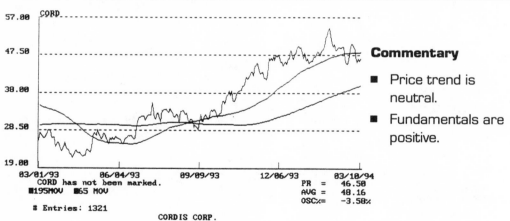

Commentary

- Price trend is neutral.
- Fundamentals are positive.

CORD has not been marked.
■195MOV ■65 MOV
PR = 46.50
AVG = 48.16
OSC%= -3.58%

Entries: 1321

CORDIS CORP.

YEAR	REVENUES	% CHANGE	NET INCOME	% CHANGE	RETURN ON EQUITY	% CHANGE
89	141.220	15.900	6.549	30.070	12.6	47.1
90	163.674	21.526	10.157	55.092	14.6	16.2
91	198.907	21.526	19.332	90.332	24.3	66.5
92	222.959	12.092	24.014	24.219	20.7	- 15.0

HEALTHINFUSION INCORPORATED

Symbol: HINF   Exchange: NMS

PRICE	RANGE	P-E RATIO	DIVIDEND	YIELD	BETA
$6\frac{7}{8}$	$5\frac{1}{2} - 10\frac{3}{4}$	11.65	0	0	2.6

LAST FOUR QUARTERS REPORTED

REVENUES	% CHANGE	NET INCOME	% CHANGE	RETURN ON EQUITY	% CHANGE
54.325	16.79	5.650	- 7.41	9.90	- 27.82

Corporate Summary

HealthInfusion Incorporated and subsidiaries is a national provider of home infusion therapy services and currently operates 31 branch facilities serving 26 states. Infusion therapy is the administration to a patient of nutrients, antibiotics, or other medications either intravenously or through a feeding tube. The company's services include educating patients and their caregivers as well as compounding prescriptions and conducting other pharmacy operations.

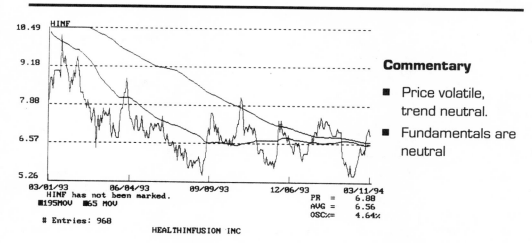

```
10.49  HINF




9.18




7.88




6.57




5.26
     03/01/93      06/04/93      09/09/93      12/06/93      03/11/94
       HINF has not been marked.                  PR  =  6.88
     ■19SMOV  ■65 MOV                              AVG =  6.56
                                                   OSC%=  4.64%
       # Entries: 968
              HEALTHINFUSION INC
```

Commentary

- Price volatile, trend neutral.
- Fundamentals are neutral

YEAR	REVENUES	% CHANGE	NET INCOME	% CHANGE	RETURN ON EQUITY	% CHANGE
89	NA	NA	NA	NA	NA	NA
90	10.388	NA	2.284	NA	27.7	NA
91	28.603	175.347	4.217	84.632	13.7	- 50.5
92	49.749	73.929	6.322	49.917	13.2	- 4.0

HEALTH MANAGEMENT ASSOCIATES INCORPORATED

Symbol: HMA   Exchange: NYS

PRICE 3/4/94	RANGE	P-E RATIO	DIVIDEND	YIELD	BETA
32³/₈	12¹/₂ - 32³/₈	27.51	0	0	1.2

LAST FOUR QUARTERS REPORTED

REVENUES	% CHANGE	NET INCOME	% CHANGE	RETURN ON EQUITY	% CHANGE
368.423	25.78	35.484	51.03	18.42	6.10

Corporate Summary

Health Management Associates Incorporated provides a broad range of general acute care health services in nonurban communities. The company is currently operating 13 general acute care hospitals and three psychiatric hospitals. The acute care hospital operations account for approximately 88 percent of net operating revenues and the psychiatric hospital operations about 12 percent.

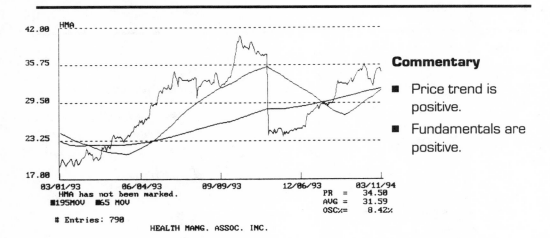

Commentary

- Price trend is positive.
- Fundamentals are positive.

HMA has not been marked.
■195MOV ■65 MOV

PR = 34.50
AVG = 31.59
OSC%=   8.42%

Entries: 790

HEALTH MANG. ASSOC. INC.

YEAR	REVENUES	% CHANGE	NET INCOME	% CHANGE	RETURN ON EQUITY	% CHANGE
89	141.970	17.992	1.980	- 67.450	12.2	- 71.2
90	191.661	35.001	4.644	134.545	22.1	81.5
91	266.140	17.990	11.991	158.204	15.8	- 28.4
92	277.961	22.915	21.881	82.479	16.2	2.3

HEALTH PROFESSIONAL INCORPORATED

Symbol: HPI   Exchange: ASE

PRICE 3/4/94	RANGE	P-E RATIO	DIVIDEND	YIELD	BETA
$^7/_8$	$^7/_8$ - 12$^3/_8$	NM	0	0	0.9

LAST FOUR QUARTERS REPORTED

REVENUES	% CHANGE	NET INCOME	% CHANGE	RETURN ON EQUITY	% CHANGE
7.994	74.35	- 2.571	NA	- 23.50	NA

Corporate Summary

Health Professionals Incorporated, along with its subsidiaries, currently operates in three businesses. The company's primary focus is the development, ownership, and innovation of patient care facilities to treat immunological and related diseases. They also engage in the study of various medical, nutritional, psychological, and pharmaceutical treatments to determine their effectiveness in treating such patients.

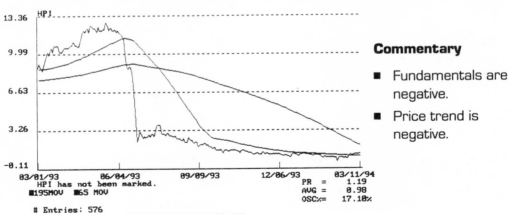

```
13.36  HPI
 9.99
 6.63
 3.26
-0.11
      03/01/93      06/04/93      09/09/93      12/06/93      03/11/94
      HPI has not been marked.                        PR  =   1.19
      ■195MOV  ■65 MOV                                AVG =   0.98
                                                      OSC%=  17.18%
      # Entries: 576
                  HEALTH PROFESSIONALS INC.
```

Commentary

- Fundamentals are negative.
- Price trend is negative.

YEAR	REVENUES	% CHANGE	NET INCOME	% CHANGE	RETURN ON EQUITY	% CHANGE
89	24.485	- 25.273	1.321	295.509	20.0	216.0
90	18.973	- 22.512	- 3.624	- 374.338	- 121.4	- 707.1
91	18.888	- 0.488	- 2.995	NA	- 36.8	NA
92	4.585	- 75.725	- 2.615	NA	- 29.8	NA

HEART LABS AMERICA INCORPORATED

Symbol: HLOA   Exchange: OTC

PRICE 3/4/94	RANGE	P-E RATIO	DIVIDEND	YIELD	BETA
$4\frac{1}{2}$	$4 - 4^{15}/_{16}$	NM	0	0	NA

LAST FOUR QUARTERS REPORTED

REVENUES	% CHANGE	NET INCOME	% CHANGE	RETURN ON EQUITY	% CHANGE
2.342	- 11.66	- 0.292	- 180.44	- 6.21	- 102.74

Corporate Summary

Heart Labs America Incorporated is currently engaged in providing mobile cardiac catheterization services to hospitals on a shared user basis. The company currently operates three mobile cardiac catheterization units, sometimes referred to as "Mobil Units." The company has been in business since 1990 and is based in Boca Raton.

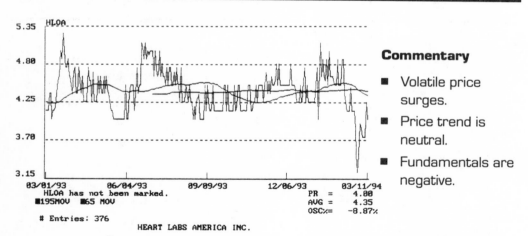

Commentary

- Volatile price surges.
- Price trend is neutral.
- Fundamentals are negative.

HLOA has not been marked.
■195MOV ■65 MOV
PR = 4.80
AVG = 4.35
OSC%= -8.87%

Entries: 376

HEART LABS AMERICA INC.

YEAR	REVENUES	% CHANGE	NET INCOME	% CHANGE	RETURN ON EQUITY	% CHANGE
89	NA	NA	NA	NA	NA	NA
90	NA	NA	NA	NA	NA	NA
91	1.462	NA	0.235	NA	- 840.4	NA
92	2.891	97.743	0.226	- 3.830	5.5	NA

HOME INTENSIVE CARE INCORPORATED

Symbol: HICI   Exchange: NMS

PRICE 3/4/94	RANGE	P-E RATIO	DIVIDEND	YIELD	BETA
NA	$5\frac{1}{4}$ - $6\frac{1}{2}$	NA	0	NA	NA

LAST FOUR QUARTERS REPORTED

REVENUES	% CHANGE	NET INCOME	% CHANGE	RETURN ON EQUITY	% CHANGE
94.210	39.39	- 12.753	- 402.71	- 50.73	- 492.21

Corporate Summary

Home Intensive Care Incorporated is currently providing health care serv-ices to its critical care patients at home. The company provides registered nurses and other professional medical personnel. Other serv-ices like respiratory therapy are also provided. The company expects to grow and to capture a good market share of the projected growth in eld-erly care needs.

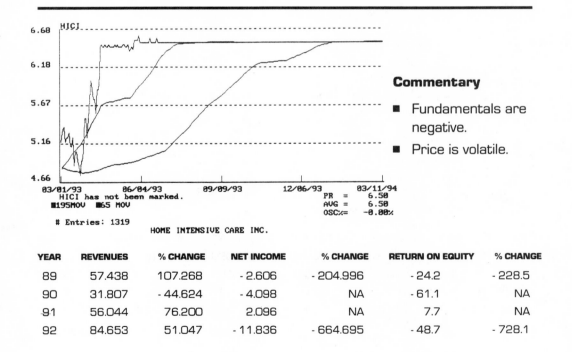

Commentary

- Fundamentals are negative.
- Price is volatile.

HICI has not been marked.
■195MOV ■65 MOV

PR = 6.50
AVG = 6.50
OSC% = -0.00%

Entries: 1319

HOME INTENSIVE CARE INC.

YEAR	REVENUES	% CHANGE	NET INCOME	% CHANGE	RETURN ON EQUITY	% CHANGE
89	57.438	107.268	- 2.606	- 204.996	- 24.2	- 228.5
90	31.807	- 44.624	- 4.098	NA	- 61.1	NA
91	56.044	76.200	2.096	NA	7.7	NA
92	84.653	51.047	- 11.836	- 664.695	- 48.7	- 728.1

HOSPITAL STAFFING SERVICES INCORPORATED

Symbol: HSS   Exchange: NYS

PRICE 3/4/94	RANGE	P-E RATIO	DIVIDEND	YIELD	BETA
$2\frac{1}{2}$	$1\frac{7}{8}$ - 5	NM	0	0	2.4

LAST FOUR QUARTERS REPORTED

REVENUES	% CHANGE	NET INCOME	% CHANGE	RETURN ON EQUITY	% CHANGE
89.95	- 24.93	- 10.475	- 464.98	- 53.63	- 648.97

Corporate Summary

Hospital Staffing Services Incorporated is a provider of home health care services offering a broad range of professional and support services to meet patients' medical and personal needs at home. The company is also a professional recruiter of registered nurses and other medical personnel, often referred to as "Travel Nurses," for provision to hospitals.

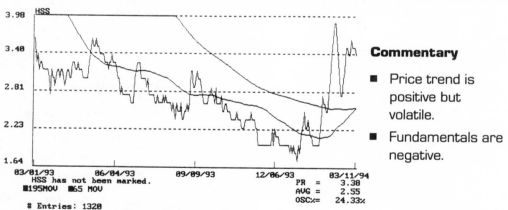

Commentary

- Price trend is positive but volatile.
- Fundamentals are negative.

HSS has not been marked.
■195MOU   ■65 MOU

PR = 3.38
AVG = 2.55
OSC%= 24.33%

Entries: 1320

HOSPITAL STAFF SERV. INC.

YEAR	REVENUES	% CHANGE	NET INCOME	% CHANGE	RETURN ON EQUITY	% CHANGE
89	24.285	62.376	1.614	107.990	14.1	- 20.0
90	38.532	58.666	1.208	- 25.155	8.9	- 37.0
91	90.121	133.886	2.711	124.421	10.0	12.5
92	120.591	33.810	- 3.185	- 217.484	- 12.8	- 227.9

IVAX CORPORATION

Symbol: IVX   Exchange: ASE

PRICE 3/4/94	RANGE	P-E RATIO	DIVIDEND	YIELD	BETA
32⅛	23¼ - 32⅛	31.81	0.02	0	0.9

LAST FOUR QUARTERS REPORTED

REVENUES	% CHANGE	NET INCOME	% CHANGE	RETURN ON EQUITY	% CHANGE
595.914	40.64	72.406	97.97	18.85	- 27.45

Corporate Summary

Ivax Corporation is a fully integrated pharmaceutical company engaged in the research, development, manufacturing, and marketing of novel and generic pharmaceuticals for human and animal use. The company's pharmaceutical business has grown through the development and acquisition of brand-name, generic, and over-the-counter products.

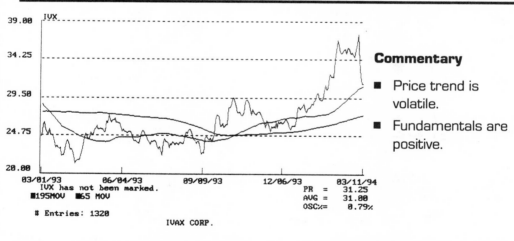

IVAX CORP.

Commentary

- Price trend is volatile.
- Fundamentals are positive.

YEAR	REVENUES	% INCREASE	NET INCOME	% INCREASE	RETURN ON EQUITY	% INCREASE
89	63.048	3.544	- 8.212	NA	- 16.1	NA
90	141.548	124.508	- 0.760	NA	- 1.3	NA
91	181.623	28.312	11.093	NA	5.5	NA
92	451.033	148.335	44.605	302.100	17.2	211.6

LINCARE HOLDINGS INCORPORATED

Symbol: LNCR   Exchange: NMS

PRICE 3/4/94	RANGE	P-E RATIO	DIVIDEND	YIELD	BETA
22	12$\frac{1}{4}$ - 24$\frac{7}{8}$	21.78	0	0	NA

LAST FOUR QUARTERS REPORTED

REVENUES	% CHANGE	NET INCOME	% CHANGE	RETURN ON EQUITY	% CHANGE
154.506	31.60	28.252	75.05	26.67	10.89

Corporate Summary

Lincare Holding Incorporated and subsidiaries is one of the nation's largest providers of oxygen and other respiratory therapy services to patients in the home. The company's customers typically suffer from chronic obstructive pulmonary disease and require supplemental oxygen or other respiratory therapy services in order to alleviate the symptoms.

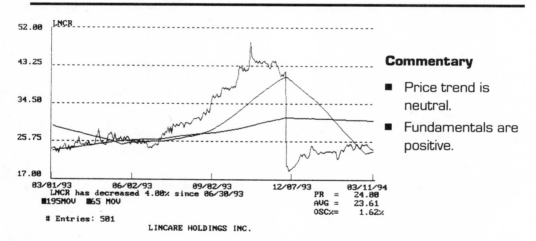

Commentary

- Price trend is neutral.

- Fundamentals are positive.

LNCR has decreased 4.00% since 06/30/93
195MOV 65 MOV

PR = 24.00
AVG = 23.61
OSC%= 1.62%

Entries: 501

LINCARE HOLDINGS INC.

YEAR	REVENUES	% CHANGE	NET INCOME	% CHANGE	RETURN ON EQUITY	% CHANGE
89	NA	NA	NA	NA	NA	NA
90	NA	NA	NA	NA	NA	NA
91	88.634	NA	2.847	NA	42.2	NA
92	117.403	32.458	16.139	466.877	19.6	- 53.8

MEDICAL TECHNOLOGY SYSTEMS INCORPORATED

Symbol: MSYS   Exchange: NMS

PRICE 3/4/94	RANGE	P-E RATIO	DIVIDEND	YIELD	BETA
9¼	7½ - 10⅞	13.81	0	0	1.2

LAST FOUR QUARTERS REPORTED

REVENUES	% CHANGE	NET INCOME	% CHANGE	RETURN ON EQUITY	% CHANGE
17.739	24.38	2.602	24.44	16.76	0.41

Corporate Summary

Medical Technology Systems Incorporated is a manufacturer and distributor of the latest medication dispensing systems. This company is based in Clearwater, Florida, and does business in the continental United States. It expects to attract some international business in developing countries.

83/01/93   06/02/93   89/02/93   12/07/93   03/11/94
MSYS has not been marked.
■195MOV ■65 MOV

PR = 7.75
AVG = 8.39
OSC%= -8.26%

\# Entries: 808

MEDICAL TECHNOLOGY SYSTEMS

Commentary

■ Price trend is neutral.

■ Fundamentals are positive.

YEAR	REVENUES	% CHANGE	NET INCOME	% CHANGE	RETURN ON EQUITY	% CHANGE
89	3.402	59.944	0.614	92.476	16.5	3.3
90	4.886	43.621	0.917	49.349	19.9	20.9
91	7.500	53.500	1.476	60.960	14.1	- 29.4
92	15.978	113.040	2.292	55.285	16.8	19.3

MEDICORE INCORPORATED

Symbol: MDK   Exchange: ASE

PRICE 3/4/94	RANGE	P-E RATIO	DIVIDEND	YIELD	BETA
1⅛	½ - 1⅛	NM	0	0	1.7

LAST FOUR QUARTERS REPORTED

REVENUES	% CHANGE	NET INCOME	% CHANGE	RETURN ON EQUITY	% CHANGE
17.993	0.78	- 1.144	NA	- 20.84	NA

Corporate Summary

Medicore Incorporated is engaged in the manufacture and distribution of medical supplies, through recently initiated consumer products division, as well as the operation of a kidney dialysis center through its subsidiary, Dialysis Corporation of America. It also engages in the manufacture, assembly, and distribution of electronic and electro-mechanical components through its majority-owned public subsidiary, Viragen, Inc.

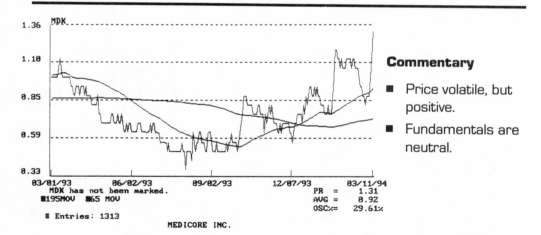

Commentary

- Price volatile, but positive.
- Fundamentals are neutral.

MDK has not been marked.
■19SMOV ■65 MOV
PR = 1.31
AVG = 0.92
OSC%= 29.61%

Entries: 1313

MEDICORE INC.

YEAR	REVENUES	% CHANGE	NET INCOME	% CHANGE	RETURN ON EQUITY	% CHANGE
89	23.938	18.935	- 0.553	NA	- 5.5	NA
90	19.397	- 18.970	- 1.809	NA	- 21.0	NA
91	17.460	- 9.986	- 1.493	NA	- 20.6	NA
92	18.322	4.937	- 0.901	NA	- 14.8	NA

NEOLENS INCORPORATED

Symbol: NEOL   Exchange: OTC

PRICE 3/4/94	RANGE	P-E RATIO	DIVIDEND	YIELD	BETA
1¼	½ - 1½	NM	0	0	1.9

LAST FOUR QUARTERS REPORTED

REVENUES	% CHANGE	NET INCOME	% CHANGE	RETURN ON EQUITY	% CHANGE
3.495	55.33	- 3.159	NA	- 439.98	NA

Corporate Summary

Neolens Incorporated is engaged in the manufacturing and marketing of ophthalmic eyeglass lenses from a plastic product known as polycarbonate. Utilizing its proprietary production method on which U.S. patents have been issued, the company believes it can produce high quality lenses which are competitively priced for the sunwear and the prescription lens markets.

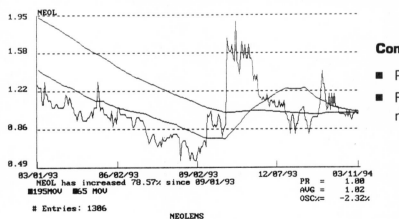

Commentary

- Price trend is flat.
- Fundamentals are negative.

NEOL has increased 78.57% since 09/01/93
■195MOV ■65 MOV

PR   =   1.00
AVG =   1.02
OSC% = -2.32%

Entries: 1306

NEOLENS

YEAR	REVENUES	% CHANGE	NET INCOME	% CHANGE	RETURN ON EQUITY	% CHANGE
89	0.382	87.255	- 2.265	NA	- 41.4	NA
90	1.122	193.717	- 2.935	NA	- 56.1	NA
91	1.860	65.775	- 2.836	NA	- 58.4	NA
92	2.597	39.642	- 4.034	NA	- 247.5	NA

NORTH AMERICAN BIOLOGICALS INCORPORATED

Symbol: NBIO   Exchange: NMS

PRICE 3/4/94	RANGE	P-E RATIO	DIVIDEND	YIELD	BETA
$4\frac{3}{8}$	$2\frac{1}{4}$ - $4\frac{3}{8}$	17.50	0	0	- 0.6

LAST FOUR QUARTERS REPORTED

REVENUES	% CHANGE	NET INCOME	% CHANGE	RETURN ON EQUITY	% CHANGE
101.574	23.34	3.405	694.24	20.68	NA

Corporate Summary

North American Biologicals Incorporated is a manufacturer and distributor of medical laboratory supplies. Demographics are working in favor of
the company. The number of people over fifty in the U.S. is projected to
rise 50 percent over the next twenty years. This type of growth should
help with the kind of supplies North American Biological provides to major
hospitals and smaller clinics.

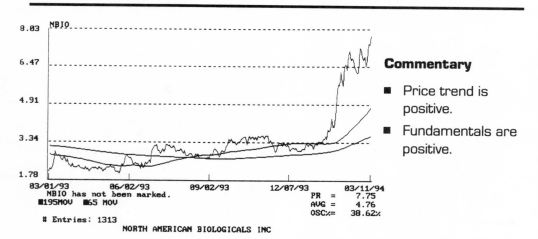

```
8.03   NBIO
6.47
4.91
3.34
1.78
    03/01/93      06/02/93      09/02/93      12/07/93      03/11/94
       NBIO has not been marked.                    PR  =    7.75
    ■19SMOV  ■65 MOV                                AVG =    4.76
                                                    OSC%=   38.62%
       # Entries: 1313
              NORTH AMERICAN BIOLOGICALS INC
```

Commentary

- Price trend is positive.

- Fundamentals are positive.

YEAR	REVENUES	% CHANGE	NET INCOME	% CHANGE	RETURN ON EQUITY	% CHANGE
89	59.225	26.712	0.815	291.827	8.4	238.0
90	72.822	22.958	2.212	171.411	18.4	117.8
91	68.230	- 6.306	2.217	0.226	14.7	- 19.9
92	82.354	20.701	- 0.573	- 125.846	- 4.1	- 127.9

OCEAN OPTIQUE DISTRIBUTORS

Symbol: OPTQ   Exchange: OTC

PRICE 3/4/94	RANGE	P-E RATIO	DIVIDEND	YIELD	BETA
$4^{5}/_{8}$	$4^{1}/_{8}$ - 6	12.43	0	0	0

LAST FOUR QUARTERS REPORTED

REVENUES	% CHANGE	NET INCOME	% CHANGE	RETURN ON EQUITY	% CHANGE
10.334	167.93	0.474	- 19.25	11.57	- 28.49

Corporate Summary

Ocean Optique Distributors is a company based in Miami, Florida, that has a niche market in eyeglass frames. This company is in the business of acquiring and distributing eyeglass frames that are manufactured and imported from developing countries. The company distribution systems and pricing strategy help maintain a healthy profit margin.

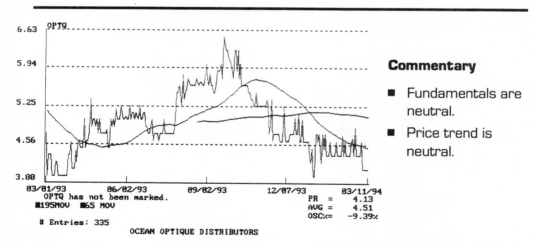

OCEAN OPTIQUE DISTRIBUTORS

Commentary

■ Fundamentals are neutral.

■ Price trend is neutral.

YEAR	REVENUES	% CHANGE	NET INCOME	% CHANGE	RETURN ON EQUITY	% CHANGE
89	NA	NA	NA	NA	NA	NA
90	NA	NA	NA	NA	NA	NA
91	2.899	NA	0.059	NA	10.6	NA
92	3.714	28.113	0.255	332.203	7.9	- 26.3

PHARMACY MANAGEMENT SERVICES

Symbol: PMSV   Exchange: NMS

PRICE 3/4/94	RANGE	P-E RATIO	DIVIDEND	YIELD	BETA
6½	5 - 7¾	19.70	0	0	2.1

LAST FOUR QUARTERS REPORTED

REVENUES	% CHANGE	NET INCOME	% CHANGE	RETURN ON EQUITY	% CHANGE
109.150	- 0.23	2.830	233.68	8.52	NA

Corporate Summary

Pharmacy Management Services and subsidiaries is a leading independent national provider of medical products and cost containment services to workers' compensation payers and claimants. The company provides substantially all of the workers' compensation claimant's needs, from the time of the job-related injury, through home care or return to employment.

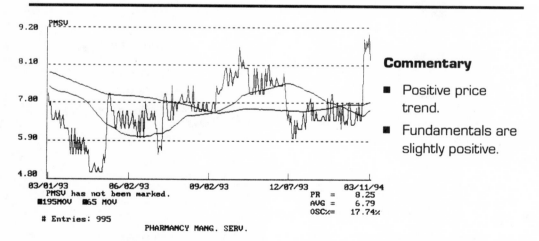

PMSV has not been marked.
■19SMOV ■6S MOV
# Entries: 995
PR = 8.25
AVG = 6.79
OSC% = 17.74%

PHARMANCY MANG. SERV.

Commentary

■ Positive price trend.

■ Fundamentals are slightly positive.

YEAR	REVENUES	% CHANGE	NET INCOME	% CHANGE	RETURN ON EQUITY	% CHANGE
89	NA	NA	NA	NA	NA	NA
90	55.681	NA	1.969	NA	6.8	NA
91	81.686	46.704	1.893	- 3.860	5.9	- 14.3
92	106.116	29.907	- 2.011	- 20.6234	- 6.7	- 214.5

RAMSAY HMO INCORPORATED

Symbol: RMO   Exchange: NYS

PRICE 3/4/94	RANGE	P-E RATIO	DIVIDEND	YIELD	BETA
42 1/8	25 - 42 1/8	22.17	0	0	2.0

LAST FOUR QUARTERS REPORTED

REVENUES	% CHANGE	NET INCOME	% CHANGE	RETURN ON EQUITY	% CHANGE
314.675	34.58	14.732	62.70	13.46	- 15.05

Corporate Summary

Ramsay HMO Incorporated is a leading managed care company in south
Florida which owns and operates a health maintenance organization with
an aggregate 132,582 members. The company provides its HMO services in the Miami (Dade County) and Ft. Lauderdale (Broward County) areas primarily through its 14 staffed model health care centers and a
modified independent practice association.

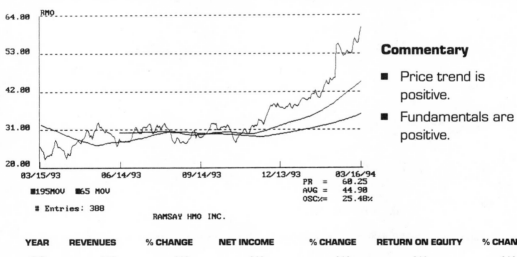

Commentary

- Price trend is positive.
- Fundamentals are positive.

RAMSAY HMO INC.

YEAR	REVENUES	% CHANGE	NET INCOME	% CHANGE	RETURN ON EQUITY	% CHANGE
89	NA	NA	NA	NA	NA	NA
90	108.308	NA	3.216	NA	17.9	NA
91	142.151	31.247	4.742	47.450	12.3	- 30.9
92	199.677	40.468	7.513	58.435	14.6	18.1

ROTECH MEDICAL CORPORATION
Symbol: ROTC   Exchange: NMS

PRICE 3/4/94	RANGE	P-E RATIO	DIVIDEND	YIELD	BETA
17½	11 -17½	21.88	0	0	2.2

LAST FOUR QUARTERS REPORTED

REVENUES	% CHANGE	NET INCOME	% CHANGE	RETURN ON EQUITY	% CHANGE
51.577	28.54	5.529	38.47	14.52	- 31.07

Corporate Summary

RoTech Medical Corporation provides home infusion therapy, home respiratory care, and other medical services and equipment. A patient base is referred to RoTech principally by primary care physicians in smaller cities and rural areas. RoTech operates strictly in the home health care market exclusive of durable medical equipment. RoTech is based in Orlando, Florida.

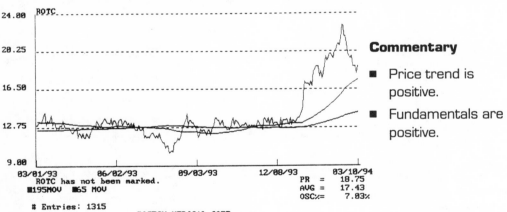

Commentary

- Price trend is positive.
- Fundamentals are positive.

ROTC has not been marked.
■195MOV ■65 MOV

PR = 18.75
AVG = 17.43
OSC%= 7.83%

Entries: 1315

ROTECH MEDICAL CORP.

YEAR	REVENUES	% CHANGE	NET INCOME	% CHANGE	RETURN ON EQUITY	% CHANGE
89	12.830	33.727	0.751	NA	27.1	NA
90	16.830	31.413	1.371	82.557	30.7	13.4
91	24.295	44.355	2.169	58.206	15.9	- 48.4
92	37.112	52.797	3.686	69.940	21.0	32.6

ROYCE LABORATORIES INCORPORATED

Symbol: RLAB   Exchange: OTC

PRICE 3/4/94	RANGE	P-E RATIO	DIVIDEND	YIELD	BETA
$7^3/_4$	$5^7/_{16}$ - $8^1/_4$	NM	0	0	1.0

LAST FOUR QUARTERS REPORTED

REVENUES	% CHANGE	NET INCOME	% CHANGE	RETURN ON EQUITY	% CHANGE
3.249	28.32	- 3.316	NA	- 67.38	NA

Corporate Summary

Royce Laboratories Incorporated is one of the largest manufacturers and distributors of pharmaceuticals in the Southeast. The company's target market is senior citizens with emphasis on guaranteed low prices, rapid service, and frequent discounts. Industry consolidation has strengthened the company's projected profits, and expanded health care will provide solid foundation for growth.

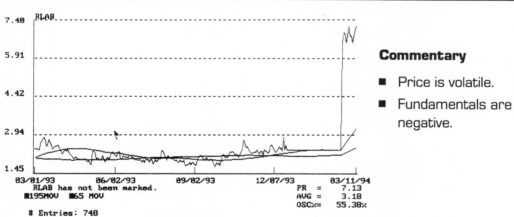

Commentary

- Price is volatile.
- Fundamentals are negative.

ROYCE LABORATORIES

YEAR	REVENUES	% CHANGE	NET INCOME	% CHANGE	RETURN ON EQUITY	% CHANGE
89	1.505	20.657	- 1.703	NA	306.3	NA
90	1.505	17.121	- 0.511	NA	56.3	- 81.6
91	1.991	32.292	- 0.187	NA	- 6.4	- 111.4
92	2.439	22.501	- 2.898	NA	- 48.9	NA

Chapter 15

Florida Manufacturing Companies

Manufacturing is boring to most investors; consequently, they avoid an area that can have big earnings and profits. Manufacturing will get more interesting if you pick a stock and it doubles! Like the restaurant industry, manufacturing has many variable options, meaning that individual companies may experience spectacular performance even when the general industry is down.

Apparel Manufacturers
No one would argue that the apparel industry under-performed the overall market for 1993. Weak consumer spending kept manufacturers conservative with production. As the economy improves and spending levels return, this industry should experience improvement.

General Manufacturing
Because the industry is so diverse, it is driven not so much by a single factor as by major economic components like GDP growth. Consequently, the industry is expected to improve as the economy picks up strength. The economic numbers are improving, but slowly.

AEROSONIC CORPORATION

Symbol: ASON   Exchange: ASE

PRICE 3/4/94	RANGE	P-E RATIO	DIVIDEND	YIELD	BETA
2 $^{15}/_{16}$	2$^3/_8$ - 3$^3/_8$	9.18	0	0	0.1

LAST FOUR QUARTERS REPORTED

REVENUES	% CHANGE	NET INCOME	% CHANGE	RETURN ON EQUITY	% CHANGE
24.274	- 10.66	1.250	- 22.98	11.23	- 31.03

Corporate Summary

Aerosonic Corporation is one of the largest manufacturers of flight instru-
mentation and ordinance equipment, supplying instruments to the military,
original equipment manufacturers, and the general aviation industry worldwide. Aerosonic was founded in 1953, employs approximately 305 people,
and is based in Clearwater, Florida.

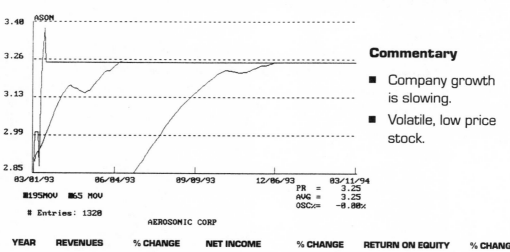

Commentary

- Company growth is slowing.
- Volatile, low price stock.

PR = 3.25
AVG = 3.25
OSC% = -0.00%

195MOV   65 MOV

Entries: 1320

AEROSONIC CORP

YEAR	REVENUES	% CHANGE	NET INCOME	% CHANGE	RETURN ON EQUITY	% CHANGE
89	11.159	13.763	0.075	- 35.345	1.1	- 36.1
90	14.069	26.078	0.435	480.000	6.1	444.4
91	29.529	109.887	1.564	259.540	18.4	199.7
92	25.889	- 12.293	1.679	7.353	15.9	- 13.4

AMERICAN SHIP BUILDING COMPANY

Symbol: ABG   Exchange: NYS

PRICE 3/4/94	RANGE	P-E RATIO	DIVIDEND	YIELD	BETA
NA	½ - 2¼	NA	0	NA	NA

LAST FOUR QUARTERS REPORTED

REVENUES	% CHANGE	NET INCOME	% CHANGE	RETURN ON EQUITY	% CHANGE
98.182	18.50	11.783	162.01	258.63	NA

Corporate Summary

American Ship Building Company is in the business of manufacturing and selling ships. The company also does repair work on ships, however the majority of the revenues generated by the company are through military contracts with the United States. The company is based in Tampa, Florida.

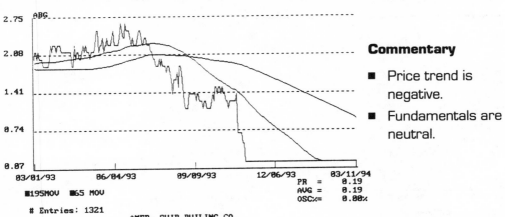

Commentary

- Price trend is negative.
- Fundamentals are neutral.

AMER. SHIP BUILING CO.

YEAR	REVENUES	% CHANGE	NET INCOME	% CHANGE	RETURN ON EQUITY	% CHANGE
89	65.782	- 6.719	- 11.971	NA	- 64.7	NA
90	74.374	13.061	- 6.421	NA	- 52.5	NA
91	73.749	- 0.840	- 4.994	NA	- 66.3	NA
92	91.488	24.053	- 12.081	NA	265.6	NA

ATLANTIS GROUP INCORPORATED

Symbol: AGH   Exchange: ASE

PRICE 3/4/94	RANGE	P-E RATIO	DIVIDEND	YIELD	BETA
5⅝	5⅛ - 6⅝	8.52	0	0	0.6

LAST FOUR QUARTERS REPORTED

REVENUES	% CHANGE	NET INCOME	% CHANGE	RETURN ON EQUITY	% CHANGE
220.163	16.65	5.065	6.90	16.31	- 3.14

Corporate Summary

Atlantis Group Incorporated, through its six operating subsidiaries, is a diversified plastics manufacturer that develops, produces, and distributes products in two principal segments: polyethylene film products and molded plastic products. The company has thirteen plastics manufacturing facilities and is based in Miami, FL.

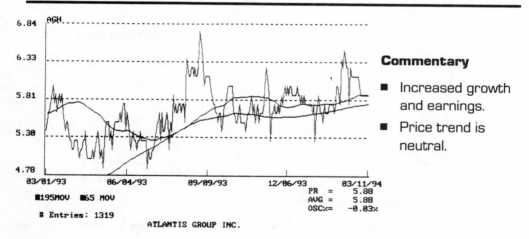

ATLANTIS GROUP INC.

Commentary

- Increased growth and earnings.
- Price trend is neutral.

YEAR	REVENUES	% CHANGE	NET INCOME	% CHANGE	RETURN ON EQUITY	% CHANGE
89	221.569	39.246	- 0.953	- 139.874	- 6.9	- 145.1
90	209.716	- 5.350	1.154	NA	9.6	NA
91	169.215	- 19.312	- 4.838	- 519.237	- 22.1	- 329.1
92	180.120	6.444	4.883	NA	17.1	NA

B/E AEROSPACE INCORPORATED

Symbol: BEAV   Exchange: NMS

PRICE 3/4/94	RANGE	P-E RATIO	DIVIDEND	YIELD	BETA
11¼	9½ - 14¾	22.06	0	0	1.4

LAST FOUR QUARTERS REPORTED

REVENUES	% CHANGE	NET INCOME	% CHANGE	RETURN ON EQUITY	% CHANGE
194.887	28.52	7.281	- 25.52	5.51	- 62.06

Corporate Summary

B/E Aerospace Incorporated designs, manufactures, sells, and services a
broad line of commercial aircraft cabin interior products. The product line
includes aircraft seats, passenger entertainment and service systems,
and galley structures and inserts. The company also provides audio and
video entertainment equipment and services to the ground transportation
industry.

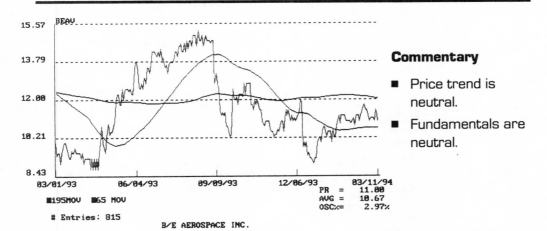

Commentary

■ Price trend is
neutral.

■ Fundamentals are
neutral.

B/E AEROSPACE INC.

YEAR	REVENUES	% CHANGE	NET INCOME	% CHANGE	RETURN ON EQUITY	% CHANGE
89	4.127	NA	- 0.637	NA	- 27.3	NA
90	22.944	455.949	2.313	NA	14.3	NA
91	24.278	5.814	4.702	103.286	20.9	46.5
92	198.019	715.631	12.150	158.401	11.3	- 46.2

BAIRNCO CORPORATION

Symbol: BZ   Exchange: NYS

PRICE 3/4/94	RANGE	P-E RATIO	DIVIDEND	YIELD	BETA
$3\frac{3}{4}$	$3\frac{3}{4}$ - 8	6.15	0.05	0.01	1.8

LAST FOUR QUARTERS REPORTED

REVENUES	% CHANGE	NET INCOME	% CHANGE	RETURN ON EQUITY	% CHANGE
157.458	- 6.05	6.501	9.87	10.08	11.76

Corporate Summary

Bairnco Corporation operates in four market sectors: electronic materials and components, replacement products and services, custom industrial products, and specialty construction products. Overall, the largest portion of the company's business is derived from the electronic materials and components division. Bairnco is based in Maitland, Florida.

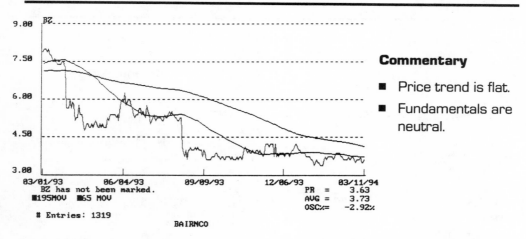

BZ has not been marked.
■19SMOV ■65 MOV

PR = 3.63
AVG = 3.73
OSC%= -2.92%

Entries: 1319

BAIRNCO

YEAR	REVENUES	% CHANGE	NET INCOME	% CHANGE	RETURN ON EQUITY	% CHANGE
89	196.943	- 13.432	7.109	- 63.101	3.5	- 59.8
90	185.910	- 5.602	- 6.963	- 197.946	- 11.6	- 427.1
91	167.645	- 9.825	4.388	NA	7.0	NA
92	164.499	- 1.877	7.498	70.875	11.5	64.2

Commentary

■ Price trend is flat.

■ Fundamentals are neutral.

CATALINA LIGHTING INCORPORATED

Symbol: LTG   Exchange: ASE

PRICE 3/4/94	RANGE	P-E RATIO	DIVIDEND	YIELD	BETA
10½	6¾ - 10½	15.22	0	0	2.9

LAST FOUR QUARTERS REPORTED

REVENUES	% CHANGE	NET INCOME	% CHANGE	RETURN ON EQUITY	% CHANGE
119.143	12.94	4.631	40.12	16.42	22.83

Corporate Summary

Catalina Lighting Incorporated designs, contract manufactures, imports, and distributes a broad line of residential and office lighting fixtures and related products under the Catalina, Dana, and Illuminada brand names. The company sells through a variety of retailers including home improvement centers, office product superstores, warehouse clubs, department stores, mass merchants, catalog showrooms, lighting showrooms, and hardware stores.

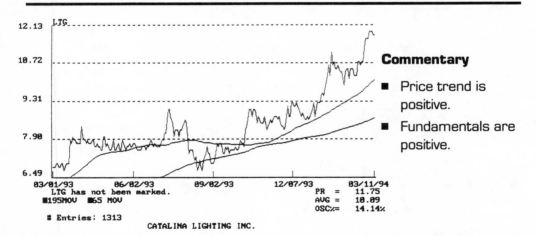

Commentary

- Price trend is positive.
- Fundamentals are positive.

LTG has not been marked.
■195MOV ■65 MOV

PR = 11.75
AVG = 10.09
OSC%= 14.14%

Entries: 1313

CATALINA LIGHTING INC.

YEAR	REVENUES	% CHANGE	NET INCOME	% CHANGE	RETURN ON EQUITY	% CHANGE
89	54.568	102.689	2.589	143.327	11.2	- 49.5
90	84.413	54.693	0.812	- 68.637	3.6	- 67.9
91	88.075	4.338	- 1.864	- 329.557	- 8.5	- 335.3
92	104.995	19.211	2.524	NA	10.2	NA

COSMO COMMUNICATION CORPORATION

Symbol: CSMO   Exchange: OTC

PRICE 3/4/94	RANGE	P-E RATIO	DIVIDEND	YIELD	BETA
$^{11}/_{16}$	$^{3}/_{8}$ - 1	NM	0	0	- 0.7

LAST FOUR QUARTERS REPORTED

REVENUES	% CHANGE	NET INCOME	% CHANGE	RETURN ON EQUITY	% CHANGE
11.758	19.80	- 0.732	NA	- 66.19	NA

Corporate Summary

Cosmo Communication Corporation manufactures, imports, markets, and distributes consumer electronic products, including digital clocks, quartz clocks, clock radios, and combination products such as clock radio telephones. As a result of significant losses, the company has eliminated most of its inventory of electronics products, saving clocks, and clock radios.

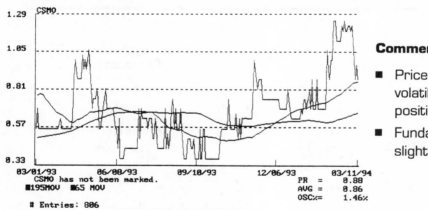

COSMO COMMUNICATIONS CORP.

Commentary

- Price trend is volatile but slightly positive.

- Fundamentals are slightly negative.

YEAR	REVENUES	% CHANGE	NET INCOME	% CHANGE	RETURN ON EQUITY	% CHANGE
89	37.669	- 14.838	- 8.365	NA	- 62.0	NA
90	22.655	- 39.858	- 10.697	NA	- 428.6	NA
91	11.304	- 50.104	- 1.922	NA	- 312.0	NA
92	9.538	- 15.623	- 1.538	NA	- 148.0	NA

DECORATOR INDUSTRIES INCORPORATED

Symbol: DII   Exchange: ASE

PRICE 3/4/94	RANGE	P-E RATIO	DIVIDEND	YIELD	BETA
9¾	7⅞ - 12	8.26	.05	.01	0.2

LAST FOUR QUARTERS REPORTED

REVENUES	% CHANGE	NET INCOME	% CHANGE	RETURN ON EQUITY	% CHANGE
27.803	30.13	2.235	104.48	27.32	47.53

Corporate Summary

Decorator Industries Incorporated, through its divisions and subsidiaries, is engaged in the production and sale of original equipment to home manufacturers, hotels, motels, and recreational vehicle manufacturers. The company has one industry segment and one class of products.

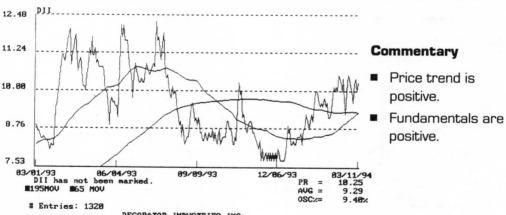

DII has not been marked.
■19SMOV ■65 MOV

PR = 10.25
AVG =   9.29
OSC%=   9.40%

Entries: 1320

DECORATOR INDUSTRIES INC.

Commentary

- Price trend is positive.
- Fundamentals are positive.

YEAR	REVENUES	% CHANGE	NET INCOME	% CHANGE	RETURN ON EQUITY	% CHANGE
89	22.030	- 27.226	0.337	151.493	6.5	146.2
90	20.712	- 5.983	0.223	- 33.828	4.1	- 36.5
91	18.072	- 12.746	0.134	- 39.910	2.7	- 35.1
92	23.605	30.616	1.529	1041.045	23.8	793.5

DIVERSIFIED COMMUNICATIONS INDUSTRIES

Symbol: DVC   Exchange: ASE

PRICE 3/4/94	RANGE	P-E RATIO	DIVIDEND	YIELD	BETA
5¼	3 - 9⅛	12.50	0	0	0.1

LAST FOUR QUARTERS REPORTED

REVENUES	% CHANGE	NET INCOME	% CHANGE	RETURN ON EQUITY	% CHANGE
12.741	104.58	0.699	103.20	29.13	37.16

Corporate Summary

Diversified Communications Industries currently operates two primary businesses. The Displays Division designs, contract manufactures, and markets proprietary and non-proprietary standard and customized clear plastic literature displays. The Cable Division engages in the design and installation of fiber optic and other cable systems.

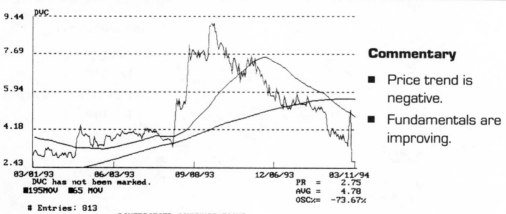

Commentary

- Price trend is negative.
- Fundamentals are improving.

DVC has not been marked.
■195MOV ■65 MOV

PR =   2.75
AVG =   4.78
OSC%= -73.67%

Entries: 813

DIVERSIFIED COMMUNICATIONS

YEAR	REVENUES	% CHANGE	NET INCOME	% CHANGE	RETURN ON EQUITY	% CHANGE
89	12.552	6.644	- 1.276	- 1181.356	- 60.0	- 1830.4
90	11.125	- 11.369	0.057	NA	2.6	NA
91	4.660	- 58.112	- 0.049	- 185.965	- 4.1	- 257.9
92	9.350	100.664	0.643	NA	35.1	NA

DIXON TICONDEROGA CO.

Symbol: DXT   Exchange: ASE

PRICE 3/4/94	RANGE	P-E RATIO	DIVIDEND	YIELD	BETA
$6\frac{1}{2}$	$4\frac{1}{4}$ - $7\frac{1}{4}$	92.86	0	0	1.2

LAST FOUR QUARTERS REPORTED

REVENUES	% CHANGE	NET INCOME	% CHANGE	RETURN ON EQUITY	% CHANGE
82.583	0.93	0.223	- 60.46	1.89	- 61.27

Corporate Summary

Dixon Ticonderoga Company, through its three main factories, is principally engaged in the production and sale of No. 2 pencils. The company
also manufactures and distributes "Wherever" pens as well as a number
of different kinds of art supplies. Dixon Ticonderoga is based in Maitland,
Florida.

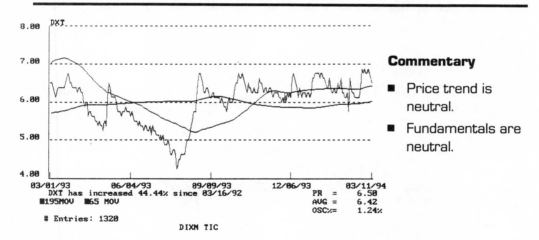

DXT has increased 44.44% since 03/16/92

PR = 6.50
AVG = 6.42
OSC%= 1.24%

■195MOV ■65 MOV

Entries: 1320

DIXN TIC

Commentary

- Price trend is
  neutral.

- Fundamentals are
  neutral.

YEAR	REVENUES	% CHANGE	NET INCOME	% CHANGE	RETURN ON EQUITY	% CHANGE
89	90.030	12.817	- 0.803	- 126.148	- 4.6	- 127.5
90	82.045	- 8.869	- 3.831	NA	- 30.8	NA
91	70.643	- 13.897	- 0.673	NA	- 5.6	NA
92	82.025	16.112	0.258	NA	2.2	NA

EMPIRE OF CAROLINA INCORPORATED

Symbol: EMP   Exchange: ASE

PRICE 3/4/94	RANGE	P-E RATIO	DIVIDEND	YIELD	BETA
6¼	6 - 8	NM	0	0	- 0.3

LAST FOUR QUARTERS REPORTED

REVENUES	% CHANGE	NET INCOME	% CHANGE	RETURN ON EQUITY	% CHANGE
42.002	- 51.38	- 2.975	NA	- 3.05	NA

Corporate Summary

Empire of Carolina Inc. is engaged in the design, manufacture, and market-ing of plastic children's toys as well as buttons for the apparel industry. Carolina's toy lines, which are designed for children ranging in age from toddlers to pre-teens, are comprised primarily of molded plastic toys such as "ride-on" toys, a variety of floor toys, and spring seasonal items.

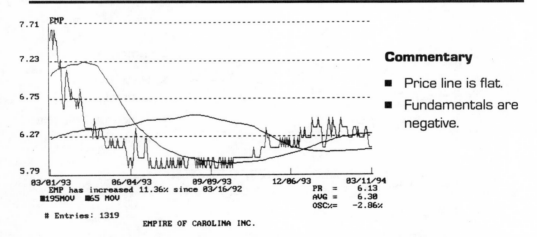

Commentary

- Price line is flat.
- Fundamentals are negative.

EMPIRE OF CAROLINA INC.

YEAR	REVENUES	% CHANGE	NET INCOME	% CHANGE	RETURN ON EQUITY	% CHANGE
89	157.920	167.122	- 12.456	- 321.637	- 35.4	- 326.8
90	215.206	91.301	- 5.248	NA	- 16.6	NA
91	153.302	3.929	7.774	NA	17.2	NA
92	130.893	- 82.363	- 2.696	- 134.680	- 4.9	- 128.7

EQUITRAC CORPORATION

Symbol: ETRC   Exchange: NMS

PRICE 3/4/94	RANGE	P-E RATIO	DIVIDEND	YIELD	BETA
5	5 - 12¼	10.00	0	0	NA

LAST FOUR QUARTERS REPORTED

REVENUES	% CHANGE	NET INCOME	% CHANGE	RETURN ON EQUITY	% CHANGE
29.443	11.55	1.876	- 19.59	9.39	- 29.41

Corporate Summary

Equitrac Corporation is a manufacturer and distributor of cost recovery systems. Special keypads and computer systems are created to meet specific accounting needs for professional firms. The target market is attorneys, C.P.A.s, and other professional firms that charge fees by the hour. The distribution of these systems is through direct sales to the firms.

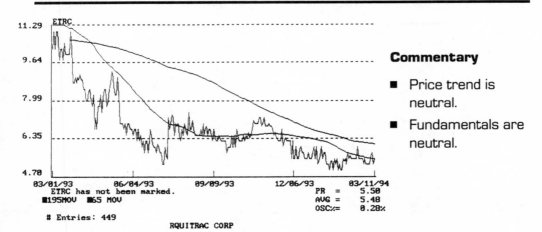

Commentary

- Price trend is neutral.
- Fundamentals are neutral.

YEAR	REVENUES	% CHANGE	NET INCOME	% CHANGE	RETURN ON EQUITY	% CHANGE
89	NA	NA	NA	NA	NA	NA
90	NA	NA	NA	NA	NA	NA
91	23.732	NA	1.750	NA	26.9	NA
92	27.475	15.772	2.44	39.657	13.0	- 51.8

FLORIDA ROCK INDUSTRIES INCORPORATED

Symbol: FRK   Exchange: ASE

PRICE 3/4/94	RANGE	P-E RATIO	DIVIDEND	YIELD	BETA
32$^1/_8$	24$^1/_4$ - 32$^1/_8$	27.93	0.25	0	0.7

LAST FOUR QUARTERS REPORTED

REVENUES	% CHANGE	NET INCOME	% CHANGE	RETURN ON EQUITY	% CHANGE
303.480	13.46	10.661	235.46	6.21	229.38

Corporate Summary

Florida Rock Industries Incorporated and its subsidiaries are principally en-gaged in the production and sale of ready mixed concrete as well as the mining, processing, and sale of sand, gravel, and crushed stone. The com-pany also produces and sells concrete block and prestressed concrete as well as other building materials. Overall, the majority of the company's busi-ness is conducted within the southeastern United States.

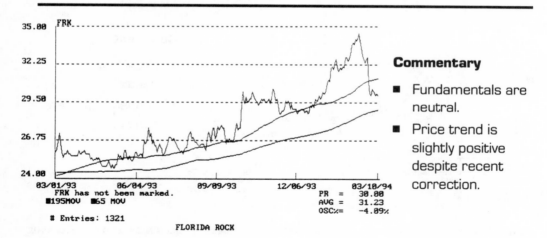

FLORIDA ROCK

FRK has not been marked.
■19SMOV ■65 MOV

PR = 30.00
AVG = 31.23
OSC%= -4.89%

Entries: 1321

Commentary

■ Fundamentals are neutral.

■ Price trend is slightly positive despite recent correction.

YEAR	REVENUES	% CHANGE	NET INCOME	% CHANGE	RETURN ON EQUITY	% CHANGE
89	420.447	2.765	23.302	- 16.246	14.6	- 25.1
90	390.546	- 7.112	17.100	- 26.616	9.9	- 31.9
91	295.726	- 24.279	2.043	- 88.053	1.2	- 87.9
92	271.821	- 8.083	3.856	88.742	2.3	89.9

GENCOR INDUSTRIES INCORPORATED

Symbol: GCOR   Exchange: NMS

PRICE 3/4/94	RANGE	P-E RATIO	DIVIDEND	YIELD	BETA
$10\frac{1}{2}$	$6\frac{3}{8}$ - 13	23.86	0	0	1.8

LAST FOUR QUARTERS REPORTED

REVENUES	% CHANGE	NET INCOME	% CHANGE	RETURN ON EQUITY	% CHANGE
52.495	9.74	0.705	- 54.58	13.74	- 49.84

Corporate Summary

Gencor Industries Incorporated designs, manufactures, and sells industrial combustion systems, electronic process control systems, fluid heat transfer systems, and asphalt production plants and components. This line of products is primarily utilized in the production of asphalt and other materials for the highway construction industry.

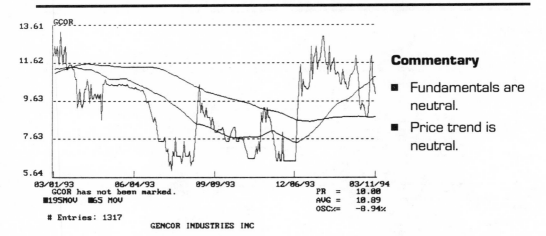

GCOR has not been marked.
■19SMOV ■65 MOV

PR = 10.00
AVG = 10.89
OSC%= -8.94%

Entries: 1317

GENCOR INDUSTRIES INC

Commentary

- Fundamentals are neutral.

- Price trend is neutral.

YEAR	REVENUES	% CHANGE	NET INCOME	% CHANGE	RETURN ON EQUITY	% CHANGE
89	54.644	- 3.794	- 6.106	- 3800.606	- 151.7	- 9526.2
90	46.217	- 15.422	- 0.771	NA	- 23.0	NA
91	38.468	- 16.767	0.676	NA	15.4	NA
92	44.853	16.598	0.045	- 93.343	1.0	- 93.5

W.R. GRACE & COMPANY

Symbol: GRA   Exchange: NYS

PRICE 3/4/94	RANGE	P-E RATIO	DIVIDEND	YIELD	BETA
45⅝	34⅝ - 45⅝	31.25	0.35	0.01	1.3

LAST FOUR QUARTERS REPORTED

REVENUES	% CHANGE	NET INCOME	% CHANGE	RETURN ON EQUITY	% CHANGE
4408.399	1.65	133.900	134.07	10.98	200.12

Corporate Summary

W.R. Grace & Company has two main business areas. The first sector works in the area of specialty chemicals including packaging and containers; catalysts and other silica-based products; construction products; water treatment; and processed chemicals. The second sector works in the area of health care, including dialysis and home care services.

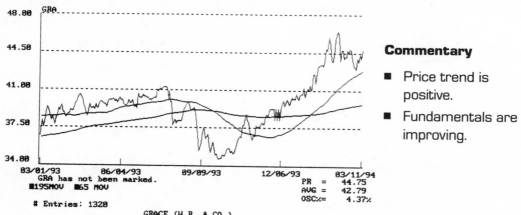

Commentary

- Price trend is positive.
- Fundamentals are improving.

GRA has not been marked.
■19SMOV ■65 MOV

PR = 44.75
AVG = 42.79
OSC%= 4.37%

Entries: 1328

GRACE (W.R. & CO.)

YEAR	REVENUES	% CHANGE	NET INCOME	% CHANGE	RETURN ON EQUITY	% CHANGE
89	6114.597	5.677	256.600	33.646	14.9	19.7
90	6754.000	10.457	202.800	-20.966	10.6	-28.5
91	6049.097	-10.473	219.200	8.087	10.9	2.0
92	5518.199	-8.776	79.400	-63.777	5.2	-52.5

INTERNATIONAL CONTAINER SYSTEMS INCORPORATED

Symbol: ICSI   Exchange: NMS

PRICE 3/4/94	RANGE	P-E RATIO	DIVIDEND	YIELD	BETA
$2\frac{5}{8}$	$2\frac{5}{8}$ - 4	12.50	0	0	- 0.4

LAST FOUR QUARTERS REPORTED

REVENUES	% CHANGE	NET INCOME	% CHANGE	RETURN ON EQUITY	% CHANGE
9.425	- 9.32	0.494	- 43.48	7.44	- 48.38

Corporate Summary

International Container Systems Incorporated is a major supplier of proprietary and patented plastic packaging systems for the transport and merchandising of disposable glass bottles, PET plastic bottles and cans of soft drinks. The company is based in Tampa, Florida.

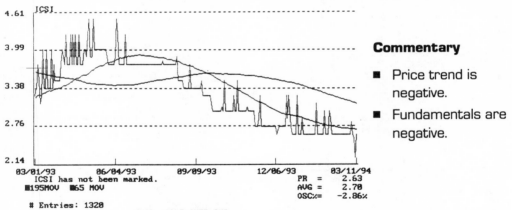

ICSI has not been marked.
■195MOV ■65 MOV

PR = 2.63
AVG = 2.70
OSC%= -2.86%

Entries: 1320

INTL. CONTAINER SYS.

Commentary

■ Price trend is negative.

■ Fundamentals are negative.

YEAR	REVENUES	% CHANGE	NET INCOME	% CHANGE	RETURN ON EQUITY	% CHANGE
89	8.974	- 27.623	- 0.095	- 106.657	- 1.4	- 106.7
90	8.086	- 9.895	0.631	NA	9.2	NA
91	14.285	76.663	1.302	106.339	22.9	149.3
92	8.630	- 39.587	0.601	- 53.840	9.7	- 57.9

JANSCO INCORPORATED

Symbol: JSKO   Exchange: OTC

PRICE 3/4/94	RANGE	P-E RATIO	DIVIDEND	YIELD	BETA
3	$2^3/_4 - 3^7/_8$	NM	0	0	- 0.3

LAST FOUR QUARTERS REPORTED

REVENUES	% CHANGE	NET INCOME	% CHANGE	RETURN ON EQUITY	% CHANGE
11.743	- 7.16	- 0.873	NA	- 16.46	NA

Corporate Summary

Jansco Incorporated, primarily through its subsidiaries, is engaged in the design, manufacturing, and sale of commercial office furniture. The company is based in Fort Lauderdale, Florida, but has manufacturing plants spread across the United States. The majority of the company's revenues are generated through sales to larger corporations.

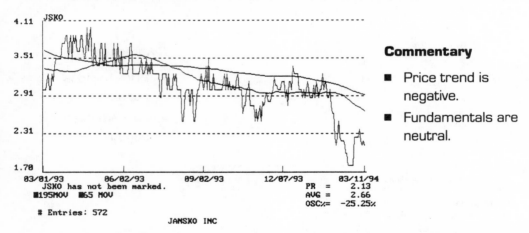

JSKO has not been marked.
■195MOV ■65 MOV
Entries: 572

PR = 2.13
AVG = 2.66
OSC%= -25.25%

JANSKO INC

Commentary

- Price trend is negative.
- Fundamentals are neutral.

YEAR	REVENUES	% CHANGE	NET INCOME	% CHANGE	RETURN ON EQUITY	% CHANGE
89	NA	NA	NA	NA	NA	NA
90	NA	NA	NA	NA	NA	NA
91	7.642	NA	- 0.882	NA	- 190.9	NA
92	13.491	76.538	0.085	NA	1.4	NA

JEWELMASTERS INCORPORATED
Symbol: JEM   Exchange: ASE

PRICE 3/4/94	RANGE	P-E RATIO	DIVIDEND	YIELD	BETA
3/4	3/4 - 1 1/4	NM	0	0	0.6

LAST FOUR QUARTERS REPORTED

REVENUES	% CHANGE	NET INCOME	% CHANGE	RETURN ON EQUITY	% CHANGE
28.498	- 13.32	- 4.575	NA	NA	NA

Corporate Summary

Jewelmasters Incorporated designs, manufactures, and sells fine jewelry through leased jewelry departments in department and specialty stores as well as through free-standing stores and outlets. A significant portion of all jewelry sold by the company is designed and hand-crafted at the company's manufacturing facilities for sale exclusively through its leased departments and retail facilities.

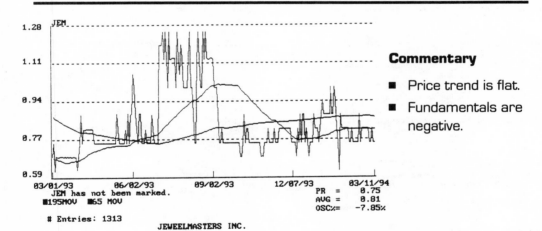

JEM has not been marked.
195MOV 65 MOV

PR = 0.75
AVG = 0.81
OSC% = -7.85%

Entries: 1313

JEWEELMASTERS INC.

Commentary

- Price trend is flat.
- Fundamentals are negative.

YEAR	REVENUES	% CHANGE	NET INCOME	% CHANGE	RETURN ON EQUITY	% CHANGE
89	65.312	18.195	0.684	47.097	4.3	41.8
90	52.769	- 19.205	- 1.086	- 258.772	- 7.6	- 275.7
91	46.062	- 12.710	- 1.494	NA	- 10.8	NA
92	31.802	- 30.958	- 2.527	NA	- 22.3	NA

KAYDON CORPORATION

Symbol: KDON   Exchange: NMS

PRICE 3/4/94	RANGE	P-E RATIO	DIVIDEND	YIELD	BETA
$20\frac{3}{8}$	$19\frac{3}{4} - 29\frac{3}{4}$	12.73	0.10	0	1.2

LAST FOUR QUARTERS REPORTED

REVENUES	% CHANGE	NET INCOME	% CHANGE	RETURN ON EQUITY	% CHANGE
184.060	0.08	27.695	8.11	18.13	6.93

Corporate Summary

Kaydon Corporation designs, manufactures, and sells custom-engineered products including bearings, filters, sealing rings, piston rings, and shaft seals. The majority of the company's revenues are generated through the exportation of replacement parts and sales to the aerospace and military industries. Kaydon is based in Clearwater, Florida.

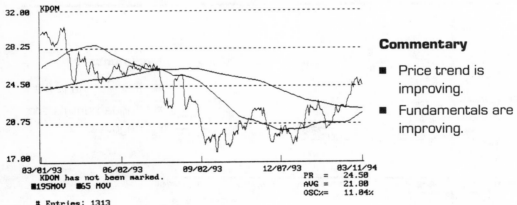

Commentary

- Price trend is improving.
- Fundamentals are improving.

KDON has not been marked.
■19SMOV ■65 MOV
PR = 24.50
AVG = 21.80
OSC%= 11.84%

Entries: 1313

KAYDON CORP.

YEAR	REVENUES	% CHANGE	NET INCOME	% CHANGE	RETURN ON EQUITY	% CHANGE
89	151.238	12.004	22.847	9.615	25.2	-15.5
90	169.442	12.037	26.009	13.840	22.9	-9.2
91	160.989	-4.989	25.455	-2.130	18.5	-19.0
92	183.904	14.234	25.618	0.640	18.8	1.7

NATIONAL BEVERAGE CORPORATION

Symbol: POPS   Exchange: NMS

PRICE 3/4/94	RANGE	P-E RATIO	DIVIDEND	YIELD	BETA
21½	17 - 22⅞	NM	0	0	0.8

LAST FOUR QUARTERS REPORTED

REVENUES	% CHANGE	NET INCOME	% CHANGE	RETURN ON EQUITY	% CHANGE
337.634	- 1.94	- 7.482	- 237.18	- 31.26	- 280.08

Corporate Summary

The National Beverage Corporation, along with its subsidiaries, manufactures, bottles, and distributes a number of different brands of soft drinks and cola, including "Shasta" and "Saygo." The company is based in Ft. Lauderdale, Florida. The majority of the company's revenues are generated by these two brands.

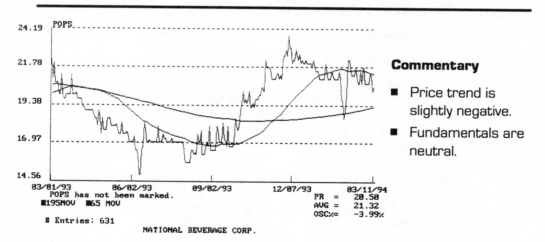

Commentary

- Price trend is slightly negative.
- Fundamentals are neutral.

POPS has not been marked.
195MOV 65 MOV

Entries: 631

PR = 20.50
AVG = 21.32
OSC%= -3.99%

NATIONAL BEVERAGE CORP.

YEAR	REVENUES	% CHANGE	NET INCOME	% CHANGE	RETURN ON EQUITY	% CHANGE
89	NA	NA	NA	NA	NA	NA
90	NA	NA	NA	NA	NA	NA
91	310.831	NA	1.807	NA	8.8	NA
92	335.791	8.030	5.625	211.289	22.1	151.7

OCEAN BIO-CHEM INCORPORATED

Symbol: OBCI   Exchange: OTC

PRICE 3/4/94	RANGE	P-E RATIO	DIVIDEND	YIELD	BETA
3	$1\frac{3}{8}$ - 3	20.00	0	0	- 0.2

LAST FOUR QUARTERS REPORTED

REVENUES	% CHANGE	NET INCOME	% CHANGE	RETURN ON EQUITY	% CHANGE
7.571	21.39	0.457	13.68	17.58	- 4.86

Corporate Summary

Ocean Bio-Chem Incorporated primarily markets and distributes a variety of appearance and maintenance products for automobiles, boats, recreational vehicles, and aircraft under the Star Brite tradename. The company's marine line of products consists of polishes, waxes, vinyl protectants, teak oils, bilge cleaners, hull cleaners, silicone sealants, polyurethane sealants, and other sealants.

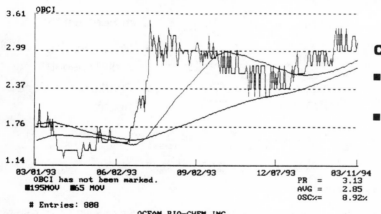

OCEAN BIO-CHEM INC.

Commentary

- Price trend is slightly positive.
- Fundamentals are improving.

YEAR	REVENUES	% CHANGE	NET INCOME	% CHANGE	RETURN ON EQUITY	% CHANGE
89	4.640	3.341	0.172	- 7.527	11.7	- 25.0
90	5.379	15.927	0.152	- 11.628	9.3	- 19.8
91	5.663	5.280	0.380	150.000	18.9	102.6
92	6.525	15.222	0.229	- 39.737	10.3	- 45.8

ORANGE-CO INCORPORATED

Symbol: OJ   Exchange: NYS

PRICE 3/4/94	RANGE	P-E RATIO	DIVIDEND	YIELD	BETA
$5\frac{1}{8}$	$4\frac{3}{4}$ - $5\frac{1}{2}$	13.14	0	0	0.3

LAST FOUR QUARTERS REPORTED

REVENUES	% CHANGE	NET INCOME	% CHANGE	RETURN ON EQUITY	% CHANGE
75.754	5.24	3.995	- 40.32	NA	NA

Corporate Summary

Orange-Co Incorporated is the product of the combination of American Agronimics and Orange-Co of Florida. The company is vertically integrated and is primarily engaged in growing, processing and marketing citrus products, including frozen orange juice concentrate and other frozen concentrated fruit juices. Orange-Co owns 22,000 acres of land in Florida.

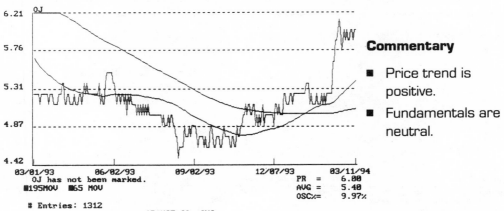

Commentary

- Price trend is positive.
- Fundamentals are neutral.

```
6.21   OJ
5.76
5.31
4.87
4.42
      03/01/93      06/02/93      09/02/93      12/07/93      03/11/94
      OJ has not been marked.                   PR  =   6.00
      ■195MOV  ■65 MOV                          AVG =   5.40
                                                OSC%=   9.97%
         # Entries: 1312
                        ORANGE-CO. INC.
```

YEAR	REVENUES	% CHANGE	NET INCOME	% CHANGE	RETURN ON EQUITY	% CHANGE
89	171.092	22.100	1.840	- 65.970	1.9	- 66.5
90	126.542	- 26.039	- 8.743	- 575.163	- 10.2	- 625.4
91	80.357	- 36.498	- 1.415	NA	- 1.7	NA
92	92.737	15.406	5.932	NA	6.7	NA

PARADISE INCORPORATED

Symbol: PARF   Exchange: OTC

PRICE 3/4/94	RANGE	P-E RATIO	DIVIDEND	YIELD	BETA
7¼	6½ - 8¼	NM	0	0.01	0.8

LAST FOUR QUARTERS REPORTED

REVENUES	% CHANGE	NET INCOME	% CHANGE	RETURN ON EQUITY	% CHANGE
18.102	-4.59	-0.124	-118.48	-1.97	-119.34

Corporate Summary

Paradise Incorporated conducts its business through two major business segments, and the primary operations of each are as follows: (1) production of candied fruit, a basic fruitcake ingredient, sold to manufacturing bakers, institutional users, and retailers for use in home baking; (2) production of plastic containers and other molded plastics for sale to various food processors.

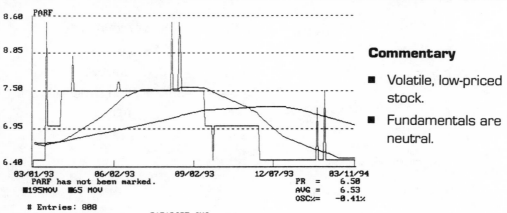

PARADISE INC.

Commentary

- Volatile, low-priced stock.
- Fundamentals are neutral.

YEAR	REVENUES	% CHANGE	NET INCOME	% CHANGE	RETURN ON EQUITY	% CHANGE
89	21.327	0.961	0.767	3.930	13.2	-8.3
90	20.315	-4.745	0.373	-51.369	6.0	-54.3
91	18.959	-6.675	0.129	-65.416	2.1	-65.9
92	19.141	0.960	0.488	278.295	7.3	255.9

PLASMA THERM INCORPORATED

Symbol: PTIS   Exchange: OTC

PRICE 3/4/94	RANGE	P-E RATIO	DIVIDEND	YIELD	BETA
$3\frac{1}{4}$	$\frac{1}{2}$ - $3\frac{7}{8}$	NM	0	0	1.7

LAST FOUR QUARTERS REPORTED

REVENUES	% CHANGE	NET INCOME	% CHANGE	RETURN ON EQUITY	% CHANGE
17.272	4.39	- 0.185	NA	- 2.18	NA

Corporate Summary

Plasma Therm Incorporated, together with its subsidiaries, is primarily engaged in the design and manufacture of thin film etching and deposition
systems which are used chiefly by manufacturers of semiconductor devices and systems. Plasma Therm is based in St. Petersburg, Florida.

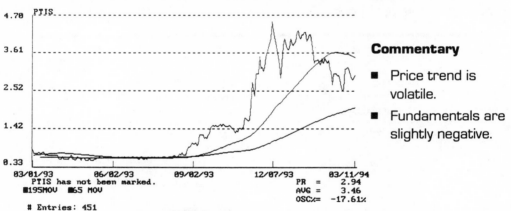

PTIS has not been marked.
■195MOV ■65 MOV
Entries: 451

PR = 2.94
AVG = 3.46
OSC% = -17.61%

PLASMA THERM INC.

Commentary

- Price trend is volatile.
- Fundamentals are slightly negative.

YEAR	REVENUES	% CHANGE	NET INCOME	% CHANGE	RETURN ON EQUITY	% CHANGE
89	28.974	33.848	1.479	264.286	17.1	193.4
90	34.355	18.572	1.756	18.729	16.0	- 6.2
91	18.733	- 45.472	- 1.391	- 179.214	- 14.5	- 190.6
92	17.497	- 6.598	- 0.028	NA	- 0.3	NA

QUIPP INCORPORATED

Symbol: QUIP   Exchange: NMS

PRICE 3/4/94	RANGE	P-E RATIO	DIVIDEND	YIELD	BETA
$2\frac{5}{8}$	$2\frac{5}{8}$ - $4\frac{1}{2}$	17.50	0	0	0.1

LAST FOUR QUARTERS REPORTED

REVENUES	% CHANGE	NET INCOME	% CHANGE	RETURN ON EQUITY	% CHANGE
14.485	- 28.31	0.225	- 72.12	2.56	- 72.27

Corporate Summary

Quipp Incorporated, through its wholly-owned subsidiary, Quipp Systems Inc., designs and manufactures materials handling equipment for the newspaper industry. The company's products generally are designed to accomplish much of the mailroom operations of a newspaper publisher. The mailroom is the area in which newspapers are stacked, bundled, and moved to the shipping docks.

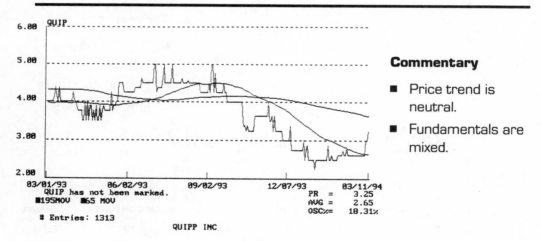

```
6.00  QUIP
5.00
4.00
3.00
2.00
      03/01/93      06/02/93      09/02/93      12/07/93      03/11/94
         QUIP has not been marked.                    PR  =   3.25
      ■19SMOV  ■65 MOV                                 AVG =   2.65
                                                       OSC%=  18.31%
      # Entries: 1313
                          QUIPP INC
```

Commentary

- Price trend is neutral.

- Fundamentals are mixed.

YEAR	REVENUES	% CHANGE	NET INCOME	% CHANGE	RETURN ON EQUITY	% CHANGE
89	12.778	- 16.429	- 0.676	- 149.128	- 8.4	- 153.3
90	12.589	- 1.479	- 0.052	NA	- 0.7	NA
91	12.976	3.074	0.094	NA	1.2	NA
92	19.794	52.543	0.679	622.341	7.7	565.0

SENSORMATIC ELECTRONICS CORPORATION

Symbol: SRM   Exchange: NYS

PRICE	RANGE	P-E RATIO	DIVIDEND	YIELD	BETA
33$\frac{1}{8}$	21$\frac{7}{8}$ - 34$\frac{5}{8}$	31.16	0.06	0	0.9

LAST FOUR QUARTERS REPORTED

REVENUES	% CHANGE	NET INCOME	% CHANGE	RETURN ON EQUITY	% CHANGE
548.635	34.41	63.217	89.84	12.11	69.24

Corporate Summary

Sensormatic Electronics Corporation manufactures, markets and services electronic article surveillance (EAS) systems and micro-processor control-led closed circuit television systems (CCTV) used to deter shoplifting and internal theft, principally in the retail industry. Manufacturing facilities are located in Deerfield Beach, Florida and Puerto Rico.

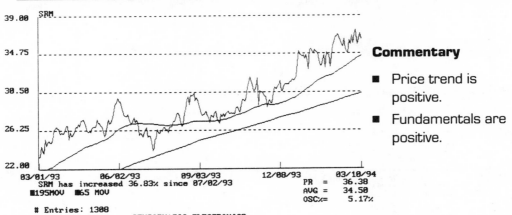

SRM has increased 36.83% since 07/02/93
■19SMOV ■6S MOV

PR = 36.38
AVG = 34.50
OSCx= 5.17%

Entries: 1388

SENSORMATIC ELECTRONICS

Commentary

■ Price trend is positive.

■ Fundamentals are positive.

YEAR	REVENUES	% CHANGE	NET INCOME	% CHANGE	RETURN ON EQUITY	% CHANGE
89	150.904	22.803	16.708	NA	8.7	NA
90	191.267	26.747	20.027	19.865	10.0	15.2
91	239.165	25.042	24.711	23.388	11.1	11.0
92	309.878	29.567	31.526	27.579	12.3	10.9

ST. JOE PAPER COMPANY

Symbol: SJP Exchange: NYS

PRICE 3/4/94	RANGE	P-E RATIO	DIVIDEND	YIELD	BETA
54$^7/_8$	38$^3/_8$ - 54$^7/_8$	288.82	0.05	0	1.0

LAST FOUR QUARTERS REPORTED

REVENUES	% CHANGE	NET INCOME	% CHANGE	RETURN ON EQUITY	% CHANGE
590.977	- 1.24	6.182	- 76.89	0.72	- 77.44

Corporate Summary

St. Joe Paper Company is currently engaged in two industries: (1) the growing and harvesting of timber, and the manufacturing, distribution and sale of forest products; (2) the transportation of goods by rail. The company also has endeavors in the growing and processing of sugar cane into raw sugar, telephone communications, and real estate.

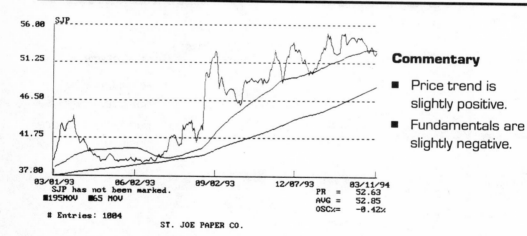

Commentary

- Price trend is slightly positive.
- Fundamentals are slightly negative.

SJP has not been marked.
■195MOV ■65 MOV

PR = 52.63
AVG = 52.85
OSC%= -0.42%

Entries: 1004

ST. JOE PAPER CO.

YEAR	REVENUES	% CHANGE	NET INCOME	% CHANGE	RETURN ON EQUITY	% CHANGE
89	635.337	- 2.488	67.241	- 18.664	8.8	- 25.1
90	610.200	- 3.956	41.290	- 38.594	5.1	- 41.3
91	582.180	- 4.592	27.588	- 33.185	3.3	- 34.9
92	591.912	1.672	15.590	- 43.490	1.9	- 44.1

STEPHAN COMPANY

Symbol: STCP   Exchange: NMS

PRICE 3/4/94	RANGE	P-E RATIO	DIVIDEND	YIELD	BETA
21	13 - 21	24.91	0	0	1.6

LAST FOUR QUARTERS REPORTED

REVENUES	% CHANGE	NET INCOME	% CHANGE	RETURN ON EQUITY	% CHANGE
15.073	8.80	2.676	14.12	27.70	- 27.36

Corporate Summary

Stephan Company, along with its subsidiaries, is in the business of developing, manufacturing, and distributing hair care and skin care products. The majority of the company's revenues are generated through its hair care division. The company is based in Ft. Lauderdale, Florida.

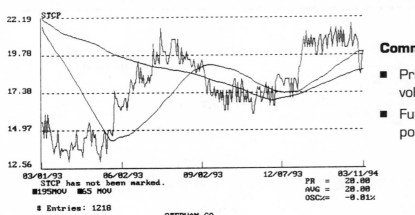

STCP has not been marked.
■195MOV ■65 MOV

PR = 20.00
AVG = 20.00
OSC%= -0.01%

Entries: 1218

STEPHAN CO.

Commentary

■ Price trend is volatile.

■ Fundamentals are positive.

YEAR	REVENUES	% CHANGE	NET INCOME	% CHANGE	RETURN ON EQUITY	% CHANGE
89	4.661	35.612	0.375	58.898	27.9	14.6
90	5.502	18.043	0.589	57.067	30.4	9.3
91	10.025	82.206	1.617	174.533	45.3	48.7
92	14.683	46.464	2.374	46.815	35.1	- 22.4

SUAVE SHOE CORPORATION
Symbol: SWV   Exchange: NYS

PRICE 3/4/94	RANGE	P-E RATIO	DIVIDEND	YIELD	BETA
3⅝	3½ - 5	NM	0	0	0.5

LAST FOUR QUARTERS REPORTED

REVENUES	% CHANGE	NET INCOME	% CHANGE	RETURN ON EQUITY	% CHANGE
29.178	- 44.31	- 5.389	- 827.26	- 36.40	- 959.06

Corporate Summary

Suave Shoe Corporation, a Florida corporation organized in 1960, and its subsidiaries, manufacture casual, athletic, and leisure footwear. The shoes are made by an injection molding process which permits automatic attachment of a plastic or rubber sole to the upper part of the shoe in a single machine operation.

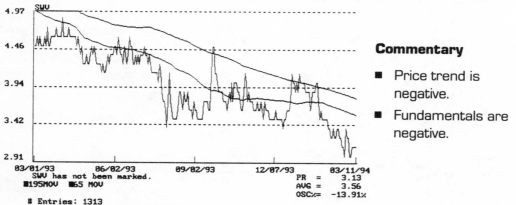

SUAVE SHOE CORP.

Commentary

- Price trend is negative.
- Fundamentals are negative.

YEAR	REVENUES	% CHANGE	NET INCOME	% CHANGE	RETURN ON EQUITY	% CHANGE
89	86.743	13.447	0.402	NA	1.9	NA
90	62.110	- 28.398	2.772	589.552	12.9	582.1
91	53.040	- 14.603	- 4.344	- 256.710	- 25.8	- 300.3
92	58.014	9.378	1.284	NA	6.9	NA

SUPERIOR SURGICAL MANUFACTURING

Symbol: SGC   Exchange: ASE

PRICE 3/4/94	RANGE	P-E RATIO	DIVIDEND	YIELD	BETA
14¾	12⅞ - 20⅞	13.29	0	0	0.3

LAST FOUR QUARTERS REPORTED

REVENUES	% CHANGE	NET INCOME	% CHANGE	RETURN ON EQUITY	% CHANGE
130.450	4.12	9.662	2.90	14.14	- 8.38

Corporate Summary

Superior Surgical Manufacturing manufactures and sells a wide range of apparel and accessories for the medical and health fields as well as for the industrial, commercial, leisure, and public safety markets. The company's principal products are uniforms and service apparel for personnel of hospitals, hotels, industrial facilities, commercial enterprises, and public and private safety and security organizations.

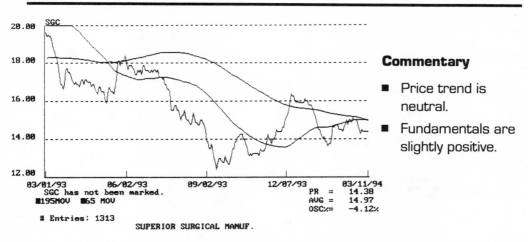

SGC has not been marked.
■19SMOV ■65 MOV

PR = 14.38
AVG = 14.97
OSC% = -4.12%

Entries: 1313

SUPERIOR SURGICAL MANUF.

Commentary

- Price trend is neutral.
- Fundamentals are slightly positive.

YEAR	REVENUES	% CHANGE	NET INCOME	% CHANGE	RETURN ON EQUITY	% CHANGE
89	113.754	1.215	7.160	1.560	16.2	- 7.6
90	123.002	8.130	8.665	21.020	18.2	12.5
91	117.503	- 4.471	8.025	- 7.386	14.7	- 19.2
92	128.666	9.500	9.914	23.539	15.7	7.0

SYMETRICS INDUSTRIES INCORPORATED

Symbol: SYMT   Exchange: OTC

PRICE 3/4/94	RANGE	P-E RATIO	DIVIDEND	YIELD	BETA
$5\frac{1}{2}$	$1\frac{1}{4}$ - $6\frac{3}{4}$	16.18	0	0	- 0.4

LAST FOUR QUARTERS REPORTED

REVENUES	% CHANGE	NET INCOME	% CHANGE	RETURN ON EQUITY	% CHANGE
6.350	74.16	0.273	1720.00	17.58	1585.23

Corporate Summary

Symetrics Industries Incorporated manufactures electronic assemblies
and systems. All electronic components, bare printed circuit boards
("PCB's"), metal parts and enclosures are purchased by the company
from third parties. Thereafter, the complete manufacturing process including soldering, wiring harnesses, cables, inspection, test, conformal coating, and environment stress screening is performed by the company.

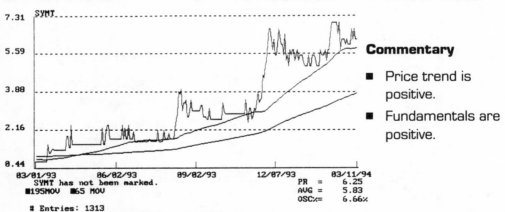

Commentary

- Price trend is positive.
- Fundamentals are positive.

SYMT has not been marked.
195MOV 65 MOV

PR = 6.25
AVG = 5.83
OSC%= 6.66%

Entries: 1313

SYMETRICS INDUSTRIES INC

YEAR	REVENUES	% CHANGE	NET INCOME	% CHANGE	RETURN ON EQUITY	% CHANGE
89	5.771	- 0.294	0.093	342.857	8.6	493.1
90	4.026	- 30.237	0.115	23.656	9.6	11.7
91	5.521	37.134	0.219	90.435	15.5	61.1
92	3.426	- 37.946	- 0.028	- 112.785	- 2.0	- 113.0

UNIROYAL TECHNOLOGY CORPORATION

Symbol: UTCI   Exchange: NMS

PRICE 3/4/94	RANGE	P-E RATIO	DIVIDEND	YIELD	BETA
$5^7/_8$	$2^7/_8 - 5^7/_8$	NM	0	0	NA

LAST FOUR QUARTERS REPORTED

REVENUES	% CHANGE	NET INCOME	% CHANGE	RETURN ON EQUITY	% CHANGE
173.361	4.71	- 1.980	- 107.25	- 5.15	NA

Corporate Summary

Uniroyal Technology Corporation is engaged in the development, manufacture, and sale of a broad range of products employing plastic and specialty chemicals technology through three operating segments: high performance plastics, coated fabrics, and specialty foams and adhesives.

Commentary

- Price trend is positive.
- Fundamentals are negative.

UTCI has not been marked.
■19SMOV ■65 MOV
Entries: 366

PR = 5.31
AVG = 5.82
OSC% = 5.49%

UNIROYAL TECHNOLOGY CORP.

YEAR	REVENUES	% CHANGE	NET INCOME	% CHANGE	RETURN ON EQUITY	% CHANGE
89	NA	NA	NA	NA	NA	NA
90	NA	NA	NA	NA	NA	NA
91	NA	NA	NA	NA	NA	NA
92	165.565	NA	27.313	NA	69.3	NA

223

WATSCO INCORPORATED CL B

Symbol: WSOB   Exchange: ASE

PRICE 3/4/94	RANGE	P-E RATIO	DIVIDEND	YIELD	BETA
14$\frac{1}{4}$	11$\frac{7}{8}$ - 15$\frac{3}{8}$	11.05	0.06	0	0.7

LAST FOUR QUARTERS REPORTED

REVENUES	% CHANGE	NET INCOME	% CHANGE	RETURN ON EQUITY	% CHANGE
218.990	16.23	4.869	86.48	11.81	6.15

Corporate Summary

Watsco Incorporated is the largest independent distributor of residential central air conditioners and related parts and supplies in the United States. The company distributes products to over 6,400 local air conditioning and heating contractors as well as to dealers servicing the residential replacement and new construction markets.

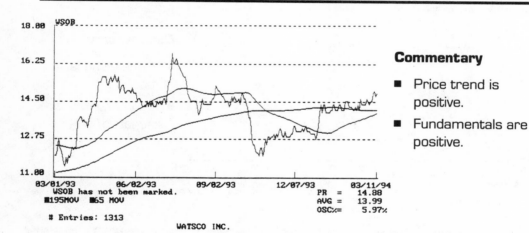

WATSCO INC.

Commentary

- Price trend is positive.
- Fundamentals are positive.

YEAR	REVENUES	% CHANGE	NET INCOME	% CHANGE	RETURN ON EQUITY	% CHANGE
89	94.318	320.012	2.029	164.883	15.9	142.1
90	117.749	24.843	1.935	- 4.633	10.2	- 35.7
91	169.318	43.796	1.990	2.842	9.6	- 6.5
92	194.633	14.951	2.918	46.633	11.5	20.9

Chapter 16

Florida Retailing Companies

You go into these companies every day and buy products. In some cases, you observe good marketing and good management. You like the store, the product, and the way it's run, and chances are other people feel the same way. When they do, they buy more, and profits go up. As profits improve, so does the company's stock. This is the classic philosophy of investing in things you know about. (It also makes shopping trips much more interesting.)

Drug Chains

Stock of the drug chains has performed weakly in early 1994. The uncertainties concerning health care changes and a slow-down in drug price inflation have been the main factors. In reality, the drugstores will likely benefit from major health care reform because more people will be covered who might not currently be able to afford expensive medications. Combine additional health insurance sales with a general increase in consumer interest in health and personal care products, and the long-term looks good for this industry. Competition will increase, so look for companies that have a special niche.

Supermarket chains

Increased competition and price-conscious shoppers have caused a decline in this industry in 1993. Supermarkets are notorious for working on a slim margin that can quickly turn negative when the economy goes down. Price cuts and new merchandise marketing will be necessary to boost the industry.

General Merchandise

This industry remained basically neutral in 1993, although a good Christmas season was helpful. The industry needs a sustained positive economy before it can make large gains.

Specialty Stores

The market outlook for 1994 looks for some improvement in this industry as the economy picks up. Some of the companies in this sector are refinancing debt to improve their bottom line and expect growth to get back on track once consumers start spending again. Stores continue to work on their own market niche, and the successful ones will prosper.

BCT INTERNATIONAL INCORPORATED

Symbol: BUCS   Exchange: OTC

PRICE 3/4/94	RANGE	P-E RATIO	DIVIDEND	YIELD	BETA
2¼	2 - 3¾	8.65	0	0	0.8

LAST FOUR QUARTERS REPORTED

REVENUES	% CHANGE	NET INCOME	% CHANGE	RETURN ON EQUITY	% CHANGE
12.522	20.88	0.641	102.21	36.61	16.75

Corporate Summary

BCT International Incorporated typically operates through the placement of business cards and stationery catalogs with commercial and retail "quick" print, office supply companies, and stationers in the trade areas of the company's plants. These catalogs are utilized by printers, office supply companies, and stationers to secure orders from their customers for thermographically printed products.

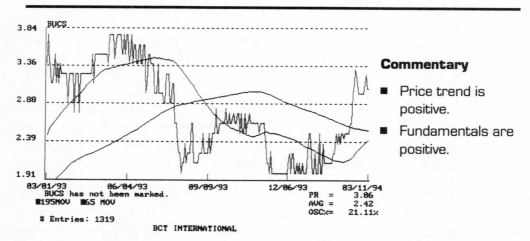

Commentary

- Price trend is positive.
- Fundamentals are positive.

```
BUCS has not been marked.
■19SMOV  ■65 MOV

# Entries: 1319

PR  =   3.86
AVG =   2.42
OSC%=  21.11%
```

BCT INTERNATIONAL

YEAR	REVENUES	% CHANGE	NET INCOME	% CHANGE	RETURN ON EQUITY	% CHANGE
89	9.358	5.561	- 2.620	- 844.318	- 143.4	- 1911.7
90	7.780	- 16.863	- 0.366	NA	- 1525.0	NA
91	8.810	13.123	- 0.703	NA	- 235.1	NA
92	10.614	20.600	0.778	NA	62.4	NA

CHECK EXPRESS INCORPORATED

Symbol: CHXS   Exchange: OTC

PRICE	RANGE	P-E RATIO	DIVIDEND	YIELD	BETA
1 $^7/_{16}$	$^7/_8$ - 1$^1/_2$	143.70	0	0	- 0.8

LAST FOUR QUARTERS REPORTED

REVENUES	% CHANGE	NET INCOME	% CHANGE	RETURN ON EQUITY	% CHANGE
3.735	- 18.87	0.033	- 82.63	0.98	- 94.41

Corporate Summary

Check Express Incorporated is a publicly-held company which, through its wholly-owned subsidiaries, owns, operates and franchises retail check cashing stores. The company owns and operates stores in Florida, South Carolina, and Indiana, and has similar franchised stores operating in 14 states. Check Express Inc. is based in Tampa, Florida.

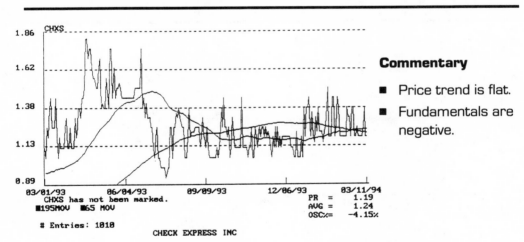

Commentary

- Price trend is flat.
- Fundamentals are negative.

CHXS has not been marked.
■195MOV ■65 MOV

PR = 1.19
AVG = 1.24
OSC%= -4.15%

Entries: 1010

CHECK EXPRESS INC

YEAR	REVENUES	% CHANGE	NET INCOME	% CHANGE	RETURN ON EQUITY	% CHANGE
89	3.402	14.123	0.018	- 70.968	1.8	- 71.5
90	3.627	6.614	0.173	861.111	14.6	708.4
91	4.400	21.312	0.008	- 95.376	0.7	- 95.4
92	3.298	- 10.727	0.141	1662.50	13.3	1885.9

CLAIRE'S STORES INCORPORATED

Symbol: CLE   Exchange: NYS

PRICE 3/4/94	RANGE	P-E RATIO	DIVIDEND	YIELD	BETA
18	$13\frac{1}{8}$ - $18\frac{1}{8}$	18.56	0.03	0	2.3

LAST FOUR QUARTERS REPORTED

REVENUES	% CHANGE	NET INCOME	% CHANGE	RETURN ON EQUITY	% CHANGE
270.404	14.39	19.764	168.10	23.54	109.40

Corporate Summary

Claire's Stores Incorporated is a leading mall-based retailer of popular-priced women's fashion accessories and trend gifts. Clarie's operates retail stores through two subsidiaries, Claire's Boutiques, Inc. and Dar Michelle, Inc. The fashion accessory stores specialize in selling popular-priced women's fashion accessories designed to appeal to females aged thirteen and up.

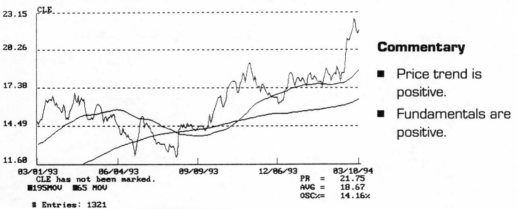

CLAIRE'S STORES INC.

Commentary

- Price trend is positive.
- Fundamentals are positive.

YEAR	REVENUES	% CHANGE	NET INCOME	% CHANGE	RETURN ON EQUITY	% CHANGE
89	190.246	49.490	19.452	174.088	35.6	68.7
90	255.199	34.142	20.453	5.146	27.8	- 22.0
91	234.162	- 8.243	5.226	- 74.449	8.2	- 70.6
92	247.987	5.904	14.551	178.435	18.9	131.8

ECKERD (JACK) CORPORATION

Symbol: ECK   Exchange: NYS

PRICE	RANGE	P-E RATIO	DIVIDEND	YIELD	BETA
19.75	19.75 - 13.88	NA	0	0	NA

LAST FOUR QUARTERS REPORTED

REVENUES	% CHANGE	NET INCOME	% CHANGE	RETURN ON EQUITY	% CHANGE
4190.021	9.30	13.873	219.90	NA	NA

Corporate Summary

Eckerd Corporation operates a retail chain of stores offering a diverse range of items, mainly nationally-known name brand items, as well as their own generic "Eckerd" brand items. The company directs its stores towards family-style, value-oriented consumers. Eckerd Corporation operates retail chains throughout the United States and became public in the third quarter of 1993.

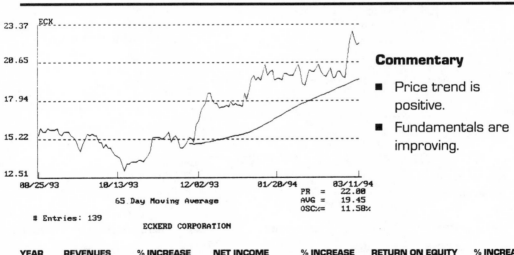

Entries: 139

ECKERD CORPORATION

PR = 22.00
AVG = 19.45
OSC% = 11.58%

Commentary

- Price trend is positive.
- Fundamentals are improving.

YEAR	REVENUES	% INCREASE	NET INCOME	% INCREASE	RETURN ON EQUITY	% INCREASE
89	3170.608	10.252	- 7.977	NA	3.8	961.5
90	3367.259	6.202	- 32.569	NA	12.9	237.9
91	3562.197	5.789	- 1.278	NA	0.5	- 96.2
92	3695.436	3.740	- 9.476	NA	3.3	590.3

HOME DEPOT INCORPORATED

Symbol: HD   Exchange: NYSE

PRICE	RANGE	P-E RATIO	DIVIDEND	YIELD	BETA
39	$38\frac{1}{2}$ - $48\frac{7}{8}$	38.61	0.30	0	1.4

LAST FOUR QUARTERS REPORTED

REVENUES	% CHANGE	NET INCOME	% CHANGE	RETURN ON EQUITY	% CHANGE
9238.763	29.24	457.401	26.053	17.06	1.969

Corporate Summary

Home Depot Incorporated operates a chain of retail "warehouse" building supply/home improvement stores in the eastern seaboard states, ranging from Connecticut to Florida, and into the states of Texas, Arizona, and California. The retail outlets average 97,000 sq. ft. in size and carry about 30,000 items.

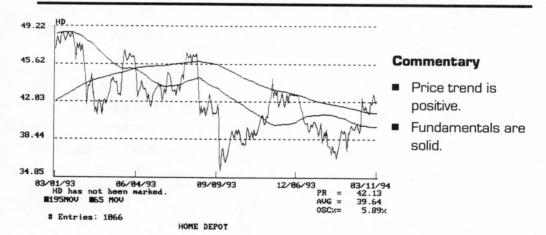

Commentary

- Price trend is positive.
- Fundamentals are solid.

HOME DEPOT

YEAR	REVENUES	% CHANGE	NET INCOME	% CHANGE	RETURN ON EQUITY	% CHANGE
89	2785.5	39.3	112.0	45.8	80.8	22.3
90	3815.4	36.9	163.4	45.9	51.7	-36.0
91	5136.7	34.6	249.2	52.5	162.1	213.5
92	7148.4	39.2	362.9	45.6	50.52	-68.8

JAN BELL MARKETING INCORPORATION

Symbol: JBM   Exchange: ASE

PRICE 3/4/94	RANGE	P-E RATIO	DIVIDEND	YIELD	BETA
$6^7/_8$	$6^7/_8$ - $20^1/_8$	NM	0	0	1.6

LAST FOUR QUARTERS REPORTED

REVENUES	% CHANGE	NET INCOME	% CHANGE	RETURN ON EQUITY	% CHANGE
290.778	2.72	- 7.079	- 155.03	- 3.16	- 154.58

Corporate Summary

Jan Bell Marketing Incorporated distributes jewelry to the wholesale membership industry and mass merchandisers. The company is currently focusing on going to retail through wholesale clubs only. Jan Bell also provides MIS support, inventory management, and market analysis to its clients.

Commentary

- Price trend is negative.
- Fundamentals are negative.

JBM has not been marked.
■19SMOV ■65 MOV

PR = 6.38
AVG = 8.15
OSC%= -27.87%

Entries: 1313

JAN BELL MARKETING INC.

YEAR	REVENUES	% CHANGE	NET INCOME	% CHANGE	RETURN ON EQUITY	% CHANGE
89	181.366	51.114	16.007	72.526	9.2	- 50.3
90	117.246	- 2.272	6.646	- 58.481	3.9	- 58.2
91	224.261	26.525	6.945	4.499	3.3	- 13.7
92	333.521	48.720	14.775	112.743	6.3	88.5

LURIA (L.) & SONS INCORPORATED

Symbol: LUR   Exchange: ASE

PRICE	RANGE	P-E RATIO	DIVIDEND	YIELD	BETA
13¾	10½ - 15	16.98	0	0	0.5

LAST FOUR QUARTERS REPORTED

REVENUES	% CHANGE	NET INCOME	% CHANGE	RETURN ON EQUITY	% CHANGE
240.253	9.64	4.303	127.79	5.31	114.63

Corporate Summary

Luria (L.) & Sons Inc. is the leading regional jewelry retailer in Florida, operating a chain of 50 stores. Luria's stores also offer china, crystal, giftware, consumer electronics, and small appliances. Luria is a niche retailer with the majority of profits being jewelry-dominated. Luria was established in 1898 and is based in Miami Lakes, FL.

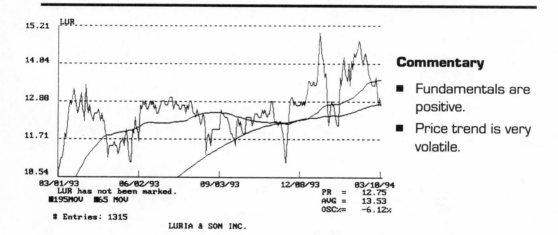

LUR has not been marked.
195MOV 65 MOV

Entries: 1315

LURIA & SON INC.

PR = 12.75
AVG = 13.53
OSC%= -6.12%

Commentary

- Fundamentals are positive.
- Price trend is very volatile.

YEAR	REVENUES	% CHANGE	NET INCOME	% CHANGE	RETURN ON EQUITY	% CHANGE
89	221.017	2.377	3.048	- 38.844	4.0	- 42.1
90	213.756	- 3.285	1.082	- 64.501	1.4	- 64.9
91	207.581	- 2.889	1.179	8.965	1.5	7.2
92	235.567	13.482	3.407	188.974	4.2	176.4

OFFICE DEPOT INCORPORATED

Symbol: ODP   Exchange: NYS

PRICE 3/4/94	RANGE	P-E RATIO	DIVIDEND	YIELD	BETA
$36\frac{1}{2}$	$19\frac{7}{8}$ - $36\frac{1}{2}$	54.48	0	0	1.6

LAST FOUR QUARTERS REPORTED

REVENUES	% CHANGE	NET INCOME	% CHANGE	RETURN ON EQUITY	% CHANGE
2579.493	48.85	63.417	67.81	11.91	10.45

Corporate Summary

Office Depot Incorporated operates the nation's largest chain of office products warehouse stores, with 228 stores in 29 states. The warehouse style stores offer approximately 5,100 brand name office products, including general office supplies, business machines, office furniture, and computer hardware and software.

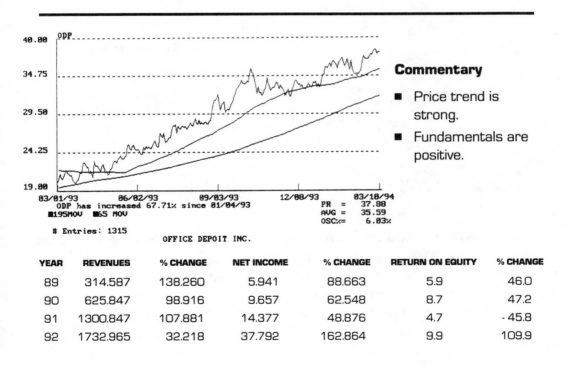

Commentary

- Price trend is strong.
- Fundamentals are positive.

ODP has increased 67.71% since 01/04/93

PR = 37.88
AVG = 35.59
OSC% = 6.03%

Entries: 1315

OFFICE DEPOIT INC.

YEAR	REVENUES	% CHANGE	NET INCOME	% CHANGE	RETURN ON EQUITY	% CHANGE
89	314.587	138.260	5.941	88.663	5.9	46.0
90	625.847	98.916	9.657	62.548	8.7	47.2
91	1300.847	107.881	14.377	48.876	4.7	- 45.8
92	1732.965	32.218	37.792	162.864	9.9	109.9

PERFUMANIA INCORPORATION

Symbol: PRFM   Exchange: NMS

PRICE 3/4/94	RANGE	P-E RATIO	DIVIDEND	YIELD	BETA
$4\frac{3}{8}$	$3\frac{3}{4}$ - $8\frac{3}{4}$	NA	0	0	- 0.8

LAST FOUR QUARTERS REPORTED

REVENUES	% CHANGE	NET INCOME	% CHANGE	RETURN ON EQUITY	% CHANGE
83.398	8.92	- 2.314	NA	- 5.84	NA

Corporate Summary

Perfumania Incorporated is a leading specialty retailer and wholesale distributor of a wide range of brand name and designer perfumes.
Perfumania operates a chain of 109 retail stores specializing in the sale
of perfumes at prices generally ranging from 20 to 60 percent below the
manufacturer's suggested retail price.

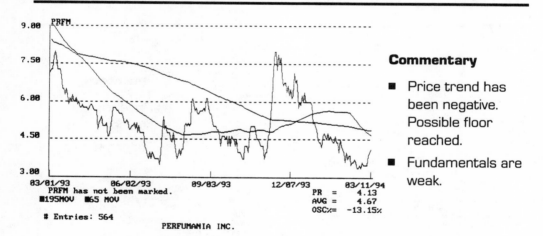

PRFM has not been marked.
■19SMOV ■6S MOV

PR = 4.13
AVG = 4.67
OSC% = -13.15%

Entries: 564

PERFUMANIA INC.

Commentary

- Price trend has been negative. Possible floor reached.

- Fundamentals are weak.

YEAR	REVENUES	% CHANGE	NET INCOME	% CHANGE	RETURN ON EQUITY	% CHANGE
89	NA	NA	NA	NA	NA	NA
90	NA	NA	NA	NA	NA	NA
91	85.737	NA	1.607	NA	10.7	NA
92	72.397	- 15.559	- 4.312	- 368.326	- 10.5	- 198.9

REPOSSESSION AUCTION INCORPORATED

Symbol: REPO   Exchange: OTC

PRICE 3/4/94	RANGE	P-E RATIO	DIVIDEND	YIELD	BETA
1	1 - 3⅜	NM	0	0	0.6

LAST FOUR QUARTERS REPORTED

REVENUES	% CHANGE	NET INCOME	% CHANGE	RETURN ON EQUITY	% CHANGE
8.721	- 2.85	- 0.099	- 131.83	- 0.98	- 132.15

Corporate Summary

Repossession Auction Incorporated does business as a vehicle auctioneer. The company is thinking about international expansion. The vehicles sold can be offered both to car dealerships as well as individual investors. Most vehicles offered are bank repossessions. As auctions become more and more popular ways to purchase vehicles, the company expects to become more profitable.

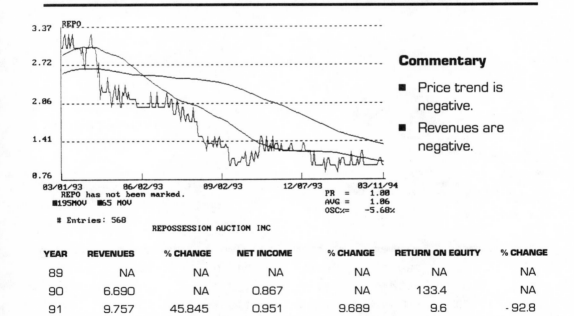

Commentary

- Price trend is negative.
- Revenues are negative.

REPO has not been marked.
■195MOV ■65 MOV
PR = 1.00
AVG = 1.06
OSC%= -5.68%

Entries: 568

REPOSSESSION AUCTION INC

YEAR	REVENUES	% CHANGE	NET INCOME	% CHANGE	RETURN ON EQUITY	% CHANGE
89	NA	NA	NA	NA	NA	NA
90	6.690	NA	0.867	NA	133.4	NA
91	9.757	45.845	0.951	9.689	9.6	- 92.8
92	9.432	- 3.331	0.165	- 82.650	1.6	- 82.9

SOUND ADVICE INCORPORATED

Symbol: SUNDE   Exchange: NMS

PRICE 3/4/94	RANGE	P-E RATIO	DIVIDEND	YIELD	BETA
6⅛	5 - 7¼	47.12	0	0	2.0

LAST FOUR QUARTERS REPORTED

REVENUES	% CHANGE	NET INCOME	% CHANGE	RETURN ON EQUITY	% CHANGE
165.209	8.74	0.458	121.55	2.32	NA

Corporate Summary

Sound Advice Incorporated is a full service specialty retailer of a broad range of high-quality, upscale entertainment and consumer electronic products. The company operates approximately 20 stores in Florida which sell home and car audio systems, large-screen televisions, video products, cellular telephones, and other personal electronics. Sound Advice is based in Dania, Florida.

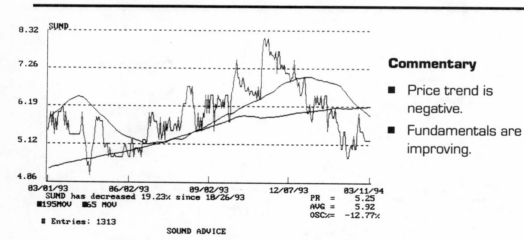

```
8.32  SUND
7.26
6.19
5.12
4.86
     03/01/93      06/02/93      09/02/93      12/07/93      03/11/94
     SUND has decreased 19.23% since 10/26/93        PR  =    5.25
     ■195MOV  ■65 MOV                                AVG =    5.92
                                                     OSC%=  -12.77%
     # Entries: 1313
                    SOUND ADVICE
```

Commentary

- Price trend is negative.
- Fundamentals are improving.

YEAR	REVENUES	% CHANGE	NET INCOME	% CHANGE	RETURN ON EQUITY	% CHANGE
89	76.614	39.911	2.892	28.762	15.5	- 29.4
90	91.511	19.444	2.582	- 10.719	12.2	- 21.6
91	117.583	28.491	2.950	14.253	12.1	- 0.8
92	137.670	17.083	- 2.929	- 199.288	- 16.2	- 234.4

SPEC'S MUSIC INCORPORATED

Symbol: SPEK   Exchange: NMS

PRICE 3/4/94	RANGE	P-E RATIO	DIVIDEND	YIELD	BETA
7	$4\frac{1}{4}$ - $7\frac{1}{2}$	28.00	0	0	1.3

LAST FOUR QUARTERS REPORTED

REVENUES	% CHANGE	NET INCOME	% CHANGE	RETURN ON EQUITY	% CHANGE
74.653	16.12	1.331	- 27.03	6.85	- 32.77

Corporate Summary

Spec's Music Incorporated is the largest specialty retailer of prerecorded music and video products in Florida. The company sells audio cassettes and compact discs, movies and music videos on VHS tape and laser disc, blank audio and video tapes, and a variety of audio and video accessories and boutique items. In addition, Spec's rents video movies.

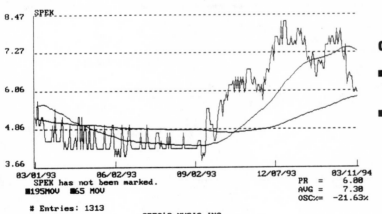

Commentary

- Price trend is volatile.
- Fundamentals are mixed.

SPEK has not been marked.
■195MOV ■65 MOV

PR = 6.00
AVG = 7.30
OSC%= -21.63%

Entries: 1313

SPEC'S MUSIC INC.

YEAR	REVENUES	% CHANGE	NET INCOME	% CHANGE	RETURN ON EQUITY	% CHANGE
89	40.152	23.427	2.231	22.920	17.7	- 0.6
90	49.359	22.930	1.995	- 10.578	13.4	- 24.5
91	59.352	20.246	1.766	- 11.479	10.6	- 20.9
92	62.834	5.867	1.930	9.287	10.6	- 0.1

SPORTS/LEISURE INCORPORATED

Symbol: SPLE   Exchange: NMS

PRICE 3/4/94	RANGE	P-E RATIO	DIVIDEND	YIELD	BETA
1$\frac{1}{2}$	$\frac{5}{8}$ - 2	NM	0	0	- 0.9

LAST FOUR QUARTERS REPORTED

REVENUES	% CHANGE	NET INCOME	% CHANGE	RETURN ON EQUITY	% CHANGE
15.453	- 18.70	- 2.054	NA	- 48.65	NA

Corporate Summary

Sports/Leisure Incorporated, based in Boca Raton, Florida, is in the business of manufacturing, marketing, and selling of sports apparel. The company has recently acquired 50 percent of Flamingo Apparel Incorporated to expand the sewing capabilities of its company. Sports/Leisure Inc. has also negotiated a two year renewable contract with Sara Lee, a subsidiary of Hayes, to manufacture and distribute women's apparel.

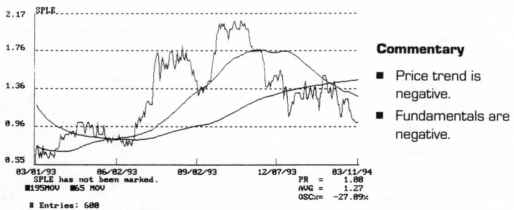

SPORTS/LEISURE INC.

Commentary

- Price trend is negative.
- Fundamentals are negative.

YEAR	REVENUES	% CHANGE	NET INCOME	% CHANGE	RETURN ON EQUITY	% CHANGE
89	NA	NA	NA	NA	NA	NA
90	7.562	NA	0.172	NA	16.4	NA
91	16.816	122.375	0.428	148.837	8.2	- 50.4
92	19.725	17.299	- 3.306	- 872.430	- 165.0	- 2123

SPORTS & RECREATION INCORPORATED

Symbol: SPRC   Exchange: NMS

PRICE 3/4/94	RANGE	P-E RATIO	DIVIDEND	YIELD	BETA
39¼	23⅛ - 39¼	50.97	0	0	NA

LAST FOUR QUARTERS REPORTED

REVENUES	% CHANGE	NET INCOME	% CHANGE	RETURN ON EQUITY	% CHANGE
203.798	29.50	9.188	115.43	8.24	96.99

Corporate Summary

Sports & Recreation Incorporated, based in Tampa, Florida, is in the business of distributing and retailing sporting goods. The company operates in the southeastern region with concentration in southwest Florida. The company has sports superstores as its main source of distribution and expects to open more stores in fiscal year 1993.

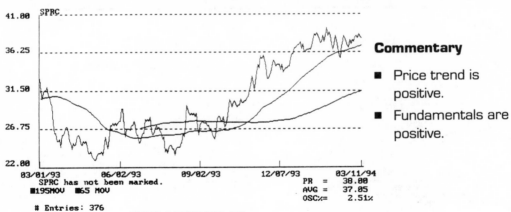

Commentary

- Price trend is positive.
- Fundamentals are positive.

SPRC has not been marked.
195MOV   65 MOV

PR = 38.00
AVG = 37.05
OSC%= 2.51%

Entries: 376

SPORTS & RECREATION INC.

YEAR	REVENUES	% INCREASE	NET INCOME	% INCREASE	RETURN ON EQUITY	% INCREASE
89	NA	NA	NA	NA	NA	NA
90	NA	NA	NA	NA	NA	NA
91	138.930	NA	2.515	NA	7.7	NA
92	167.355	20.460	5.470	117.495	5.2	- 33.1

STEIN MART INCORPORATED

Symbol: SMRT   Exchange: NMS

PRICE 3/4/94	RANGE	P-E RATIO	DIVIDEND	YIELD	BETA
17$\frac{1}{4}$	15$\frac{5}{8}$ - 23$\frac{1}{2}$	26.54	0	0	NA

LAST FOUR QUARTERS REPORTED

REVENUES	% CHANGE	NET INCOME	% CHANGE	RETURN ON EQUITY	% CHANGE
323.369	27.13	15.451	6.33	27.51	- 22.87

Corporate Summary

Stein Mart Incorporated operates a 55-store retail chain offering fashion-able, current season, primarily branded merchandise comparable in quality and presentation to that of traditional department and fine spe-cialty stores at prices competitive with off-price retail chains. Stein Mart caters to fashion-conscious, value-oriented customers who would usually shop at department stores.

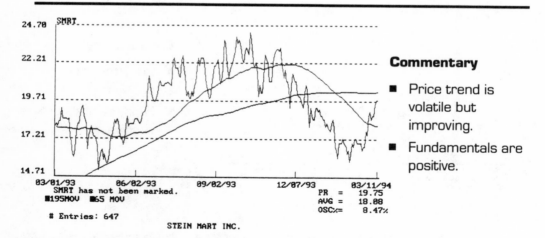

Commentary

- Price trend is volatile but improving.

- Fundamentals are positive.

STEIN MART INC.

YEAR	REVENUES	% CHANGE	NET INCOME	% CHANGE	RETURN ON EQUITY	% CHANGE
89	NA	NA	NA	NA	NA	NA
90	NA	NA	NA	NA	NA	NA
91	225.389	NA	12.554	NA	39.8	NA
92	278.254	23.455	13.921	10.889	27.7	- 30.3

SUNSHINE-JR STORES

Symbol: SJS   Exchange: ASE

PRICE 3/4/94	RANGE	P-E RATIO	DIVIDEND	YIELD	BETA
$8^7/8$	$2^7/8$ - $8^7/8$	NM	0	0	0

LAST FOUR QUARTERS REPORTED

REVENUES	% CHANGE	NET INCOME	% CHANGE	RETURN ON EQUITY	% CHANGE
218.824	- 1.65	- 8.250	NA	- 69.94	NA

Corporate Summary

Sunshine-Jr. Stores Incorporated is in the business of operating supermarkets and convenience stores. The company operates all convenience stores under the trade name "Jr. Food Stores." The convenience stores are located and designed to attract customers on an eighteen to twenty-four hour basis seven days per week. All stores are self-service outlets, offering gasoline and food as well as merchandise.

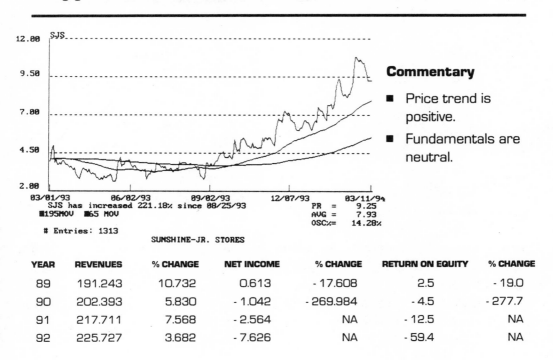

Commentary

- Price trend is positive.
- Fundamentals are neutral.

SJS has increased 221.18% since 08/25/93
195MOV 65 MOV

PR = 9.25
AVG = 7.93
OSC% = 14.28%

Entries: 1313

SUNSHINE-JR. STORES

YEAR	REVENUES	% CHANGE	NET INCOME	% CHANGE	RETURN ON EQUITY	% CHANGE
89	191.243	10.732	0.613	- 17.608	2.5	- 19.0
90	202.393	5.830	- 1.042	- 269.984	- 4.5	- 277.7
91	217.711	7.568	- 2.564	NA	- 12.5	NA
92	225.727	3.682	- 7.626	NA	- 59.4	NA

WAL-MART STORES

Symbol: WMT   Exchange: NYS

PRICE 3/4/94	RANGE	P-E RATIO	DIVIDEND	YIELD	BETA
26½	24⅝ - 32½	27.46	.03	0	1.2

LAST FOUR QUARTERS REPORTED

REVENUES	% CHANGE	NET INCOME	% CHANGE	RETURN ON EQUITY	% CHANGE
64105.797	23.28	2214.852	19.88	22.26	- 2.97

Corporate Summary

Wal-Mart Stores Incorporated is the world's largest retailer. The company operates an expanding chain of modern discount retail stores in cities and towns across the United States. The company targets its retail units towards value-oriented consumers. Additionally, Wal-Mart operates chains of Sam's Wholesale Clubs in metropolitan areas.

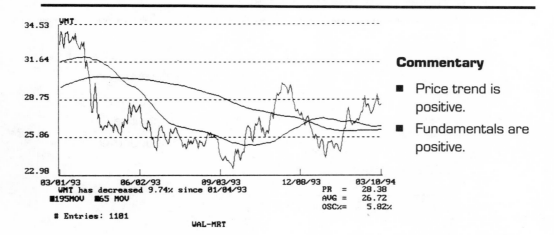

WMT has decreased 9.74% since 01/04/93

PR = 28.38
AVG = 26.72
OSC% = 5.82%

■19SMOV ■65 MOV

Entries: 1101

WAL-MRT

Commentary

■ Price trend is positive.

■ Fundamentals are positive.

YEAR	REVENUES	% CHANGE	NET INCOME	% CHANGE	RETURN ON EQUITY	% CHANGE
89	25810.598	24.997	1075.900	28.508	27.1	- 2.5
90	32601.500	26.311	1291.024	19.995	24.1	- 11.3
91	43886.898	34.616	1608.476	24.589	23.0	- 4.4
92	55483.699	26.424	1994.794	24.018	22.77	- 1.0

WILSON BROTHERS

Symbol: WLB   Exchange: REG

PRICE 3/4/94	RANGE	P-E RATIO	DIVIDEND	YIELD	BETA
NA	$^1/_8$ - $^{13}/_{16}$	NA	0	NA	NA

LAST FOUR QUARTERS REPORTED

REVENUES	% CHANGE	NET INCOME	% CHANGE	RETURN ON EQUITY	% CHANGE
SF	SF	SF	NA	NA	NA

Corporate Summary

Wilson Brothers, located in Miami Beach, Florida, is in the business of manufacturing and distributing glass and ceramic products. The major target industry is construction and they do business throughout the U.S. The company is in the process of streamlining operations and is hoping to take advantage of the growth of Florida real estate construction.

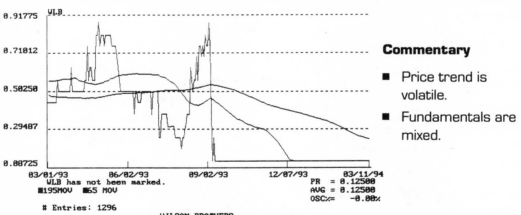

Commentary

- Price trend is volatile.

- Fundamentals are mixed.

WLB has not been marked.
195MOV   65 MOV
Entries: 1296

PR = 0.12500
AVG = 0.12500
OSC% = -0.00%

WILSON BROTHERS

YEAR	REVENUES	% CHANGE	NET INCOME	% CHANGE	RETURN ON EQUITY	% CHANGE
89	7.470	26.567	0.670	NA	9.8	NA
90	14.258	90.870	- 0.782	- 216.716	- 12.9	- 231.8
91	13.744	- 3.605	- 0.968	NA	- 19.0	NA
92	10.730	- 21.930	- 2.352	NA	- 85.5	NA

WINDMERE CORPORATION

Symbol: WND   Exchange: NYS

PRICE	RANGE	P-E RATIO	DIVIDEND	YIELD	BETA
$8\frac{1}{8}$	$6\frac{5}{8}$ - $8\frac{1}{4}$	13.77	0	0	1.1

LAST FOUR QUARTERS REPORTED

REVENUES	% CHANGE	NET INCOME	% CHANGE	RETURN ON EQUITY	% CHANGE
179.275	3.99	9.536	369.52	6.74	336.64

Corporate Summary

Windmere Corporation is a manufacturer and distributor of personal care appliances and related products, health care appliances, fans, heaters, and air filtration devices for the home, as well as other small household appliances. The company designs and manufactures its appliances for sale to distributors and professional salon owners located primarily in the United States and Canada, with developing distribution in Western Europe.

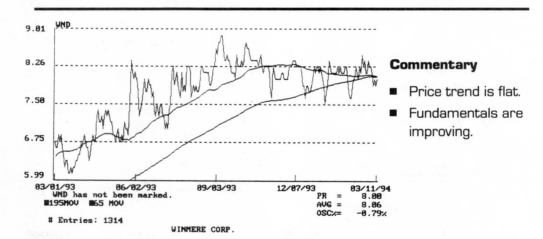

Commentary

■ Price trend is flat.
■ Fundamentals are improving.

YEAR	REVENUES	% CHANGE	NET INCOME	% CHANGE	RETURN ON EQUITY	% CHANGE
89	178.698	- 7.566	7.688	- 76.418	6.7	- 81.5
90	154.859	- 13.340	- 3.729	- 148.504	- 3.4	- 150.2
91	141.608	- 8.557	- 9.488	NA	- 9.5	NA
92	175.450	23.898	4.686	NA	3.5	NA

WINN-DIXIE STORES INCORPORATED

Symbol: WIN   Exchange: NYS

PRICE	RANGE	P-E RATIO	DIVIDEND	YIELD	BETA
50	50 - 74½	15.72	0.36	0.1	1.0

LAST FOUR QUARTERS REPORTED

REVENUES	% CHANGE	NET INCOME	% CHANGE	RETURN ON EQUITY	% CHANGE
11040.159	5.34	239.709	3.16	24.09	- 1.57

Corporate Summary

Winn-Dixie Stores Incorporated is the nation's fifth largest supermarket chain, and the largest supermarket chain in the Sunbelt. The company operates about 1,200 supermarkets under the names "Winn-Dixie" and "Marketplace," as well as distribution centers, processing and manufacturing plants, and a truck fleet. Winn-Dixie is based in Jacksonville, Florida.

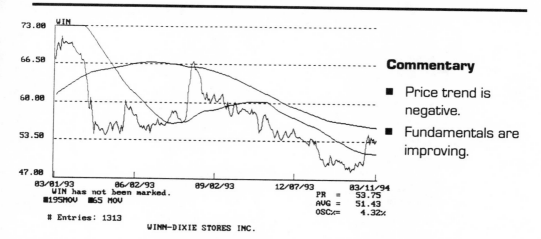

Commentary

- Price trend is negative.
- Fundamentals are improving.

WIN has not been marked.
■195MOV ■65 MOV
PR = 53.75
AVG = 51.43
OSC%= 4.32%

Entries: 1313

WINN-DIXIE STORES INC.

YEAR	REVENUES	% CHANGE	NET INCOME	% CHANGE	RETURN ON EQUITY	% CHANGE
89	9151.144	1.592	134.545	15.297	17.2	6.9
90	9744.492	6.484	152.530	13.367	18.8	9.2
91	10074.296	3.385	170.931	12.064	19.9	6.0
92	10337.296	2.611	216.419	26.612	22.7	14.4

Chapter 17

Florida Environmental Companies

The slow economy has had a major impact on this industry, which relies heavily on industrial customers. Before the environmental industry improves, its customers must experience improvement in their respective businesses, and thus we expect this industry to lag behind any upswing in the economy.

At the present time, with stock prices at historical lows, an opportunity exists for bargain hunting. I encourage caution, however, because of the expected time lag for a turnaround. Investors should wait for earning improvements.

Long-term analysis is positive, since we expect to see more environmental legislation introduced by the current administration.

I know of people who invest only in environmental stocks out of a desire to support a clean environment. I applaud their attitude, but from an investment standpoint, they may be using faulty logic. You aren't investing if you are putting money in a company for reasons other than making a profit. If your goal is to help the environment, invest wisely to make more money; then, if you like, donate the additional money to environmental causes.

The environmental industry had a difficult 1993, and 1994 won't prove any kinder. In a weak economy, many companies are forced to spend money in other areas before addressing environmental concerns. No doubt future legislation will help these companies recover, but until that occurs, things will be slow.

ENVIROQ CORPORATION
Symbol: EROQ   Exchange: NMS

PRICE 3/4/94	RANGE	P-E RATIO	DIVIDEND	YIELD	BETA
3¼	2⅞ - 4⅛	NM	0	0	1.2

LAST FOUR QUARTERS REPORTED

REVENUES	% CHANGE	NET INCOME	% CHANGE	RETURN ON EQUITY	% CHANGE
18.896	24.21	- 0.316	NA	- 2.69	NA

Corporate Summary

Enviroq Corporation is primarily in the business of protecting the environment by solving infrastructure problems in water and wastewater
systems for industry and government. The company is the leading supplier
of non-disruptive pipeline reconstruction and repair in Alabama, Florida,
Georgia, North Carolina, and South Carolina.

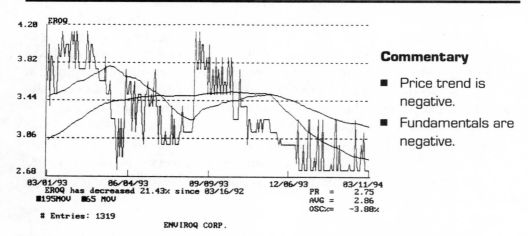

ENVIROQ CORP.

Commentary

■ Price trend is negative.

■ Fundamentals are negative.

YEAR	REVENUES	% CHANGE	NET INCOME	% CHANGE	RETURN ON EQUITY	% CHANGE
89	20.101	30.154	1.496	17.425	13.6	1.5
90	20.779	3.373	1.262	- 15.642	10.3	- 24.3
91	15.755	- 24.178	- 0.943	- 174.723	- 8.0	- 178.3
92	15.291	- 2.945	- 0.463	NA	- 4.0	NA

KIMMINS ENVIRONMENTAL SERVICE CORPORATION

Symbol: KVN   Exchange: NYS

PRICE 3/4/94	RANGE	P-E RATIO	DIVIDEND	YIELD	BETA
$2^5/_8$	$2^1/_8$ - $2^3/_4$	12.50	0	0	1.1

LAST FOUR QUARTERS REPORTED

REVENUES	% CHANGE	NET INCOME	% CHANGE	RETURN ON EQUITY	% CHANGE
79.155	6.17	2.728	546.48	11.64	NA

Corporate Summary

Kimmins Environmental Service Corporation is a solid waste management and specialty contracting company that provides a full range of solid waste handling services and project-oriented services for the remediation of sites and facilities. The company is based in Tampa, Florida.

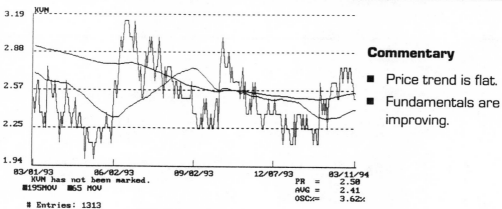

```
3.19  KVN
2.88
2.57
2.25
1.94
     03/01/93      06/02/93      09/02/93      12/07/93      03/11/94
        KVN has not been marked.                    PR  =    2.50
     ■195MOV  ■65 MOV                               AVG =    2.41
                                                    OSC%=    3.62%
        # Entries: 1313
                    KIMMINS ENV. SERV.
```

Commentary

- Price trend is flat.
- Fundamentals are improving.

YEAR	REVENUES	% CHANGE	NET INCOME	% CHANGE	RETURN ON EQUITY	% CHANGE
89	107.462	35.326	3.613	127.090	22.9	75.8
90	107.245	- 0.202	- 1.790	- 149.543	- 9.0	- 139.4
91	100.646	- 6.153	2.593	NA	11.5	NA
92	87.442	- 13.119	0.061	- 97.648	0.3	- 97.5

LICON INTERNATIONAL INCORPORATED

Symbol: LCON   Exchange: OTC

PRICE 3/4/94	RANGE	P-E RATIO	DIVIDEND	YIELD	BETA
$^{13}/_{16}$	$^{13}/_{16}$ - 4	NM	0	0	- 1.2

LAST FOUR QUARTERS REPORTED

REVENUES	% CHANGE	NET INCOME	% CHANGE	RETURN ON EQUITY	% CHANGE
2.597	- 36.90	- 4.081	NA	- 342.65	NA

Corporate Summary

Licon International Incorporated was formed to establish, acquire, and manage businesses in the environmental sector, including water, wastewater, liquid processing, and other environmental services and remediation equipment. The company is engaged in the design, assembly, and marketing of equipment used to concentrate and purify hazardous and non-hazardous liquid wastes.

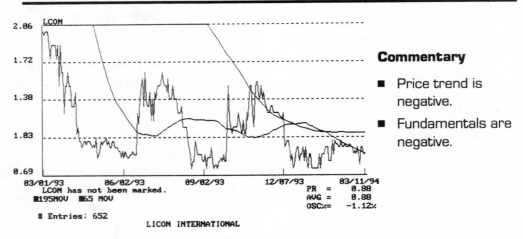

Commentary

■ Price trend is negative.

■ Fundamentals are negative.

LCON has not been marked.
■195MOV ■65 MOV

PR = 0.88
AVG = 0.88
OSCx= -1.12%

Entries: 652

LICON INTERNATIONAL

YEAR	REVENUES	% CHANGE	NET INCOME	% CHANGE	RETURN ON EQUITY	% CHANGE
89	NA	NA	NA	NA	NA	NA
90	1.140	NA	- 0.641	NA	225.7	NA
91	3.295	189.035	- 1.356	NA	- 36.8	- 116.3
92	4.602	39.666	- 3.837	NA	- 272.3	NA

PLANTS FOR TOMORROW INCORPORATED

Symbol: PFTI   Exchange: OTC

PRICE 3/4/94	RANGE	P-E RATIO	DIVIDEND	YIELD	BETA
$\frac{1}{4}$	$\frac{1}{4}$ - $2\frac{3}{16}$	NM	0	0	- 1.3

LAST FOUR QUARTERS REPORTED

REVENUES	% CHANGE	NET INCOME	% CHANGE	RETURN ON EQUITY	% CHANGE
6.837	101.62	- 1.872	NA	- 56.90	NA

Corporate Summary

Plants For Tomorrow Incorporated specializes in the propagation and growing of more than 400 species of terrestrial and aquatic plants and plant seeds that are native to Florida, and is the sole source of supply for certain varieties. The company has nurseries throughout Florida and is based in Loxahatchee, Florida.

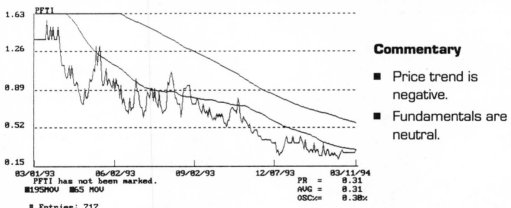

1.63 PFTI
1.26
0.89
0.52
0.15
03/01/93   06/02/93   09/02/93   12/07/93   03/11/94
PFTI has not been marked.
■19SMOV ■65 MOV
Entries: 717
PLANTS FOR TOMORROW INC.

PR = 0.31
AVG = 0.31
OSC%= 0.30%

Commentary

- Price trend is negative.
- Fundamentals are neutral.

YEAR	REVENUES	% CHANGE	NET INCOME	% CHANGE	RETURN ON EQUITY	% CHANGE
89	NA	NA	NA	NA	NA	NA
90	1.844	NA	0.107	NA	19.7	NA
91	2.091	13.395	- 0.094	- 187.850	- 4.8	- 124.6
92	4.060	94.165	- 1.422	NA	- 38.8	NA

QUADREX CORPORATION

Symbol: QUAD   Exchange: NMS

PRICE 3/4/94	RANGE	P-E RATIO	DIVIDEND	YIELD	BETA
$3\frac{3}{4}$	$3\frac{5}{8}$ - 13	NM	0	0	1.5

LAST FOUR QUARTERS REPORTED

REVENUES	% CHANGE	NET INCOME	% CHANGE	RETURN ON EQUITY	% CHANGE
43.428	- 10.54	- 26.581	- 1951.04	- 389.75	- 6347.14

Corporate Summary

Quadrex Corporation is in the business of converting wastes into resources. Its business activities are all focused on the taking, converting or
recycling of waste materials into resources which improve the environment or which contribute to the production of energy. In particular, the
company is focusing in the areas of decontamination, waste collection, recycling, and various aspects of energy development.

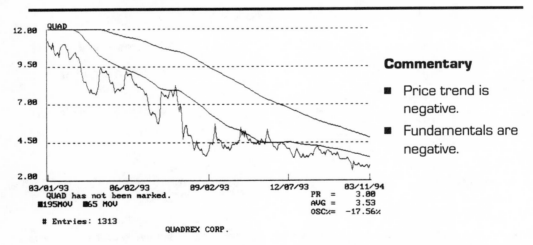

QUAD has not been marked.
■195MOV ■65 MOV

PR =   3.00
AVG =   3.53
OSC%= -17.56%

\# Entries: 1313

QUADREX CORP.

Commentary

- Price trend is negative.
- Fundamentals are negative.

YEAR	REVENUES	% CHANGE	NET INCOME	% CHANGE	RETURN ON EQUITY	% CHANGE
89	40.598	- 1.274	- 9.968	NA	- 284.6	NA
90	33.169	- 18.299	0.347	NA	6.0	NA
91	43.356	30.712	1.621	367.147	8.7	44.1
92	49.067	13.172	- 1.962	- 221.036	- 9.7	- 211.4

VIROGROUP INCORPORATED

Symbol: VIRO   Exchange: NMS

PRICE 3/4/94	RANGE	P-E RATIO	DIVIDEND	YIELD	BETA
$3\frac{5}{8}$	$2\frac{1}{4}$ - $9\frac{3}{4}$	NM	0	0	1.6

LAST FOUR QUARTERS REPORTED

REVENUES	% CHANGE	NET INCOME	% CHANGE	RETURN ON EQUITY	% CHANGE
27.137	20.17	- 13.336	- 1039.82	- 180.34	- 1718.85

Corporate Summary

Virogroup Incorporated, formerly Missimer & Associates, provides a wide range of environmental services to assess and remediate groundwater and soil contamination, to design and monitor solid waste landfills, to protect air quality, to assure regulatory compliance, and to develop groundwater resources.

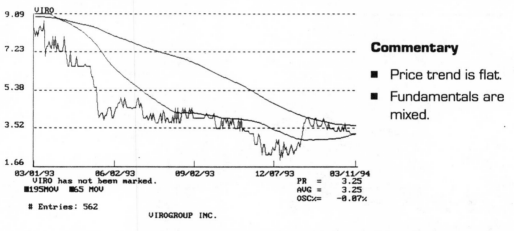

VIRO has not been marked.
■195MOV ■65 MOV
PR = 3.25
AVG = 3.25
OSC%= -0.07%

Entries: 562

VIROGROUP INC.

Commentary

■ Price trend is flat.
■ Fundamentals are mixed.

YEAR	REVENUES	% CHANGE	NET INCOME	% CHANGE	RETURN ON EQUITY	% CHANGE
89	NA	NA	NA	NA	NA	NA
90	NA	NA	NA	NA	NA	NA
91	10.839	NA	0.667	NA	53.3	NA
92	19.187	77.018	1.204	80.510	9.8	- 81.7

WASTE TECHNOLOGY CORPORATION

Symbol: WTEK   Exchange: OTC

PRICE 3/4/94	RANGE	P-E RATIO	DIVIDEND	YIELD	BETA
1¼	$^{15}/_{16}$ - 2¼	3.47	0	0	1.4

LAST FOUR QUARTERS REPORTED

REVENUES	% CHANGE	NET INCOME	% CHANGE	RETURN ON EQUITY	% CHANGE
7.511	-1.31	0.732	159.80	59.80	NA

Corporate Summary

Waste Technology Corporation, along with its subsidiaries, works in the area of waste disposal, industrial coating, and energy conservation. The company's main business is the manufacturing and sales of balers, which are machines used to compress and compact various waste materials. The company manufactures approximately 50 different models of balers for use with different materials.

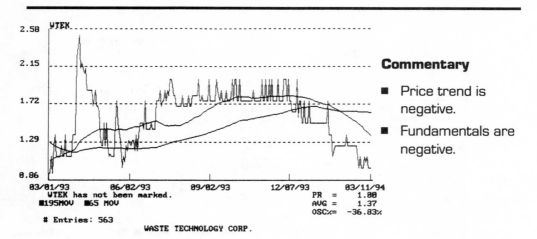

Commentary

- Price trend is negative.
- Fundamentals are negative.

WTEK has not been marked.
195MOV 65 MOV

Entries: 563

PR = 1.00
AVG = 1.37
OSC%= -36.83%

WASTE TECHNOLOGY CORP.

YEAR	REVENUES	% CHANGE	NET INCOME	% CHANGE	RETURN ON EQUITY	% CHANGE
89	6.922	23.850	0.428	217.037	10.6	147.2
90	7.631	10.243	0.406	-5.140	10.3	-3.4
91	10.820	41.790	0.385	-5.172	9.1	-11.0
92	6.716	-37.930	-0.838	-317.662	-120.6	-1420.7

Chapter 18

Florida Leisure Companies

Florida's diverse leisure industry contains everything from sports clothes to cruise lines and entertainment parks. Indeed, this diversity makes general predictions for the industry difficult. Nationally, gaming stocks have done the best, but in Florida, specialty companies like Blockbuster have been quite successful.

For the near future, I forsee improvement in the industry as a whole and continued success for some specific companies whose unique products make marketing easier.

The long-term picture holds great prospects for some of these companies. Disney continues to announce exciting projects into the next century. Despite problems with its EuroDisney venture, the company continues to produce.

Blockbuster is another future-sited company. Realizing that the rental video market may face a dim future, Blockbuster is rapidly diversifying into an entertainment conglomerate. They realize that the company that controls the production of movies will have a great deal to say about their distribution. Consequently, they are expanding to become a production giant.

ACTION PRODUCTS INTERNATIONAL INCORPORATED

Symbol: APII   Exchange: OTC

PRICE 3/4/94	RANGE	P-E RATIO	DIVIDEND	YIELD	BETA
$2\frac{1}{2}$	$2\frac{1}{8} - 3\frac{5}{8}$	31.25	0	0	- 1.1

LAST FOUR QUARTERS REPORTED

REVENUES	% CHANGE	NET INCOME	% CHANGE	RETURN ON EQUITY	% CHANGE
4.076	- 17.69	0.075	7400.23	2.98	7227.13

Corporate Summary

Action Products International Incorporated markets a wide range of space, education, and consumer products to museums, space bases, and corporations for resale. The company is the largest single supplier of goods and services to gift shops at museums, zoos, planetariums, arboretums, botanical gardens, and science centers in the United States.

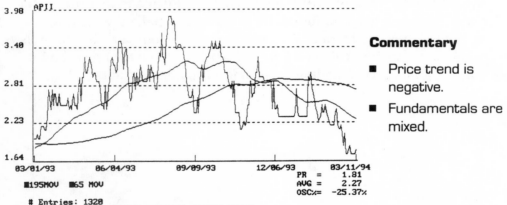

Commentary

- Price trend is negative.
- Fundamentals are mixed.

ACTION PRODUCTS INTERNATIONAL

YEAR	REVENUES	% CHANGE	NET INCOME	% CHANGE	RETURN ON EQUITY	% CHANGE
89	3.338	- 16.592	- 0.145	- 270.588	- 10.0	- 287.2
90	3.971	18.963	- 0.085	NA	- 6.3	NA
91	4.324	8.889	.0106	NA	5.5	NA
92	4.952	14.524	0.001	- 99.057	0.0	- 99.2

BLOCKBUSTER ENTERTAINMENT CORPORATION

Symbol: BV   Exchange: NYS

PRICE 3/4/94	RANGE	P-E RATIO	DIVIDEND	YIELD	BETA
27⅝	17⅝ - 33⅜	24.89	0.03	0	0.7

LAST FOUR QUARTERS REPORTED

REVENUES	% CHANGE	NET INCOME	% CHANGE	RETURN ON EQUITY	% CHANGE
2227.003	69.25	243.646	64.33	18.24	- 15.03

Corporate Summary

Blockbuster Entertainment Corporation's principal businesses are home video and music retailing. Through its domestic and international home video divisions, the company is the largest home video retailer in the world with over 30 million members and 3,127 video stores in the Blockbuster system. In addition, the company is a partner with the Virgin Retail Group in the ownership and operation of 15 music "Megastores" in Australia, the United States, and six countries in Europe.

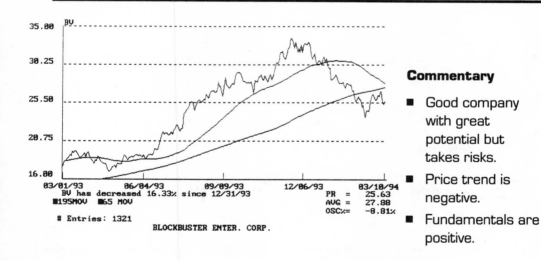

BV has decreased 16.33% since 12/31/93
195MOV 65 MOV

PR = 25.63
AVG = 27.88
OSC% = -8.81%

Entries: 1321

BLOCKBUSTER ENTER. CORP.

Commentary

- Good company with great potential but takes risks.
- Price trend is negative.
- Fundamentals are positive.

YEAR	REVENUES	% CHANGE	NET INCOME	% CHANGE	RETURN ON EQUITY	% CHANGE
89	402.538	194.053	44.152	184.888	21.2	39.3
90	632.670	57.170	68.654	55.495	21.8	2.8
91	868.003	37.197	93.681	36.454	19.4	- 11.2
92	1200.494	38.305	142.034	51.615	18.1	- 6.4

CARNIVAL CRUISE LINES INCORPORATED

Symbol: CCL   Exchange: NYS

PRICE	RANGE	P-E RATIO	DIVIDEND	YIELD	BETA
49$\frac{1}{2}$	32$\frac{3}{4}$ - 49$\frac{1}{2}$	22.00	0.14	0	1.6

LAST FOUR QUARTERS REPORTED

REVENUES	% CHANGE	NET INCOME	% CHANGE	RETURN ON EQUITY	% CHANGE
1556.899	5.65	318.131	12.90	19.93	- 3.75

Corporate Summary

Carnival Cruise Lines Incorporated, together with its subsidiaries, is the world's largest multiple-night cruise line. The company offers a broad range of cruise products, serving the contemporary cruise market through Carnival Cruise Lines, the premium market through Holland America Line, and the luxury market through Windstar Cruises and the company's joint venture, Seabourn Cruise Lines.

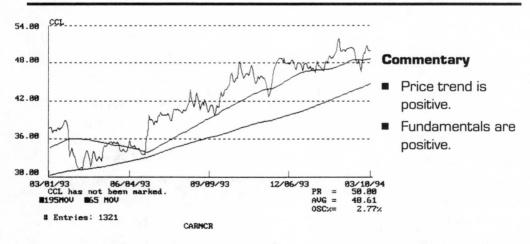

Commentary

- Price trend is positive.

- Fundamentals are positive.

YEAR	REVENUES	% CHANGE	NET INCOME	% CHANGE	RETURN ON EQUITY	% CHANGE
89	1147.675	91.365	193.605	- 1.420	21.7	- 17.0
90	1391.332	21.230	206.202	6.507	19.9	- 8.2
91	1404.704	0.961	253.842	23.095	21.7	8.9
92	1473.614	4.906	281.773	11.011	20.3	- 6.1

CRUISE AMERICA INCORPORATED

Symbol: RVR   Exchange: ASE

PRICE 3/4/94	RANGE	P-E RATIO	DIVIDEND	YIELD	BETA
5	$4^3/_4 - 6^1/_8$	NM	0	0	1.6

LAST FOUR QUARTERS REPORTED

REVENUES	% CHANGE	NET INCOME	% CHANGE	RETURN ON EQUITY	% CHANGE
103.240	9.89	- 0.195	- 132.50	- 0.61	- 132.31

Corporate Summary

Cruise America Incorporated, primarily through its subsidiaries, is in the business of purchasing pre-manufactured motorhomes and other recreational vehicles for the purpose of renting and selling to outside users. The majority of the company's revenues are generated by the renting of recreational vehicles. The company is based in Miami, Florida.

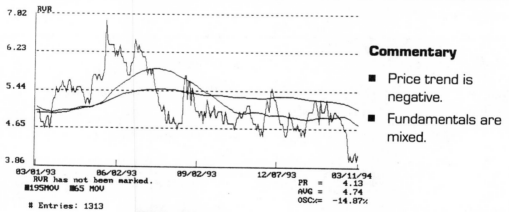

Commentary

- Price trend is negative.
- Fundamentals are mixed.

CRUISE AMERICA INC.

YEAR	REVENUES	% CHANGE	NET INCOME	% CHANGE	RETURN ON EQUITY	% CHANGE
89	72.017	17.500	- 1.072	NA	- 4.3	NA
90	69.908	- 2.928	3.521	NA	13.3	NA
91	75.463	7.946	- 0.512	- 114.541	- 2.0	- 114.8
92	106.763	41.477	- 0.800	NA	- 3.2	NA

DISNEY (WALT) COMPANY

Symbol: DIS   Exchange: NYS

PRICE 3/4/94	RANGE	P-E RATIO	DIVIDEND	YIELD	BETA
47¼	37½ - 47¼	33.75	.06	0	1.3

LAST FOUR QUARTERS REPORTED

REVENUES	% CHANGE	NET INCOME	% CHANGE	RETURN ON EQUITY	% CHANGE
8865.129	11.10	764.764	- 13.46	15.20	- 19.07

Corporate Summary

Disney (Walt) Company currently operates a number of theme parks including Disneyland (CA), Walt Disney World (FL), Epcot Center, Disney MGM Studios, and EuroDisney (the company owns a 49% stake in EuroDisney). Additionally Disney supplies entertainment for theaters, TV, and video as well as publishes books and records music, the majority of which is marketed towards children. The company also owns and operates the Disney Channel.

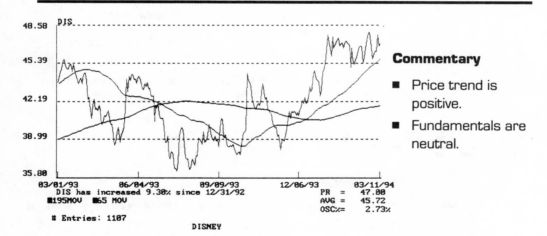

48.58   DIS

45.39

42.19

38.99

35.88

03/01/93   06/04/93   09/09/93   12/06/93   03/11/94
DIS has increased 9.30% since 12/31/92   PR = 47.00
■195MOV ■65 MOV   AVG = 45.72
                                              OSC%= 2.73%

\# Entries: 1107

DISNEY

Commentary

- Price trend is positive.

- Fundamentals are neutral.

YEAR	REVENUES	% CHANGE	NET INCOME	% CHANGE	RETURN ON EQUITY	% CHANGE
89	4594.296	33.625	703.300	34.732	23.1	4.4
90	5843.699	27.195	824.000	17.162	23.6	2.2
91	6182.398	5.796	636.600	- 22.743	16.4	- 30.4
92	7504.000	21.377	816.700	28.291	17.36	5.6

EUROPA CRUISES CORPORATION

Symbol: KRUZ   Exchange: OTC

PRICE 3/4/94	RANGE	P-E RATIO	DIVIDEND	YIELD	BETA
1⅝	1³⁄₁₆ - 5⅛	NM	0	0	0.4

LAST FOUR QUARTERS REPORTED

REVENUES	% CHANGE	NET INCOME	% CHANGE	RETURN ON EQUITY	% CHANGE
12.371	- 14.69	- 3.003	- 349.42	- 72.99	- 469.16

Corporate Summary

Europa Cruises Corporation promotes and operates cruise vessels which provide moderately-priced day and evening cruises. The company's cruises include a variety of shipboard activities such as dining, casino operations, sightseeing, live music, and other entertainment. The company's business strategy is to emphasize the cruise experience over the destination.

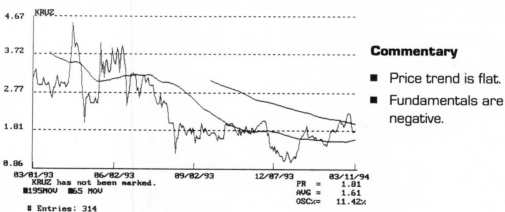

KRUZ has not been marked.
195MOV   65 MOV

Entries: 314

PR = 1.81
AVG = 1.61
OSC% = 11.42%

Commentary

- Price trend is flat.
- Fundamentals are negative.

EUROPA CRUISES CORP

YEAR	REVENUES	% CHANGE	NET INCOME	% CHANGE	RETURN ON EQUITY	% CHANGE
89	7.435	15.022	0.222	- 58.349	5.4	- 96.6
90	10.549	41.883	- 2.143	- 1065.315	- 109.1	- 2118.1
91	9.997	- 5.233	0.824	NA	15.9	NA
92	14.287	42.913	- 1.191	- 244.539	- 23.5	- 248.2

FLANIGAN'S ENTERPRISES INCORPORATED

Symbol: BDL   Exchange: ASE

PRICE 3/4/94	RANGE	P-E RATIO	DIVIDEND	YIELD	BETA
5¾	5¾ - 14¾	5.81	0	0	2.6

LAST FOUR QUARTERS REPORTED

REVENUES	% CHANGE	NET INCOME	% CHANGE	RETURN ON EQUITY	% CHANGE
18.835	10.37	1.039	20.12	93.52	- 75.35

Corporate Summary

Flanigan's Enterprises Incorporated owns and/or operates retail package liquor stores, restaurants, and lounges (known as "Big Daddy's"), and entertainment-oriented clubs. The company operates 14 units and has interests in eight additional units which have been franchised by the company. Flanigan's Enterprises Inc. was established in 1959 and is based in Fort Lauderdale, Florida.

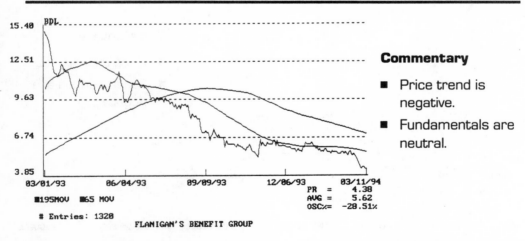

Commentary

- Price trend is negative.
- Fundamentals are neutral.

FLANIGAN'S BENEFIT GROUP

YEAR	REVENUES	% CHANGE	NET INCOME	% CHANGE	RETURN ON EQUITY	% CHANGE
89	31.673	- 0.145	- 1.184	NA	- 103.1	NA
90	27.785	- 12.275	- 0.270	NA	- 30.8	NA
91	22.355	- 19.543	- 1.514	NA	238.1	NA
92	17.065	- 23.664	0.865	NA	379.4	59.4

HOME SHOPPING NETWORK INCORPORATED

Symbol: HSN   Exchange: NYS

PRICE	RANGE	P-E RATIO	DIVIDEND	YIELD	BETA
14¼	6⅛ - 14⅞	712.50	0	0	1.0

LAST FOUR QUARTERS REPORTED

REVENUES	% CHANGE	NET INCOME	% CHANGE	RETURN ON EQUITY	% CHANGE
SF	SF	SF	NA	SF	SF

Corporate Summary

Home Shopping Network is a holding company, the subsidiaries of which conduct the day-to-day operations of the company's various business activities. The company's main business is electronic retailing conducted by Home Shopping Club, Inc. Home Shopping Network is based in St. Petersburg, FL.

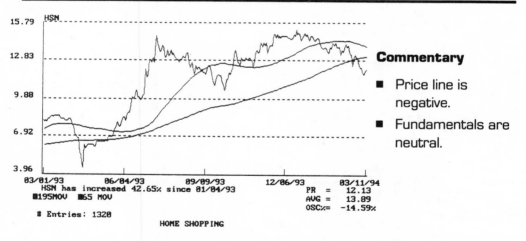

Commentary

- Price line is negative.
- Fundamentals are neutral.

HSN has increased 42.65% since 01/04/93
■195MOV ■65 MOV
PR = 12.13
AVG = 13.89
OSC%= -14.59%
Entries: 1320

HOME SHOPPING

YEAR	REVENUES	% CHANGE	NET INCOME	% CHANGE	RETURN ON EQUITY	% CHANGE
89	774.342	6.062	- 22.075	- 222.762	- 15.8	- 225.7
90	1008.272	30.210	32.464	NA	18.3	NA
91	1078.547	6.970	- 9.599	- 129.568	- 5.9	- 132.4
92	1097.787	1.784	37.405	NA	22.0	NA

JILLIAN'S ENTERTAINMENT CORPORATION

Symbol: QBAL   Exchange: OTC

PRICE 3/4/94	RANGE	P-E RATIO	DIVIDEND	YIELD	BETA
$7/8$	$3/4$ - $1\,3/16$	NM	0	0	2.0

LAST FOUR QUARTERS REPORTED

REVENUES	% CHANGE	NET INCOME	% CHANGE	RETURN ON EQUITY	% CHANGE
4.485	50.00	- 0.510	NA	- 13.36	NA

Corporate Summary

Jillian's Entertainment Corporation is in the business of acquiring and operating billiard clubs located in various cities throughout the United States and internationally. The company's billiard clubs offer a wide variety of entertainment and food services and are designed to attract a broader segment of the population than traditional pool halls.

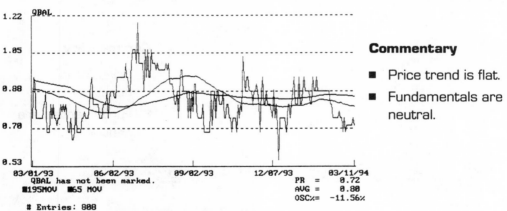

```
1.22  QBAL
1.05
0.88
0.70
0.53
     03/01/93    06/02/93    09/02/93    12/07/93    03/11/94
        QBAL has not been marked.            PR  =   0.72
     195MOV  65 MOV                          AVG =   0.88
                                             OSC%=  -11.56%
     # Entries: 808
              JILLIAN'S ENTERTAINMENT CORP.
```

Commentary

- Price trend is flat.
- Fundamentals are neutral.

YEAR	REVENUES	% CHANGE	NET INCOME	% CHANGE	RETURN ON EQUITY	% CHANGE
89	0.998	- 54.009	- 0.328	NA	- 4.7	NA
90	2.226	123.046	- 0.991	NA	- 21.1	NA
91	2.890	29.829	- 1.061	NA	- 32.3	NA
92	3.304	14.325	0.065	- 0.328	1.6	NA

NDL PRODUCTS INCORPORATED

Symbol: NDLP   Exchange: OTC

PRICE 3/4/94	RANGE	P-E RATIO	DIVIDEND	YIELD	BETA
1 1/8	1 - 2 1/8	NM	0	0	0.3

LAST FOUR QUARTERS REPORTED

REVENUES	% CHANGE	NET INCOME	% CHANGE	RETURN ON EQUITY	% CHANGE
10.940	10.39	- 0.443	- 253.82	- 16.96	- 280.61

Corporate Summary

NDL Products Incorporated is in the business of manufacturing, marketing, and selling sports medicine products, fitness equipment, and accessories for physical fitness. The company manufactures and sells over 60 varieties of neoprene and elastic athletic supports, supporters, pads, and wraps principally under the trade names NDL, Dr. Bone Savers, GRID, Hitman, and Flex-Aid.

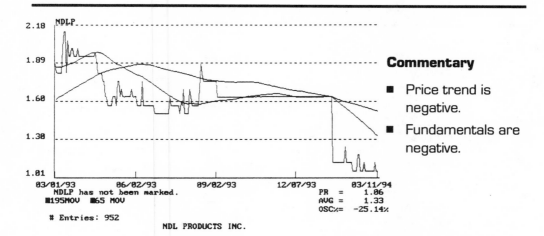

Commentary

- Price trend is negative.
- Fundamentals are negative.

NDLP has not been marked.
■195MOV ■65 MOV

PR = 1.06
AVG = 1.33
OSC%= -25.14%

Entries: 952

NDL PRODUCTS INC.

YEAR	REVENUES	% CHANGE	NET INCOME	% CHANGE	RETURN ON EQUITY	% CHANGE
89	7.320	96.616	- 0.025	- 110.638	- 1.1	- 110.1
90	8.426	15.109	- 0.215	NA	- 9.9	NA
91	10.188	20.911	0.472	NA	17.8	NA
92	10.620	4.240	0.417	- 11.653	13.7	- 23.2

NUTMEG INDUSTRIES INCORPORATED

Symbol: NTM   Exchange: NYS

PRICE 3/4/94	RANGE	P-E RATIO	DIVIDEND	YIELD	BETA
17³⁄₈	9³⁄₄ - 17³⁄₈	22.57	0	0	2.6

LAST FOUR QUARTERS REPORTED

REVENUES	% CHANGE	NET INCOME	% CHANGE	RETURN ON EQUITY	% CHANGE
185.259	19.10	14.461	36.05	15.03	13.51

Corporate Summary

Nutmeg Industries Incorporated is one of the leading producers of spectator sportswear under licenses granted by the four major American professional sports leagues (Major League Baseball, National Basketball Association, National Football League, National Hockey League), and most major American colleges and universities. The majority of the products are sold to department stores, sporting goods stores, and specialty retailers.

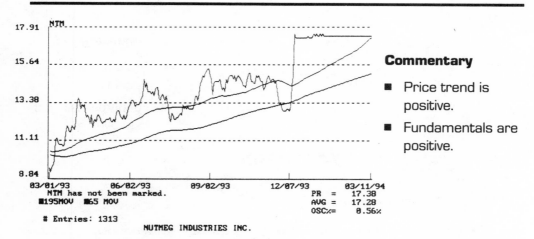

NUTMEG INDUSTRIES INC.

Commentary

- Price trend is positive.
- Fundamentals are positive.

YEAR	REVENUES	% CHANGE	NET INCOME	% CHANGE	RETURN ON EQUITY	% CHANGE
89	50.706	26.364	0.181	- 94.377	0.7	- 97.9
90	74.211	46.355	2.016	1013.812	7.8	1086.8
91	122.373	64.899	6.799	237.252	9.5	21.5
92	159.989	30.739	11.435	68.451	13.5	42.6

OMNI FILMS INTERNATIONAL INCORPORATED

Symbol: OFII   Exchange: NMS

PRICE 3/4/94	RANGE	P-E RATIO	DIVIDEND	YIELD	BETA
9	$2\frac{5}{8} - 9\frac{5}{8}$	NM	0	0	0.5

LAST FOUR QUARTERS REPORTED

REVENUES	% CHANGE	NET INCOME	% CHANGE	RETURN ON EQUITY	% CHANGE
7.167	- 33.45	- 0.877	- 491.52	- 14.92	- 549.93

Corporate Summary

Omni Films International Incorporated is a vertically integrated entertainment technology company specializing in the design, manufacture, installation, and service of advanced 70mm large-screen cinema and motion simulation theater systems for amusement and theme parks and other specialized markets. The company also produces and licenses short duration specialty films for use in such theater systems.

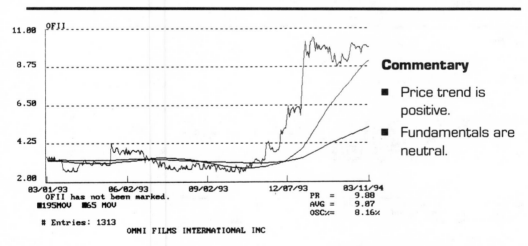

OMNI FILMS INTERNATIONAL INC

OFII has not been marked.
■195MOV ■65 MOV

PR = 9.88
AVG = 9.07
OSC%= 8.16%

Entries: 1313

Commentary

- Price trend is positive.
- Fundamentals are neutral.

YEAR	REVENUES	% CHANGE	NET INCOME	% CHANGE	RETURN ON EQUITY	% CHANGE
89	2.849	- 18.250	- 0.379	- 225.082	- 16.0	- 139.2
90	8.438	196.174	0.968	NA	29.0	NA
91	7.298	- 13.510	0.042	- 95.661	0.6	- 98.0
92	10.362	41.984	0.381	807.143	5.2	769.1

PATTEN CORPORATION

Symbol: PAT   Exchange: NYS

PRICE 3/4/94	RANGE	P-E RATIO	DIVIDEND	YIELD	BETA
$3\frac{1}{8}$	$2\frac{7}{8}$ - $4\frac{3}{8}$	14.27	0	0	1.8

LAST FOUR QUARTERS REPORTED

REVENUES	% CHANGE	NET INCOME	% CHANGE	RETURN ON EQUITY	% CHANGE
67.633	- 4.16	4.113	26.67	8.30	16.07

Corporate Summary

The Patten Corporation's primary business is to acquire undeveloped rural properties ranging in size from approximately 40 to 8,000 acres and to subdivide those properties into two- to 35-acre parcels. The company markets and sells the subdivided parcels primarily to residents of metropolitan areas who seek rural land to satisfy a desire for property ownership and for hunting, fishing, camping, and possible future vacation or retirement.

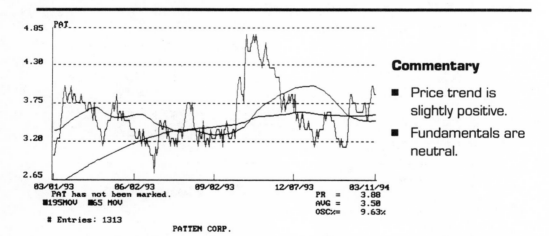

Commentary

- Price trend is slightly positive.

- Fundamentals are neutral.

YEAR	REVENUES	% CHANGE	NET INCOME	% CHANGE	RETURN ON EQUITY	% CHANGE
89	120.369	- 21.712	- 15.394	- 266.143	- 20.8	- 320.7
90	81.658	32.160	- 32.189	NA	76.6	NA
91	61.615	- 24.545	1.368	NA	3.2	NA
92	63.540	3.124	3.457	152.705	7.4	133.9

SERVICO INCORPORATED

Symbol: SER   Exchange: ASE

PRICE 3/4/94	RANGE	P-E RATIO	DIVIDEND	YIELD	BETA
$7\frac{1}{4}$	$3\frac{5}{8}$ - $7\frac{1}{4}$	30.21	0	0	NA

LAST FOUR QUARTERS REPORTED

REVENUES	% CHANGE	NET INCOME	% CHANGE	RETURN ON EQUITY	% CHANGE
127.266	3.23	1.777	- 96.69	5.06	NA

Corporate Summary

Servico Incorporated owns and manages hotels nationwide and is based in West Palm Beach, Florida. The company's hotels range in size from 100 to 595 rooms, and substantially all of the hotels are "full service" properties offering lodging, food, beverage, and meeting facilities. Servico currently owns or manages 31 hotels containing 6,382 rooms in 15 states.

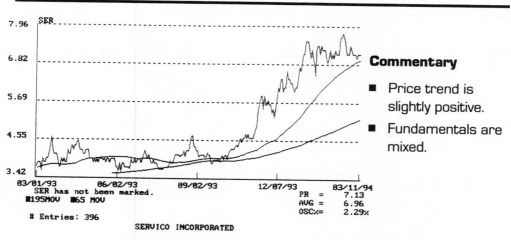

Commentary

- Price trend is slightly positive.
- Fundamentals are mixed.

SER has not been marked.
■195MOV ■65 MOV

PR = 7.13
AVG = 6.96
OSC%= 2.29%

Entries: 396

SERVICO INCORPORATED

YEAR	REVENUES	% CHANGE	NET INCOME	% CHANGE	RETURN ON EQUITY	% CHANGE
89	155.302	- 6.161	- 24.837	NA	268.0	NA
90	152.105	- 2.059	- 192.834	NA	95.4	- 64.4
91	135.151	- 11.146	174.706	NA	- 637.7	- 768.4
92	123.285	- 8.780	53.683	- 69.272	168.8	NA

SILVER KING COMMUNICATIONS INCORPORATED

Symbol: SKTV   Exchange: OTC

PRICE 3/4/94	RANGE	P-E RATIO	DIVIDEND	YIELD	BETA
10¾	3¾ - 18	NM	0	0	NA

LAST FOUR QUARTERS REPORTED

REVENUES	% CHANGE	NET INCOME	% CHANGE	RETURN ON EQUITY	% CHANGE
46.117	0.97	- 4.326	NA	- 123.32	NA

Corporate Summary

Silver King Communications Incorporated, through eleven wholly-owned subsidiaries, owns and operates twelve independent full-power UHF television broadcast stations, including one television satellite station. The stations serve metropolitan television markets, including eight of the twelve largest television markets in the United States. The stations are carried on a substantially full-time basis on cable systems.

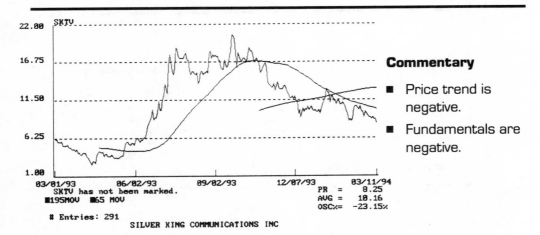

SILVER KING COMMUNICATIONS INC

Commentary

- Price trend is negative.
- Fundamentals are negative.

YEAR	REVENUES	% CHANGE	NET INCOME	% CHANGE	RETURN ON EQUITY	% CHANGE
89	NA	NA	NA	NA	NA	NA
90	NA	NA	NA	NA	NA	NA
91	NA	NA	NA	NA	NA	NA
92	46.776	NA	- 15.222	NA	17.5	NA

VIDEO JUKEBOX NETWORK INCORPORATED

Symbol: JUKE   Exchange: OTC

PRICE 3/4/94	RANGE	P-E RATIO	DIVIDEND	YIELD	BETA
3$^7/_8$	$^9/_{16}$ - 3$^7/_8$	NM	0	0	2.6

LAST FOUR QUARTERS REPORTED

REVENUES	% CHANGE	NET INCOME	% CHANGE	RETURN ON EQUITY	% CHANGE
13.919	- 5.54	- 2.964	NA	- 100.82	NA

Corporate Summary

Video Jukebox Network Incorporated provides viewer interactive television services. The company's programming network, known as "The Jukebox Network," operates twenty-four hours per day, seven days per week. Viewers of "The Jukebox Network" channel are able to choose a specific music video to be shown on the television by dialing a 900 number.

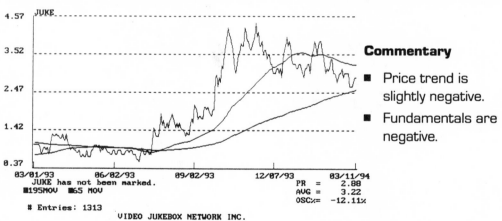

Commentary

- Price trend is slightly negative.
- Fundamentals are negative.

JUKE has not been marked.
■195MOV ■65 MOV

PR = 2.88
AVG = 3.22
OSC% = -12.11%

Entries: 1313

VIDEO JUKEBOX NETWORK INC.

YEAR	REVENUES	% CHANGE	NET INCOME	% CHANGE	RETURN ON EQUITY	% CHANGE
89	3.793	234.775	- 2.161	NA	- 61.1	NA
90	13.583	258.107	- 1.230	NA	- 16.1	NA
91	15.333	12.884	- 2.687	NA	- 49.9	NA
92	14.140	- 7.781	- 4.809	NA	- 1147.7	NA

Chapter 19

Florida Automotive Companies

The automobile industry had a strong 1993, and the S & P Automobile Index remained near its high in January 1994. There has been some recent fallback in prices, but this can probably be considered a period of consolidation rather than a trend reversal. Florida doesn't have any auto manufacturing companies and is limited to the service area of this industry.

Auto Parts

The year 1993 was good for auto parts companies as a group. Further gains are likely in 1994 as the industry expands domestically and overseas.

Discount Auto Parts is Florida's leader in this area. They have done a great job of expansion throughout Florida, but will face stiff competition as they move nationally. This is a big market, and the dominant company ultimately will receive great rewards.

ASSIX INTERNATIONAL INCORPORATED

Symbol: ASIXE   Exchange: NMS

PRICE 3/4/94	RANGE	P-E RATIO	DIVIDEND	YIELD	BETA
NA	$^3/_{16}$ - $2^1/_2$	NA	0	NA	NA

LAST FOUR QUARTERS REPORTED

REVENUES	% CHANGE	NET INCOME	% CHANGE	RETURN ON EQUITY	% CHANGE
6.329	- 7.01	- 3.612	NA	- 360.12	NA

Corporate Summary

Assix International Incorporated is in the business of marketing ride-related automotive services through tire dealer retail service outlets. The principal ride-related service the company presently markets is the "Accu-Balance" complete wheel balancing program using its "Tire Matching" technology, believed to be a technologically superior form of wheel balancing. "AccuBalance" is sold to the general public through licensed dealers.

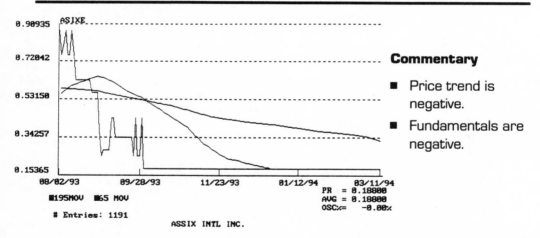

Commentary

- Price trend is negative.
- Fundamentals are negative.

ASSIX INTL INC.

YEAR	REVENUES	% CHANGE	NET INCOME	% CHANGE	RETURN ON EQUITY	% CHANGE
89	2.804	65.428	0.479	36.080	14.6	- 31.4
90	6.677	138.124	1.345	180.793	26.4	80.6
91	8.271	23.873	0.172	- 87.212	2.1	- 92.1
92	6.504	- 21.364	- 9.793	- 5793.604	619.8	29.5

DISCOUNT AUTO PARTS

Symbol: DAP   Exchange: NYS

PRICE 3/4/94	RANGE	P-E RATIO	DIVIDEND	YIELD	BETA
$27\frac{1}{2}$	$23\frac{5}{8}$ - $29\frac{1}{4}$	29.25	0	0	NA

LAST FOUR QUARTERS REPORTED

REVENUES	% CHANGE	NET INCOME	% CHANGE	RETURN ON EQUITY	% CHANGE
191.174	18.71	13.179	-2.70	14.65	-16.78

Corporate Summary

Discount Auto Parts operates one of the nation's largest chains of auto-motive products and accessories retail stores. The retail outlets offer a number of high quality, name brand automotive parts for auto repair and servicing as well as a number of automotive accessories and options.

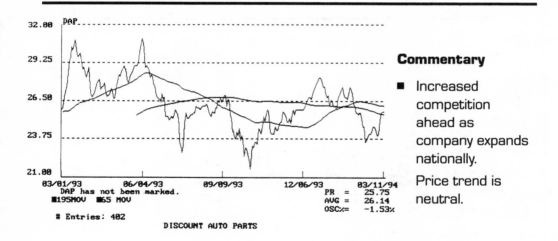

DISCOUNT AUTO PARTS

Commentary

- Increased competition ahead as company expands nationally.

Price trend is neutral.

YEAR	REVENUES	% CHANGE	NET INCOME	% CHANGE	RETURN ON EQUITY	% CHANGE
89	NA	NA	NA	NA	NA	NA
90	NA	NA	NA	NA	NA	NA
91	NA	NA	NA	NA	NA	NA
92	141.206	NA	12.226	NA	34.5	NA

FRP PROPERTIES INCORPORATED

Symbol: FRPP   Exchange: NMS

PRICE 3/4/94	RANGE	P-E RATIO	DIVIDEND	YIELD	BETA
14¾	12¼ - 14¾	22.35	0	0	0.2

LAST FOUR QUARTERS REPORTED

REVENUES	% CHANGE	NET INCOME	% CHANGE	RETURN ON EQUITY	% CHANGE
47.995	10.78	2.733	- 5.92	4.56	- 8.08

Corporate Summary

FRP Properties Incorporated and its subsidiaries are engaged in the transportation and real estate businesses. The majority of the company's revenues are generated through the transportation and hauling of liquid and dry bulk commodities as well as the mining of owned properties. However, FRP does have endeavors in industrial rental properties as well.

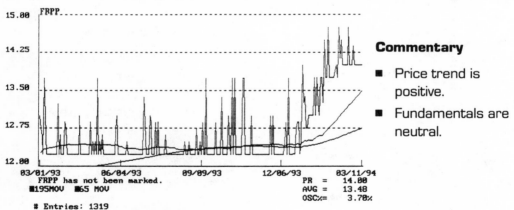

FRPP has not been marked.
■195MOV ■65 MOV

PR = 14.00
AVG = 13.48
OSC%= 3.70%

Entries: 1319

Commentary

- Price trend is positive.
- Fundamentals are neutral.

FRP PROPERTIES INC

YEAR	REVENUES	% CHANGE	NET INCOME	% CHANGE	RETURN ON EQUITY	% CHANGE
89	32.376	4.862	2.120	- 30.171	3.9	- 31.9
90	41.624	28.564	2.175	2.594	4.0	2.0
91	42.775	2.765	2.589	19.034	4.6	15.9
92	42.995	0.514	2.847	9.965	4.9	6.0

HOLIDAY RV SUPERSTORES INCORPORATED

Symbol: RVEE   Exchange: NMS

PRICE 3/4/94	RANGE	P-E RATIO	DIVIDEND	YIELD	BETA
2	$1\frac{1}{4} - 2\frac{3}{8}$	15.39	0	0	1.2

LAST FOUR QUARTERS REPORTED

REVENUES	% CHANGE	NET INCOME	% CHANGE	RETURN ON EQUITY	% CHANGE
45.767	11.83	0.970	657.81	8.82	584.36

Corporate Summary

Holiday RV Superstores Incorporated is a multi-store retail chain engaged in the retail sales and service of recreational vehicles and recreational boats. The company currently operates six sales and service dealerships, one of which is located in the heart of the Walt Disney World tourist area in Orlando, Florida. Each of the company's full service dealerships is equipped to repair virtually any type of recreational vehicle.

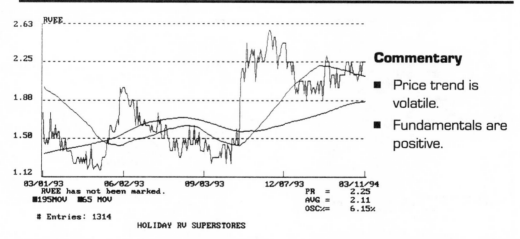

Commentary

■ Price trend is volatile.

■ Fundamentals are positive.

```
2.63  RVEE
2.25
1.88
1.58
1.12
     03/01/93      06/02/93      09/03/93      12/07/93      03/11/94
        RVEE has not been marked.                   PR  =  2.25
     ■19SMOV  ■65 MOV                               AVG =  2.11
                                                    OSC%=  6.15%
        # Entries: 1314
              HOLIDAY RV SUPERSTORES
```

YEAR	REVENUES	% CHANGE	NET INCOME	% CHANGE	RETURN ON EQUITY	% CHANGE
89	40.942	25.385	1.043	- 0.477	11.0	- 18.2
90	40.755	- 0.457	0.757	- 27.421	7.4	- 33.0
91	35.771	- 12.229	- 0.412	- 154.425	- 4.2	- 156.5
92	40.927	14.414	0.128	NA	1.3	NA

RT INDUSTRIES INCORPORATED

Symbol: RTIC   Exchange: OTC

PRICE 3/4/94	RANGE	P-E RATIO	DIVIDEND	YIELD	BETA
2½	2½ - 4¼	125.00	0	0	NA

LAST FOUR QUARTERS REPORTED

REVENUES	% CHANGE	NET INCOME	% CHANGE	RETURN ON EQUITY	% CHANGE
18.649	9.10	0.101	- 91.74	1.47	- 91.88

Corporate Summary

RT Industries Incorporated, through its five subsidiaries, is engaged in the manufacture and sale of motor vehicle parts. The company specializes in the manufacture of brake shoes, brake pads, and spark plug wires. Additionally, the majority of the company's revenues are generated from the sale of parts to warehouses and not to retail outlets. RT Industries is based in Boca Raton, Florida, although the company exports parts throughout the world.

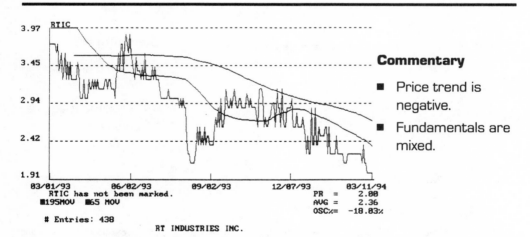

Commentary

- Price trend is negative.
- Fundamentals are mixed.

RTIC has not been marked.
■19SMOV ■65 MOV
PR = 2.00
AVG = 2.36
OSC% = -18.03%

Entries: 438

RT INDUSTRIES INC.

YEAR	REVENUES	% CHANGE	NET INCOME	% CHANGE	RETURN ON EQUITY	% CHANGE
89	NA	NA	NA	NA	NA	NA
90	NA	NA	NA	NA	NA	NA
91	16.221	NA	0.952	NA	31.0	NA
92	17.021	4.932	0.853	- 10.399	13.1	- 57.8

Chapter 20

Florida Technology Companies

High-tech and stock volatility often go together. On the one hand, high-tech stocks can have dramatic moves upon the discovery of a new product or the design of a new system; on the other hand, a company's products can become outdated quickly.

Computers

Stocks in the computer sector reflect the volatility of this rapidly changing industry. Dramatic shifts can cause tremendous profits or losses in individual stocks. For the long-term, this is an industry on the move. However, investors must be cautious of shakeups and be prepared to act quickly.

Electronics

The overall industry wound up positive for 1993 and continued expansion is expected in 1994. The electronics industry is not as volatile as computers, but caution is recommended.

ALL AMERICAN SEMICONDUCTOR INCORPORATED

Symbol: SEMIW   Exchange: NMS

PRICE 3/4/94	RANGE	P-E RATIO	DIVIDEND	YIELD	BETA
2⁷/₈	1¼ - 2⁷/₈	19.17	0	0	0.5

LAST FOUR QUARTERS REPORTED

REVENUES	% CHANGE	NET INCOME	% CHANGE	RETURN ON EQUITY	% CHANGE
61.737	31.20	1.290	120.14	10.55	52.48

Corporate Summary

All American Semiconductor Incorporated, along with its subsidiaries, is engaged in the distribution of electronic components manufactured by others. The company distributes a full range of semiconductors, including transistors, diodes, integrated circuits, memory chips and microprocessors, as well as passive products, such as capacitors, resistors, sockets, connectors, and cables.

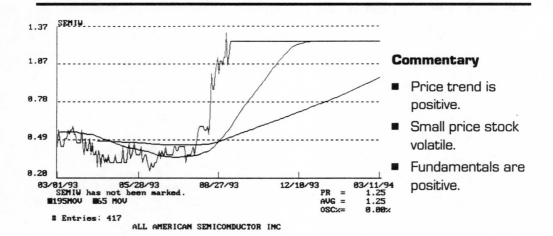

ALL AMERICAN SEMICONDUCTOR INC

Commentary

- Price trend is positive.

- Small price stock volatile.

- Fundamentals are positive.

YEAR	REVENUES	% CHANGE	NET INCOME	% CHANGE	RETURN ON EQUITY	% CHANGE
89	37.076	12.036	- 0.205	- 119.769	- 4.6	- 120.5
90	41.315	11.433	0.018	NA	0.4	NA
91	45.332	9.723	0.117	550.00	2.5	533.6
92	49.015	8.125	0.756	546.154	8.9	251.5

BLOC DEVELOPMENT CORPORATION

Symbol: BDEV   Exchange: NMS

PRICE 3/4/94	RANGE	P-E RATIO	DIVIDEND	YIELD	BETA
$2^{1}\!/\!_{16}$	$1^{13}\!/\!_{16} - 3^{1}\!/\!_{16}$	51.55	0	0	0.5

LAST FOUR QUARTERS REPORTED

REVENUES	% CHANGE	NET INCOME	% CHANGE	RETURN ON EQUITY	% CHANGE
70.652	21.89	0.833	111.39	12.25	NA

Corporate Summary

BLOC Development Corporation is engaged in the data-based direct marketing of business productivity and utility software, hardware, and peripherals. Additionally, it engages in the development and marketing of graphics-based forms automation software. The company conducts its data-based direct marketing efforts through its operating subsidiaries Tiger Direct, Inc., and Fulfillment Center, Inc., and its graphics-based division through BLOC Development Corporation.

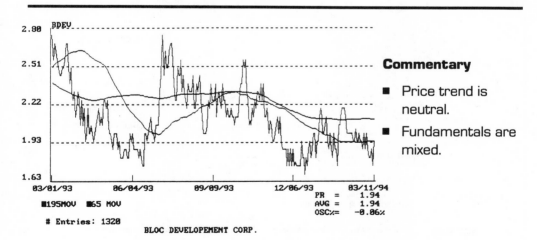

BLOC DEVELOPEMENT CORP.

Commentary

- Price trend is neutral.
- Fundamentals are mixed.

YEAR	REVENUES	% CHANGE	NET INCOME	% CHANGE	RETURN ON EQUITY	% CHANGE
89	11.344	159.885	1.196	140.644	13.7	- 10.3
90	26.262	131.506	0.770	- 35.619	5.2	- 62.1
91	43.404	65.273	- 2.149	- 379.091	- 15.1	- 390.4
92	61.394	41.448	- 7.640	NA	- 154.4	NA

BOCA RESEARCH INCORPORATED

Symbol: BOCI   Exchange: NMS

PRICE 3/4/94	RANGE	P-E RATIO	DIVIDEND	YIELD	BETA
7¼	6⅝ - 14	8.95	0	0	NA

LAST FOUR QUARTERS REPORTED

REVENUES	% CHANGE	NET INCOME	% CHANGE	RETURN ON EQUITY	% CHANGE
59.146	NA	6.316	NA	19.79	NA

Corporate Summary

Boca Research Incorporated designs, manufactures, markets, and supports board-level enhancement products that expand the capabilities and
performance of IBM and IBM-compatible personal computers. The company's line of enhancement products are designed as expansion boards
for existing systems and add-on boards for newly manufactured systems
and can be used with all major IBM and IBM-compatible PCs.

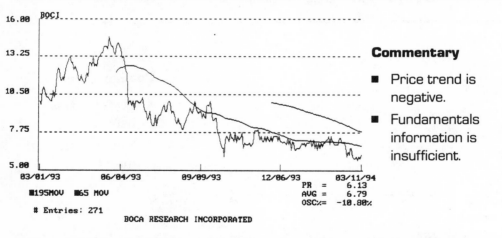

Commentary

- Price trend is negative.

- Fundamentals information is insufficient.

```
PR  =    6.13
AVG =    6.79
OSC%=  -10.80%
```

■195MOV ■65 MOV

\# Entries: 271

BOCA RESEARCH INCORPORATED

YEAR	REVENUES	% CHANGE	NET INCOME	% CHANGE	RETURN ON EQUITY	% CHANGE
89	NA	NA	NA	NA	NA	NA
90	NA	NA	NA	NA	NA	NA
91	NA	NA	NA	NA	NA	NA
92	44.554	NA	5.843	NA	42.7	NA

CMS DATA CORPORATION

Symbol: LAWR   Exchange: NMS

PRICE 3/4/94	RANGE	P-E RATIO	DIVIDEND	YIELD	BETA
$1^7/_{16}$	1 - 2	NM	0	0	1.0

LAST FOUR QUARTERS REPORTED

REVENUES	% CHANGE	NET INCOME	% CHANGE	RETURN ON EQUITY	% CHANGE
15.233	13.63	- 1.570	NA	- 15.76	NA

Corporate Summary

CMS Data Corporation is a software developer and systems integrator
which designs, markets, installs, and supports integrated turnkey law office computer systems. CMS Data Corporation's main goal is to provide
law firms and corporate and governmental law departments with highly integrated software applications. The company is a subsidiary of The
Quartex Corporation, a publicly-held software developer.

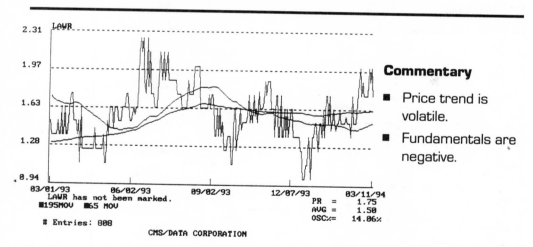

CMS/DATA CORPORATION

Commentary

- Price trend is volatile.
- Fundamentals are negative.

YEAR	REVENUES	% CHANGE	NET INCOME	% CHANGE	RETURN ON EQUITY	% CHANGE
89	NA	NA	NA	NA	NA	NA
90	12.506	NA	1.434	NA	23.7	NA
91	14.059	12.418	0.521	- 63.668	6.2	- 73.8
92	12.697	- 9.688	- 1.606	- 408.253	- 23.2	- 471.8

COMPUTER PRODUCTS INCORPORATED

Symbol: CPRD   Exchange: NMS

PRICE 3/4/94	RANGE	P-E RATIO	DIVIDEND	YIELD	BETA
$2^5/_{16}$	$2^1/_8$ - $3^1/_4$	77.07	0	0	0.9

LAST FOUR QUARTERS REPORTED

REVENUES	% CHANGE	NET INCOME	% CHANGE	RETURN ON EQUITY	% CHANGE
123.790	7.83	0.597	- 70.18	1.82	- 71.99

Corporate Summary

Computer Products Incorporated designs, develops, manufactures, and markets electronic products and systems. The company works in three main product areas: 1) power conversion products for electronic equipment requiring a precise and constant voltage level for proper operation, 2) process automation hardware and software systems, and 3) high performance single-board computers, systems and subsystems for real-time applications.

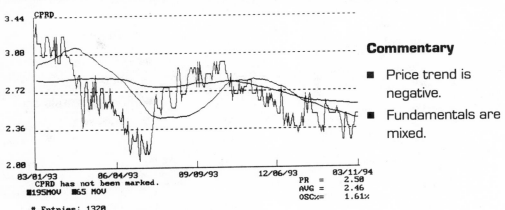

Commentary

- Price trend is negative.
- Fundamentals are mixed.

```
CPRD
3.44 ----------------------------------------
3.08 ----------------------------------------
2.72 ----------------------------------------
2.36 ----------------------------------------
2.00
   03/01/93    06/04/93    09/09/93    12/06/93   03/11/94
   CPRD has not been marked.              PR  =  2.50
   ■19SMOV ■65 MOV                        AVG =  2.46
                                          OSC%=  1.61%
   # Entries: 1320
            COMPUTER PRODUCTS INC.
```

YEAR	REVENUES	% CHANGE	NET INCOME	% CHANGE	RETURN ON EQUITY	% CHANGE
89	119.513	- .3282	4.071	NA	12.4	NA
90	107.458	- 10.087	4.061	- 0.246	10.1	- 18.2
91	83.240	- 22.537	- 4.234	- 204.260	- 14.8	- 246.9
92	114.799	37.913	2.002	NA	6.5	NA

DBA SYSTEMS INCORPORATED

Symbol: DBAS   Exchange: NMS

PRICE 3/4/94	RANGE	P-E RATIO	DIVIDEND	YIELD	BETA
6⅞	3¾ - 6⅞	18.58	0	0	0.3

LAST FOUR QUARTERS REPORTED

REVENUES	% CHANGE	NET INCOME	% CHANGE	RETURN ON EQUITY	% CHANGE
30.663	- 14.10	1.462	- 30.18	6.57	- 36.41

Corporate Summary

DBA Systems Incorporated is in the business of providing near earth tracking analysis of spacecraft from NASA. Recently, the company has been predominantly involved in providing hardware and software systems for applications in the military defense industry. DBA also has ventures in the areas of commercial graphic arts, remote sensing, and medical markets.

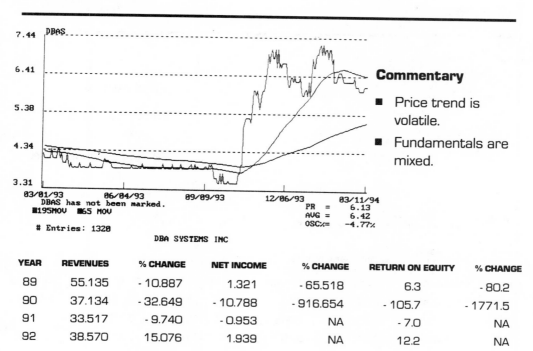

Commentary

- Price trend is volatile.
- Fundamentals are mixed.

YEAR	REVENUES	% CHANGE	NET INCOME	% CHANGE	RETURN ON EQUITY	% CHANGE
89	55.135	- 10.887	1.321	- 65.518	6.3	- 80.2
90	37.134	- 32.649	- 10.788	- 916.654	- 105.7	- 1771.5
91	33.517	- 9.740	- 0.953	NA	- 7.0	NA
92	38.570	15.076	1.939	NA	12.2	NA

DIGITAL PRODUCTS CORPORATION

Symbol: DIPC   Exchange: NMS

PRICE 3/4/94	RANGE	P-E RATIO	DIVIDEND	YIELD	BETA
$1\frac{1}{2}$	$1\frac{3}{8}$ - $4\frac{1}{2}$	NM	0	0	- 0.8

LAST FOUR QUARTERS REPORTED

REVENUES	% CHANGE	NET INCOME	% CHANGE	RETURN ON EQUITY	% CHANGE
9.132	- 6.61	- 10.126	NA	- 129.82	NA

Corporate Summary

Digital Products Incorporated and its subsidiaries are the developers, manufacturers, and distributors of telecomputer products and technology, as well as computer software programs. The company also provides post-sale support services for the same products, as well as technology, and software programs. In connection with the sale of its products, technology and services, it may act as a dealer of computer hardware and other software products.

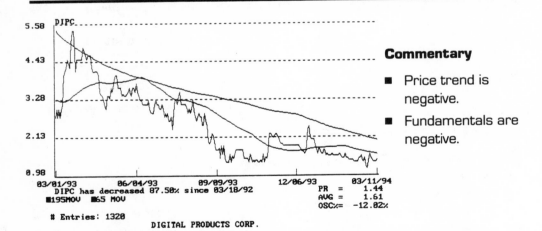

Commentary

- Price trend is negative.
- Fundamentals are negative.

DIPC has decreased 87.50% since 03/18/92
195MOV 65 MOV
PR = 1.44
AVG = 1.61
OSC% = -12.02%

Entries: 1320

DIGITAL PRODUCTS CORP.

YEAR	REVENUES	% CHANGE	NET INCOME	% CHANGE	RETURN ON EQUITY	% CHANGE
89	3.454	2.341	- 0.465	- 392.453	- 22.8	- 247.8
90	4.107	18.906	- 1.943	NA	- 53.5	NA
91	8.688	111.541	- 0.767	NA	- 2.8	NA
92	8.915	2.613	- 6.716	NA	- 45.2	NA

EVANS ENVIRONMENTAL CORPORATION

Symbol: ECOS   Exchange: OTC

PRICE	RANGE	P-E RATIO	DIVIDEND	YIELD	BETA
$2^5/_{16}$	$1^7/_8$ - 6	NM	0	0	- 5.8

LAST FOUR QUARTERS REPORTED

REVENUES	% CHANGE	NET INCOME	% CHANGE	RETURN ON EQUITY	% CHANGE
SF	SF	SF	NA	SF	NA

Corporate Summary

Evans Environmental Corporation maintains two unique divisions operated through its wholly-owned subsidiaries: an environmental division (Evans Environmental), and a cable products division (ABC Cable Products, Inc.). The company is based in Miami, Florida.

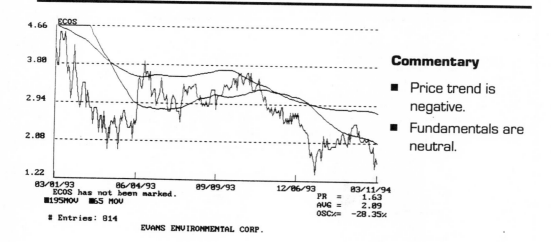

Commentary

■ Price trend is negative.

■ Fundamentals are neutral.

ECOS has not been marked.
■195MOV ■65 MOV

PR = 1.63
AVG = 2.89
OSC%= -28.35%

Entries: 814

EVANS ENVIRONMENTAL CORP.

YEAR	REVENUES	% CHANGE	NET INCOME	% CHANGE	RETURN ON EQUITY	% CHANGE
89	5.517	7.439	- 0.141	- 393.750	- 5.6	- 410.3
90	5.139	- 6.852	- 0.247	NA	- 11.4	NA
91	2.383	- 53.629	- 0.455	NA	- 35.9	NA
92	3.582	50.315	0.050	NA	1.8	NA

FDP CORPORATION

Symbol: FDPC   Exchange: NMS

PRICE 3/4/94	RANGE	P-E RATIO	DIVIDEND	YIELD	BETA
$4^3/_4$	$3^7/_8$ - $4^3/_4$	118.75	0	0	0.1

LAST FOUR QUARTERS REPORTED

REVENUES	% CHANGE	NET INCOME	% CHANGE	RETURN ON EQUITY	% CHANGE
17.473	- 2.72	0.151	- 78.67	0.87	- 77.98

Corporate Summary

Financial Data Planning (FDP) Corporation is in the business of developing new computer software products, or enhancing existing ones, and successfully marketing its software and related services. The company is currently a value-added dealer of computer equipment for Hewlett-Packard. FDP is based in Miami, Florida.

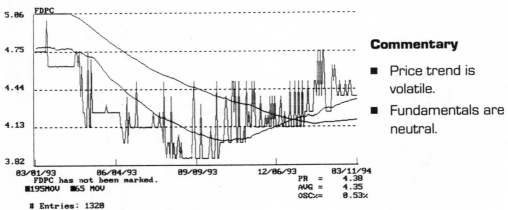

Commentary

- Price trend is volatile.
- Fundamentals are neutral.

YEAR	REVENUES	% CHANGE	NET INCOME	% CHANGE	RETURN ON EQUITY	% CHANGE
89	14.651	4.560	- 0.100	- 119.724	- 0.6	- 120.7
90	16.763	14.415	0.472	NA	2.8	NA
91	16.314	- 2.679	- 0.275	- 158.263	- 1.6	- 158.4
92	17.542	7.527	0.616	NA	3.5	NA

GEONEX CORPORATION

Symbol: GEOX   Exchange: NMS

PRICE 3/4/94	RANGE	P-E RATIO	DIVIDEND	YIELD	BETA
$1\frac{1}{2}$	$1\frac{1}{2} - 3\frac{3}{16}$	NM	0	0	1.3

LAST FOUR QUARTERS REPORTED

REVENUES	% CHANGE	NET INCOME	% CHANGE	RETURN ON EQUITY	% CHANGE
52.162	- 15.33	- 11.234	NA	- 247.34	NA

Corporate Summary

Geonex Corporation, based in St. Petersburg, is in the business of using aerial technology, as well as additional techniques, to develop above- and below-ground maps. The majority of the company's domestic revenues are generated through contracts with utility companies and Department of Defense contracts. Geonex has offices throughout the world and does a large portion of its business internationally.

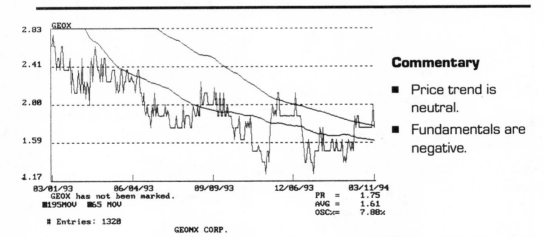

Commentary

- Price trend is neutral.

- Fundamentals are negative.

GEOX has not been marked.
■195MOV ■65 MOV

PR = 1.75
AVG = 1.61
OSC%= 7.88%

Entries: 1320

GEONX CORP.

YEAR	REVENUES	% CHANGE	NET INCOME	% CHANGE	RETURN ON EQUITY	% CHANGE
89	27.655	32.606	1.367	303.245	11.3	249.0
90	44.197	59.816	1.460	6.803	10.4	- 8.0
91	67.758	53.309	1.970	34.962	7.2	- 30.9
92	55.765	- 17.700	- 19.536	- 1091.675	- 236.1	- 3388.4

HARRIS CORPORATION

Symbol: HRS   Exchange: NBB

PRICE 3/4/94	RANGE	P-E RATIO	DIVIDEND	YIELD	BETA
48$\frac{3}{8}$	25$\frac{1}{4}$ - 48$\frac{3}{8}$	16.02	0.28	0.01	1.7

LAST FOUR QUARTERS REPORTED

REVENUES	% CHANGE	NET INCOME	% CHANGE	RETURN ON EQUITY	% CHANGE
3179.929	3.94	119.673	17.75	10.30	10.45

Corporate Summary

Harris Corporation, along with its subsidiaries, is a worldwide company focused on four core businesses: advanced electronic systems,
semiconductors, communications, and an office equipment distribution
network. The executive offices of Harris Corporation are located in Melbourne.

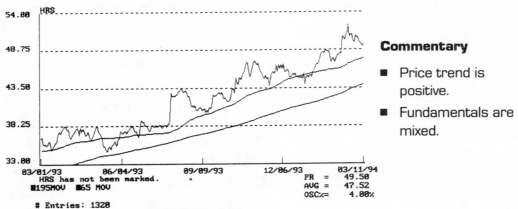

```
54.00   HRS
48.75
43.50
38.25
33.00
        03/01/93      06/04/93      09/09/93      12/06/93    03/11/94
        HRS has not been marked.                      PR  =   49.50
        195MOV   65 MOV                               AVG =   47.52
                                                      OSC%=    4.00%
     # Entries: 1320
                    HARRIS CORPORATION
```

Commentary

■ Price trend is positive.

■ Fundamentals are mixed.

YEAR	REVENUES	% CHANGE	NET INCOME	% CHANGE	RETURN ON EQUITY	% CHANGE
89	2213.649	7.325	116.165	77.658	12.3	82.3
90	3052.686	37.903	130.691	12.505	12.1	- 1.60
91	3040.126	- 0.411	19.455	- 85.114	1.90	- 84.3
92	3003.971	- 1.189	87.489	349.699	8.2	332.8

HEICO CORPORATION

Symbol: HEI   Exchange: ASE

PRICE 3/4/94	RANGE	P-E RATIO	DIVIDEND	YIELD	BETA
$12\frac{3}{8}$	$9\frac{1}{4}$ - $14\frac{3}{8}$	53.80	0.08	0	0.4

LAST FOUR QUARTERS REPORTED

REVENUES	% CHANGE	NET INCOME	% CHANGE	RETURN ON EQUITY	% CHANGE
25.882	19.11	0.534	192.07	2.09	NA

Corporate Summary

Heico Corporation is principally engaged in two business segments: the manufacture, overhaul, and sale of aerospace products and services; and the acquisition, development, operation, and management of high technology medical facilities. The company was established in 1957 and is based in Hollywood, Florida.

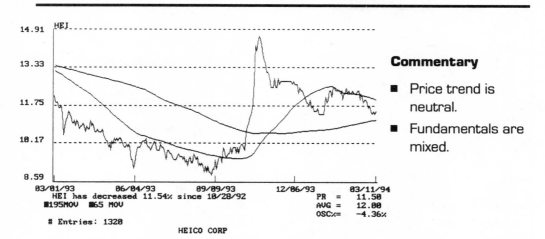

HEICO CORP

Commentary

- Price trend is neutral.
- Fundamentals are mixed.

YEAR	REVENUES	% CHANGE	NET INCOME	% CHANGE	RETURN ON EQUITY	% CHANGE
89	26.239	- 38.665	1.721	- 30.772	4.7	- 22.4
90	26.239	- 0.884	1.961	13.945	6.3	34.7
91	25.368	- 3.319	2.363	20.500	8.2	29.3
92	21.729	- 14.345	- 0.580	- 124.545	- 2.3	- 127.7

INTERNATIONAL AIRLINE SUPPORT GROUP

Symbol: IASG   Exchange: NMS

PRICE 3/4/94	RANGE	P-E RATIO	DIVIDEND	YIELD	BETA
$2\frac{3}{8}$	$2\frac{3}{8}$ - 6	NM	0	0	1.1

LAST FOUR QUARTERS REPORTED

REVENUES	% CHANGE	NET INCOME	% CHANGE	RETURN ON EQUITY	% CHANGE
22.268	- 32.22	- 2.014	- 180.56	- 29.18	- 202.64

Corporate Summary

International Airline Support Group, with its headquarters based in Miami,
Florida, is involved primarily in the purchase and sale of parts for commercial jet aircraft, many of which are no longer in production but still widely
operated by air cargo companies and passenger airlines throughout the
world.

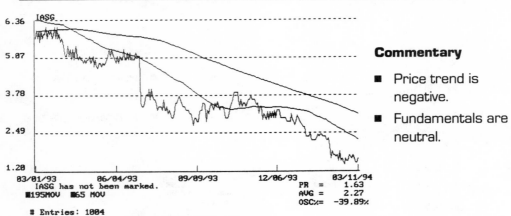

INTL. AIRLINE SUPP. GRP.

IASG has not been marked.
■195MOV ■65 MOV

PR = 1.63
AVG = 2.27
OSC% = -39.89%

Entries: 1004

Commentary

- Price trend is negative.
- Fundamentals are neutral.

YEAR	REVENUES	% CHANGE	NET INCOME	% CHANGE	RETURN ON EQUITY	% CHANGE
89	NA	NA	NA	NA	NA	NA
90	10.067	NA	0.554	NA	17.8	NA
91	21.521	113.778	1.412	154.874	31.2	75.4
92	26.527	23.261	1.984	40.510	28.0	- 10.1

INTERNATIONAL RECOVERY CORPORATION

Symbol: INT   Exchange: NYS

PRICE 3/4/94	RANGE	P-E RATIO	DIVIDEND	YIELD	BETA
15	$10^{3}/_{4}$ - $15^{3}/_{4}$	12.71	0	0	1.2

LAST FOUR QUARTERS REPORTED

REVENUES	% CHANGE	NET INCOME	% CHANGE	RETURN ON EQUITY	% CHANGE
257.751	8.04	5.581	- 1.71	14.96	- 9.00

Corporate Summary

International Recovery Corporation is involved in two principal businesses. The company markets aviation fuel and recycles used oil. International Recovery presently conducts its aviation fueling business through four subsidiaries with offices in Miami, Florida, and Gatwick airport near London, England, while the used oil recycling business is run from five states in the United States.

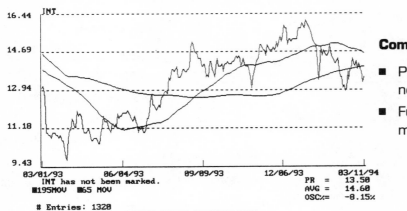

Commentary

- Price trend is neutral.
- Fundamentals are mixed.

```
INT has not been marked.            PR  =  13.50
195MOV  65 MOV                      AVG =  14.60
                                    OSC%=  -8.15%
# Entries: 1320
        INTERNATIONAL RECOVERY CORP
```

YEAR	REVENUES	% CHANGE	NET INCOME	% CHANGE	RETURN ON EQUITY	% CHANGE
89	142.209	120.647	3.964	77.519	19.0	- 31.3
90	234.280	64.743	4.806	21.241	18.4	- 3.2
91	205.454	- 12.304	5.880	22.347	18.0	- 2.3
92	254.767	24.002	5.262	- 10.510	15.3	- 14.9

KREISLER MANUFACTURING CORPORATION

Symbol: KRSL   Exchange: OTC

PRICE 3/4/94	RANGE	P-E RATIO	DIVIDEND	YIELD	BETA
7½	7 - 8¼	NM	0	0	0.5

LAST FOUR QUARTERS REPORTED

REVENUES	% CHANGE	NET INCOME	% CHANGE	RETURN ON EQUITY	% CHANGE
4.424	- 29.41	- 0.615	NA	- 9.94	NA

Corporate Summary

Kreisler Manufacturing Corporation is a wholly-owned subsidiary of Kreisler Industrial Corporation, which manufactures precision metal components and assemblies for use in military and commercial aircraft engines. The company has been in business since 1938 and is based in St. Petersburg, Florida.

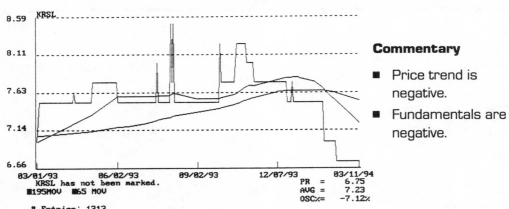

Commentary

- Price trend is negative.
- Fundamentals are negative.

KRSL has not been marked.
195MOV 65 MOV
PR = 6.75
AVG = 7.23
OSC% = -7.12%
Entries: 1313

KREISLER MANUFACTURING CORP.

YEAR	REVENUES	% CHANGE	NET INCOME	% CHANGE	RETURN ON EQUITY	% CHANGE
89	7.326	- 0.462	0.741	- 2.500	9.7	- 12.0
90	8.225	12.271	0.602	- 18.758	7.3	- 24.7
91	6.182	- 24.839	0.530	- 11.960	7.6	3.4
92	6.028	- 2.491	- 0.359	- 167.736	- 5.4	- 171.4

OPTO MECHANIK INCORPORATED

Symbol: OPTO   Exchange: NMS

PRICE 3/4/94	RANGE	P-E RATIO	DIVIDEND	YIELD	BETA
$2^3/_4$	$2^1/_2$ - $4^3/_8$	NM	0	0	0.1

LAST FOUR QUARTERS REPORTED

REVENUES	% CHANGE	NET INCOME	% CHANGE	RETURN ON EQUITY	% CHANGE
30.627	- 6.39	- 3.879	- 550.52	- 35.06	- 531.67

Corporate Summary

Opto Mechanik Incorporated specializes in building optical and electro-optical devices for use in fire control applications for various weapons systems. The company's main products consist of day and night periscopes used on tanks, panoramic telescopes used on howitzers, and other sighting systems including a target acquisition relay system.

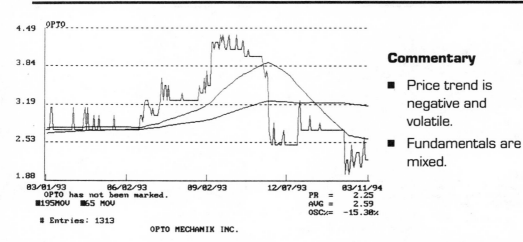

OPTO has not been marked.
■195MOU ■65 MOU
Entries: 1313

PR = 2.25
AVG = 2.59
OSC%= -15.30%

OPTO MECHANIK INC.

Commentary

- Price trend is negative and volatile.
- Fundamentals are mixed.

YEAR	REVENUES	% CHANGE	NET INCOME	% CHANGE	RETURN ON EQUITY	% CHANGE
89	30.256	12.321	0.925	13.081	8.4	- 2.1
90	39.174	29.475	0.986	6.595	8.2	- 2.4
91	32.198	- 17.808	- 2.311	- 334.381	- 23.8	- 390.1
92	32.622	1.317	0.720	NA	6.9	NA

PRISM GROUP INCORPORATED

Symbol: PRSM   Exchange: OTC

PRICE 3/4/94	RANGE	P-E RATIO	DIVIDEND	YIELD	BETA
$2\frac{3}{8}$	$1\frac{3}{4}$ - $4\frac{1}{2}$	NM	0	0	NA

LAST FOUR QUARTERS REPORTED

REVENUES	% CHANGE	NET INCOME	% CHANGE	RETURN ON EQUITY	% CHANGE
18.322	54.93	-0.763	-1078.21	-25.75	-1054.77

Corporate Summary

Prism Group Incorporated provides order processing, manufacturing, and product delivery services to medium size software publishers, and over-flow order processing, manufacturing, and product delivery services to the larger software publishers by acquiring software manufacturing firms in the U.S. and internationally.

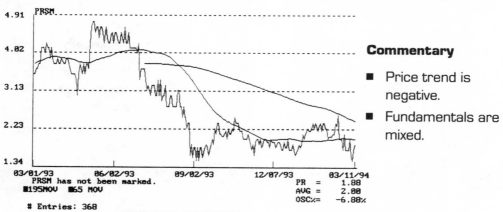

PRISM GROUP INCORPORATED

Commentary

- Price trend is negative.
- Fundamentals are mixed.

YEAR	REVENUES	% CHANGE	NET INCOME	% CHANGE	RETURN ON EQUITY	% CHANGE
89	NA	NA	NA	NA	NA	NA
90	NA	NA	NA	NA	NA	NA
91	2.102	NA	-0.125	NA	-5.4	NA
92	14.729	600.714	0.084	NA	2.6	NA

REFLECTONE INCORPORATED

Symbol: RFTN   Exchange: NMS

PRICE 3/4/94	RANGE	P-E RATIO	DIVIDEND	YIELD	BETA
11$\frac{1}{4}$	7$\frac{1}{8}$ - 11^{13}⁄16	13.65	0	0	- 0.1

LAST FOUR QUARTERS REPORTED

REVENUES	% CHANGE	NET INCOME	% CHANGE	RETURN ON EQUITY	% CHANGE
65.792	- 1.34	2.262	227.51	17.82	NA

Corporate Summary

Reflectone Incorporated is a Florida corporation whose principal business is conducted through its training devices segment and involves the design and manufacture of flight simulators, weapon system trainers, maintenance trainers, part-task trainers, and other sophisticated training devices for U.S. Government, commercial, and international customers.

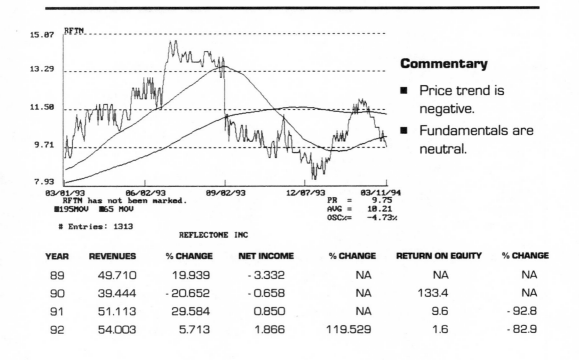

Commentary

■ Price trend is negative.

■ Fundamentals are neutral.

RFTN has not been marked.
■195MOV ■65 MOV

PR =   9.75
AVG =   10.21
OSC%=   -4.73%

Entries: 1313

REFLECTONE INC

YEAR	REVENUES	% CHANGE	NET INCOME	% CHANGE	RETURN ON EQUITY	% CHANGE
89	49.710	19.939	- 3.332	NA	NA	NA
90	39.444	- 20.652	- 0.658	NA	133.4	NA
91	51.113	29.584	0.850	NA	9.6	- 92.8
92	54.003	5.713	1.866	119.529	1.6	- 82.9

SOLITRON DEVICES INCORPORATED

Symbol: SOD   Exchange: NYS

PRICE 3/4/94	RANGE	P-E RATIO	DIVIDEND	YIELD	BETA
3	2 - 6$\frac{7}{8}$	NM	0	0	- 0.4

LAST FOUR QUARTERS REPORTED

REVENUES	% CHANGE	NET INCOME	% CHANGE	RETURN ON EQUITY	% CHANGE
SF	SF	SF	NA	SF	NA

Corporate Summary

Solitron Devices Incorporated, based in West Palm Beach, Florida, is a leading manufacturer and distributor of semiconductor products including connectors, transistors, and other devices. The majority of the revenues generated by Solitron are obtained from sales to companies who have direct contracts with the government.

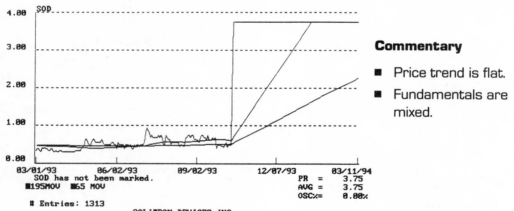

SOD has not been marked.
■19SMOV ■65 MOV

PR = 3.75
AVG = 3.75
OSC% = 0.00%

Entries: 1313

SOLITRON DEVICES INC.

Commentary

■ Price trend is flat.
■ Fundamentals are mixed.

YEAR	REVENUES	% CHANGE	NET INCOME	% CHANGE	RETURN ON EQUITY	% CHANGE
89	36.308	- 5.147	- 9.786	NA	- 77.1	NA
90	36.857	1.512	- 1.424	NA	- 12.6	NA
91	30.035	- 18.509	- 8.363	NA	- 730.4	NA
92	22.608	- 24.728	- 16.489	NA	107.5	NA

TECH DATA CORPORATION

Symbol: TECD   Exchange: NMS

PRICE 3/4/94	RANGE	P-E RATIO	DIVIDEND	YIELD	BETA
37¾	23 - 37¾	24.51	0	0	1.1

LAST FOUR QUARTERS REPORTED

REVENUES	% CHANGE	NET INCOME	% CHANGE	RETURN ON EQUITY	% CHANGE
1372.117	53.26	27.108	49.18	13.31	- 19.91

Corporate Summary

Tech Data Corporation is a leading distributor of personal computer products. The company offers comprehensive product lines in software, networking and communications, mass storage, peripherals, and computer systems. Tech Data serves more than 35,000 value-added resellers and retail dealers from 11 distribution centers throughout the United States and Canada.

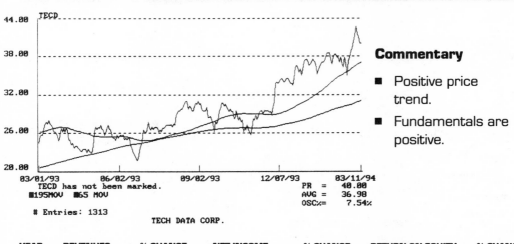

Commentary

- Positive price trend.
- Fundamentals are positive.

TECD has not been marked.
■195MOV ■65 MOV

PR = 40.00
AVG = 36.98
OSC%= 7.54%

Entries: 1313

TECH DATA CORP.

YEAR	REVENUES	% CHANGE	NET INCOME	% CHANGE	RETURN ON EQUITY	% CHANGE
89	348.037	41.060	3.061	- 61.061	6.8	- 63.8
90	441.777	26.934	6.653	117.347	12.9	89.3
91	646.961	46.445	11.887	78.671	12.6	- 2.6
92	978.832	51.302	19.782	66.417	17.2	36.8

TECHNOLOGY RESEARCH CORPORATION

Symbol: TRCI   Exchange: OTC

PRICE 3/4/94	RANGE	P-E RATIO	DIVIDEND	YIELD	BETA
$2^7/_{16}$	$1^3/_8 - 2^7/_{16}$	14.52	0	0	0.9

LAST FOUR QUARTERS REPORTED

REVENUES	% CHANGE	NET INCOME	% CHANGE	RETURN ON EQUITY	% CHANGE
19.614	86.02	2.324	131.71	25.14	- 16.69

Corporate Summary

Technology Research Corporation (TRC) is an international company with engineering, design, and manufacturing capabilities for electrical control and measurement devices. Since the company was founded in 1981, Technology Research Corp. has focused on a strong military product base and has adapters, extension cord models, and modules for original equipment manufacturers (OEM).

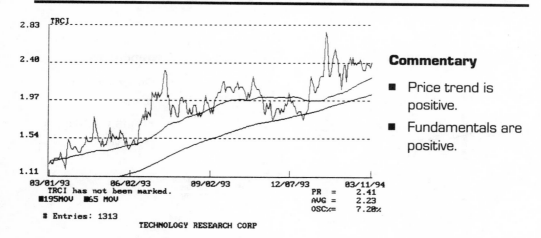

2.83 TRCI

2.40

1.97

1.54

1.11

03/01/93   06/02/93   09/02/93   12/07/93   03/11/94

TRCI has not been marked.
■195MOV ■65 MOV

PR = 2.41
AVG = 2.23
OSC%= 7.28%

Entries: 1313

TECHNOLOGY RESEARCH CORP

Commentary

■ Price trend is positive.

■ Fundamentals are positive.

YEAR	REVENUES	% CHANGE	NET INCOME	% CHANGE	RETURN ON EQUITY	% CHANGE
89	7.400	- 3.909	- 0.850	NA	- 25.3	NA
90	6.578	- 11.108	- 0.655	NA	- 24.2	NA
91	8.194	24.567	0.124	NA	4.3	NA
92	12.875	57.127	1.655	1234.677	35.7	727.4

UNIQUEST INCORPORATED

Symbol: UQST   Exchange: OTC

PRICE 3/4/94	RANGE	P-E RATIO	DIVIDEND	YIELD	BETA
$1^3/_4$	$1^9/_{16}$ - $4^1/_4$	NM	0	0	0.4

LAST FOUR QUARTERS REPORTED

REVENUES	% CHANGE	NET INCOME	% CHANGE	RETURN ON EQUITY	% CHANGE
32.945	57.25	- 22.468	NA	- 172.08	NA

Corporate Summary

The focus of Uniquest Incorporated is on providing system application solutions to consumer-oriented industries. The company has six operating units which serve different consumer markets. The six markets are: health care, retail, hospitality, restaurant, distribution and utility, and government. The installation, training, and support for all the divisions is provided by Uniquest Professional Services Organization.

Commentary

■ Price trend is slightly positive.

■ Fundamentals are mixed.

UQST has not been marked.
■195MOV ■65 MOV

PR = 1.81
AVG = 1.56
OSC% = 14.18%

Entries: 711

UNIQUEST

YEAR	REVENUES	% CHANGE	NET INCOME	% CHANGE	RETURN ON EQUITY	% CHANGE
89	2.043	- 15.718	- 1.806	NA	449.3	1472.9
90	3.275	60.303	0.313	NA	306.9	- 31.7
91	4.063	24.061	- 0.977	- 412.141	- 58.0	- 118.9
92	10.865	167.413	- 0.663	NA	- 7.7	NA

Chapter 21

Florida Telecommunications Companies

The telecommunications industry has been one of the leaders for 1993, and we can feel positive about its future. The information age is upon us. Changes are coming in the way we shop, learn, and entertain at home, and this industry will lead the way. Isolated stocks can have tremendous growth in short time periods. All that being said, however, an investor can not jump blindly into this industry. One thing that is also certain about hot industries is that they can also have burn-out periods.

The Florida telecommunications industry is primarily equipment- or service-related. Within the telecommunications industry as a whole, this was the slowest segment. International opportunities may increase as more countries invest in their telecommunications infrastructure.

BURNUP & SIMS INCORPORATED

Symbol: BSIM   Exchange: NMS

PRICE 3/4/94	RANGE	P-E RATIO	DIVIDEND	YIELD	BETA
$8\frac{1}{16}$	$1\frac{15}{16}$ - $8\frac{1}{16}$	NM	0	0	0.9

LAST FOUR QUARTERS REPORTED

REVENUES	% CHANGE	NET INCOME	% CHANGE	RETURN ON EQUITY	% CHANGE
139.157	- 4.57	- 8.886	NA	- 25.70	NA

Corporate Summary

Burnup & Sims Incorporated and its subsidiaries provide a wide range of cable design and maintenance services to telephone, CATV, and utility service customers throughout the United States. In addition, the company is one of the principal manufacturers of power supplies for the CATV industry and provides commercial printing and graphic arts services.

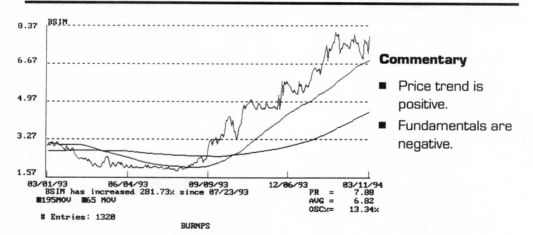

BSIM has increased 281.73% since 07/23/93
■195MOV ■65 MOV

PR =   7.88
AVG =   6.82
OSC%=   13.34%

Entries: 1320

BURNPS

Commentary

■ Price trend is positive.

■ Fundamentals are negative.

YEAR	REVENUES	% CHANGE	NET INCOME	% CHANGE	RETURN ON EQUITY	% CHANGE
89	192.712	8.035	0.785	- 91.503	- 1.8	- 91.7
90	175.236	- 9.068	- 0.782	- 199.618	- 1.8	- 239.9
91	153.521	- 12.392	- 1.047	NA	- 2.5	NA
92	140.987	- 8.164	- 9.308	NA	- 27.6	NA

COMCENTRAL CORPORATION

Symbol: COMC   Exchange: OTC

PRICE 3/4/94	RANGE	P-E RATIO	DIVIDEND	YIELD	BETA
$2\frac{5}{8}$	$5 - \frac{5}{8}$	NM	0	0	0.7

LAST FOUR QUARTERS REPORTED

REVENUES	% CHANGE	NET INCOME	% CHANGE	RETURN ON EQUITY	% CHANGE
2.915	- 71.26	- 1.747	- 846.58	- 55.20	- 809.55

Corporate Summary

ComCentral Corporation is an "operator service company" that provides long distance telecommunications services. Operator service companies are long distance telephone companies that serve the pay phone, hotel, prison, and hospital markets and provide credit card and operator assisted long distance telephone services.

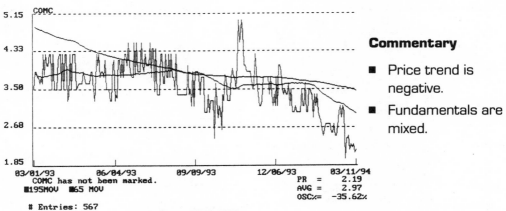

Commentary

■ Price trend is negative.

■ Fundamentals are mixed.

```
5.15  COMC
4.33
3.58
2.68
1.85
      83/01/93      06/04/93      09/09/93      12/06/93    83/11/94
        COMC has not been marked.                    PR  =   2.19
      ■19SMOV  ■65 MOV                               AVG =   2.97
                                                     OSC%=  -35.62%
        # Entries: 567
```

COMCENTRAL CORPORATION

YEAR	REVENUES	% CHANGE	NET INCOME	% CHANGE	RETURN ON EQUITY	% CHANGE
89	NA	NA	NA	NA	NA	NA
90	0.780	NA	- 0.231	NA	537.2	NA
91	4.275	448.077	- 0.186	NA	- 11.6	- 102.2
92	9.997	133.848	0.476	NA	11.6	NA

DYCOM INDUSTRIES INCORPORATED

Symbol: DY   Exchange: NYS

PRICE 3/4/94	RANGE	P-E RATIO	DIVIDEND	YIELD	BETA
$3\frac{1}{2}$	$2\frac{1}{4}$ - $4\frac{1}{2}$	NM	0	0	0.9

LAST FOUR QUARTERS REPORTED

REVENUES	% CHANGE	NET INCOME	% CHANGE	RETURN ON EQUITY	% CHANGE
129.254	- 3.59	- 30.969	NA	- 225.80	NA

Corporate Summary

Dycom Industries Incorporated is in the business of providing a range of services to large companies in the telecommunications and electric utility industries, private enterprise, and governmental units. The services provided by the company can be categorized into three broad groups: telecommunications services, utility line locating services, and electrical services.

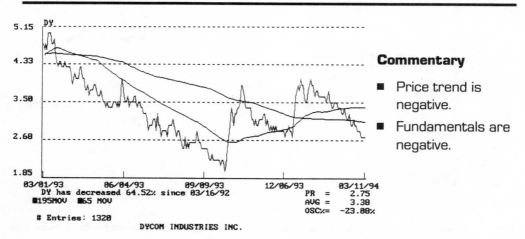

Commentary

- Price trend is negative.
- Fundamentals are negative.

DY has decreased 64.52% since 03/16/92
■195MOV ■65 MOV
PR = 2.75
AVG = 3.38
OSC%= -23.88%

\# Entries: 1320

DYCOM INDUSTRIES INC.

YEAR	REVENUES	% CHANGE	NET INCOME	% CHANGE	RETURN ON EQUITY	% CHANGE
89	118.864	2.490	5.642	24.878	18.3	- 1.6
90	165.398	39.149	9.584	69.869	16.6	- 9.3
91	147.323	- 10.928	- 1.691	- 117.644	- 3.4	- 120.3
92	134.028	- 9.024	- 4.573	NA	- 10.1	NA

INTERMEDIA COMMUNICATIONS OF FLORIDA
Symbol: ICIX   Exchange: NMS

PRICE 3/4/94	RANGE	P-E RATIO	DIVIDEND	YIELD	BETA
13	7¼ - 17⅛	NM	0	0	NA

LAST FOUR QUARTERS REPORTED

REVENUES	% CHANGE	NET INCOME	% CHANGE	RETURN ON EQUITY	% CHANGE
7.722	14.81	- 1.343	NA	- 6.69	NA

Corporate Summary
Intermedia Communications of Florida manufactures and distributes inter-active voice response systems. The target market focus is on companies that have a high volume of call-ins, i.e., minimum of 50,000 calls a day. Most customers are order-taking companies or direct discount teleretailers. The company is based in Tampa, Florida.

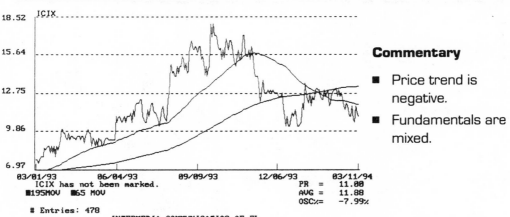

Commentary
- Price trend is negative.
- Fundamentals are mixed.

```
ICIX has not been marked.    PR  = 11.00
195MOV  65 MOV               AVG = 11.88
                             OSC%= -7.99%
# Entries: 478
INTERMEDIA COMMUNICATIOS OF FL
```

YEAR	REVENUES	% CHANGE	NET INCOME	% CHANGE	RETURN ON EQUITY	% CHANGE
89	NA	NA	NA	NA	NA	NA
90	NA	NA	NA	NA	NA	NA
91	5.184	NA	- 0.959	NA	12.7	NA
92	7.030	35.610	- 0.235	NA	- 1.1	- 108.7

PEOPLES TELEPHONE CO. INCORPORATED

Symbol: PTEL   Exchange: NMS

PRICE 3/4/94	RANGE	P-E RATIO	DIVIDEND	YIELD	BETA
10	$8^3/16$ - 13	28.33	0	0	1.3

LAST FOUR QUARTERS REPORTED

REVENUES	% CHANGE	NET INCOME	% CHANGE	RETURN ON EQUITY	% CHANGE
108.641	62.74	4.893	73.27	9.36	- 29.91

Corporate Summary

Peoples Telephone Company Incorporated, through acquisition and internal growth, is the largest independent operator of public pay telephones in the United States. All of the company's public pay telephones are electronically linked to the company's centralized, proprietary management information system located at the company headquarters in Miami, Florida.

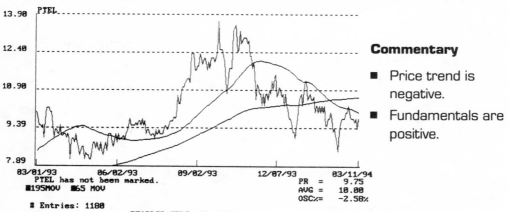

PEOPLES TELE. CO. INC.

Commentary

- Price trend is negative.
- Fundamentals are positive.

YEAR	REVENUES	% CHANGE	NET INCOME	% CHANGE	RETURN ON EQUITY	% CHANGE
89	19.113	47.386	1.038	31.726	11.3	17.50
90	34.745	81.787	0.447	- 56.936	4.8	- 57.7
91	55.876	60.817	1.882	321.029	15.3	220.1
92	74.898	34.043	3.254	72.901	11.8	- 22.7

PRECISION SYSTEMS INCORPORATED

Symbol: PSYS   Exchange: OTC

PRICE 3/4/94	RANGE	P-E RATIO	DIVIDEND	YIELD	BETA
$3\frac{1}{2}$	$2\frac{5}{8}$ - $5\frac{3}{8}$	NM	0	0	NA

LAST FOUR QUARTERS REPORTED

REVENUES	% CHANGE	NET INCOME	% CHANGE	RETURN ON EQUITY	% CHANGE
13.453	- 37.93	- 10.044	NA	- 39.45	NA

Corporate Summary

Precision Systems Incorporated distributes interactive voice response systems to companies that require high volume call-handling capability to run multiple applications on a single, centrally-managed platform even in a geographically distributed environment. The company also provides computer-to-telephone integration for high-level systems integration and capacity planning.

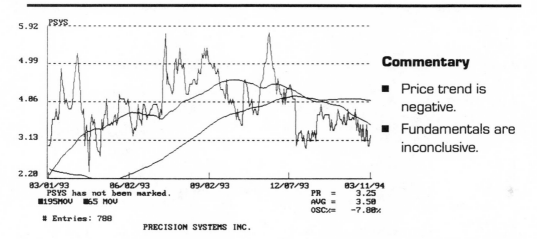

Commentary

- Price trend is negative.

- Fundamentals are inconclusive.

PSYS has not been marked.
■195MOV ■65 MOV

PR = 3.25
AVG = 3.50
OSC%= -7.80%

Entries: 788

PRECISION SYSTEMS INC.

YEAR	REVENUES	% CHANGE	NET INCOME	% CHANGE	RETURN ON EQUITY	% CHANGE
89	NA	NA	NA	NA	NA	NA
90	NA	NA	NA	NA	NA	NA
91	NA	NA	NA	NA	NA	NA
92	18.645	NA	- 2.698	NA	- 7.6	NA

RESTOR INDUSTRIES INCORPORATED

Symbol: REST   Exchange: NMS

PRICE 3/4/94	RANGE	P-E RATIO	DIVIDEND	YIELD	BETA
2	1⁵⁄₁₆ - 2¹⁄₂	NM	0	0	- 0.7

LAST FOUR QUARTERS REPORTED

REVENUES	% CHANGE	NET INCOME	% CHANGE	RETURN ON EQUITY	% CHANGE
17.607	15.41	- 3.378	NA	- 276.66	NA

Corporate Summary

Restor Industries Incorporated provides electronics manufacturing, repair, and modification services to telecommunications, access control, transportation, and other technology companies. The company's principal operations are based in Orlando, Florida with regional repair, distribution, and engineering operations also established in Texas, Kentucky, Indiana, and Oregon.

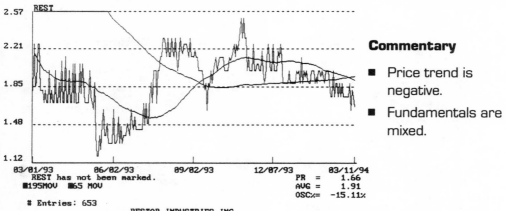

RESTOR INDUSTRIES INC

Commentary

- Price trend is negative.
- Fundamentals are mixed.

YEAR	REVENUES	% CHANGE	NET INCOME	% CHANGE	RETURN ON EQUITY	% CHANGE
89	NA	NA	NA	NA	NA	NA
90	11.718	NA	- 0.009	NA	- 0.9	NA
91	19.535	66.706	0.495	NA	7.0	NA
92	16.946	- 13.253	- 3.298	- 766.263	236.9	3294.5

SUNAIR ELECTRONICS INCORPORATED

Symbol: SNRU   Exchange: ASE

PRICE 3/4/94	RANGE	P-E RATIO	DIVIDEND	YIELD	BETA
2¼	2¼ - 4	13.23	0	0	0.5

LAST FOUR QUARTERS REPORTED

REVENUES	% CHANGE	NET INCOME	% CHANGE	RETURN ON EQUITY	% CHANGE
5.055	- 41.90	0.650	- 51.49	4.91	- 54.46

Corporate Summary

Sunair Electronics Incorporated is engaged in the design, manufacture, and sale of high frequency single-sideband communications equipment utilized for long-range voice and data communications in the fixed station, airborne, mobile, and marine "para-military" applications. The company has both U.S. and international outfits for strategic military and other operations.

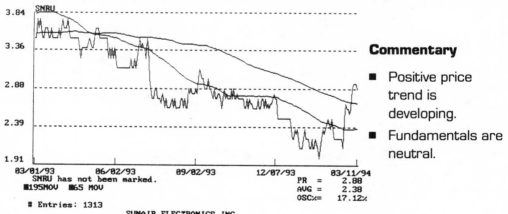

Commentary

- Positive price trend is developing.
- Fundamentals are neutral.

SNRU has not been marked.
■19SMOV ■65 MOV

PR = 2.88
AVG = 2.38
OSC%= 17.12%

Entries: 1313

SUNAIR ELECTRONICS INC.

YEAR	REVENUES	% CHANGE	NET INCOME	% CHANGE	RETURN ON EQUITY	% CHANGE
89	4.466	- 13.533	0.389	- 60.707	3.3	- 62.0
90	4.165	- 6.740	- 0.561	- 244.216	- 5.0	- 251.4
91	4.582	10.012	- 0.332	NA	- 3.0	NA
92	8.010	74.815	1.137	NA	9.2	NA

TELTRONICS INCORPORATED

Symbol: TELT   Exchange: OTC

PRICE 3/4/94	RANGE	P-E RATIO	DIVIDEND	YIELD	BETA
$7/8$	$1/2 - 1 1/4$	NM	0	0	0

LAST FOUR QUARTERS REPORTED

REVENUES	% CHANGE	NET INCOME	% CHANGE	RETURN ON EQUITY	% CHANGE
11.929	- 40.95	- 0.010	- 115.87	- 0.15	- 114.23

Corporate Summary

Teltronics Incorporated designs, manufactures, distributes, and markets electronic peripheral hardware and application software products to the telecommunications market. The company also provides customer loca-tion and long distance management equipment. Teltronics has a strong in-ternational marketing strategy which includes a sister company in the U.K.

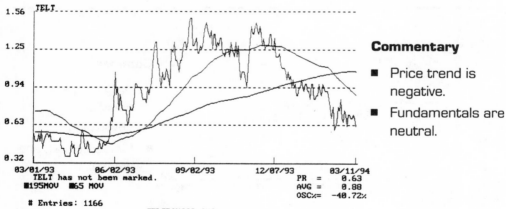

Commentary

- Price trend is negative.
- Fundamentals are neutral.

TELT has not been marked.
■195MOV ■65 MOV

PR = 0.63
AVG = 0.88
OSC%= -40.72%

Entries: 1166

TELTRONICS INC.

YEAR	REVENUES	% CHANGE	NET INCOME	% CHANGE	RETURN ON EQUITY	% CHANGE
89	7.324	59.680	0.370	3.689	8.0	- 91.3
90	11.695	17.657	0.199	46.245	10.4	30.5
91	13.760	17.657	0.276	- 46.216	3.1	- 69.8
92	20.016	45.465	34.336	38.693	4.5	42.7

Chapter 22

Florida Transportation Companies

The Florida companies in this industry are mixed, with revenues also coming from other sources. Only Ryder is a pure transportation company.

The trucking industry was extremely volatile in 1993, falling almost 30 percent early in the year, and then staging a dramatic comeback in the second half of the year. I don't expect the pace to continue and expect a pullback at some point. Having already seen a big rally, 1994 should be neutral.

GENERAL PARCEL SERVICES INCORPORATED

Symbol: GPSX   Exchange: OTC

PRICE 3/4/94	RANGE	P-E RATIO	DIVIDEND	YIELD	BETA
$4\frac{1}{4}$	$3 - 6\frac{3}{4}$	NM	0	0	0.2

LAST FOUR QUARTERS REPORTED

REVENUES	% CHANGE	NET INCOME	% CHANGE	RETURN ON EQUITY	% CHANGE
15.591	10.77	- 0.550	NA	- 29.79	NA

Corporate Summary

General Parcel Services Incorporated is in the parcel shipping and delivery business, providing pickup and delivery of packages principally for business shippers. The company has concentrated on tailoring its services to the commercial or business shipper.

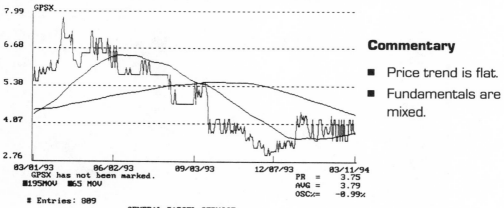

GPSX has not been marked.
■195MOV ■65 MOV

PR = 3.75
AVG = 3.79
OSC%= -0.99%

Entries: 809

GENERAL PARCEL SERVICE

Commentary

- Price trend is flat.
- Fundamentals are mixed.

YEAR	REVENUES	% CHANGE	NET INCOME	% CHANGE	RETURN ON EQUITY	% CHANGE
89	4.938	NA	- 1.486	NA	- 94.2	NA
90	8.201	66.079	- 2.555	NA	3361.8	NA
91	12.617	53.847	- 1.884	NA	- 6728.6	- 300.1
92	13.892	10.105	- 1.268	NA	- 125.5	NA

RYDER SYSTEM INCORPORATED

Symbol: R   Exchange: NYS

PRICE 3/4/94	RANGE	P-E RATIO	DIVIDEND	YIELD	BETA
26⁷⁄₈	26¹⁄₂ - 33¹⁄₈	18.79	.15	.01	1.4

LAST FOUR QUARTERS REPORTED

REVENUES	% CHANGE	NET INCOME	% CHANGE	RETURN ON EQUITY	% CHANGE
4217.029	4.91	111.105	26.91	8.74	36.04

Corporate Summary

Ryder Systems Incorporated, through its subsidiaries, engages primarily in full service leasing and short-term rental of trucks. Additionally, the company engages in dedicated logistics services, public transit management and student transportation, transportation by truck of automobiles, repair and overhaul of aircraft and helicopter turbine and turboprop engines, and the sale and leasing of aircraft parts to the worldwide aviation industry. Ryder was established in 1955 and is based in Miami, FL.

R has not been marked.
■195MOV ■65 MOV

PR = 26.63
AVG = 26.72
OSC%= -0.35%

Entries: 1313

RYDER SYSTEM INC.

Commentary

- Slightly negative price.
- Fundamentals are positive.

YEAR	REVENUES	% CHANGE	NET INCOME	% CHANGE	RETURN ON EQUITY	% CHANGE
89	5073.425	0.872	52.189	- 61.243	3.8	- 58.4
90	5162.332	1.752	82.216	57.535	6.2	64.4
91	5061.098	- 1.961	65.720	- 20.064	5.1	- 17.5
92	5191.519	2.577	117.926	79.437	8.6	68.0

Chapter 23

Florida Communications Companies

The stocks in this section are a combination of publishing and communications. Investing in these Florida companies will allow you to participate in everything from *The National Enquirer* to videotape production.

Publishing

The publishing industry as a group substantially outpaced the general market, and that growth is expected to continue. The determining factor on its continued pace may well be the general economy and whether advertising sales pick up as projected.

Newspapers

The newspaper industry has shown signs of life after a moderate performance in 1993.

Broadcast Media

The outlook for broadcast is favorable, particularly as it relates to anything in the cable industry.

ENQUIRER/STAR GROUP INCORPORATED

Symbol: ENQ   Exchange: NYS

PRICE 3/4/94	RANGE	P-E RATIO	DIVIDEND	YIELD	BETA
18⁷⁄₈	15 - 19	29.96	0.05	0	1.6

LAST FOUR QUARTERS REPORTED

REVENUES	% CHANGE	NET INCOME	% CHANGE	RETURN ON EQUITY	% CHANGE
291.588	2.82	25.988	30.09	8.35	23.57

Corporate Summary

Enquirer/Star Group, Inc. operates through its subsidiaries as a leading publisher in the field of personality journalism. The company publishes **National Enquirer**, **Star**, **Weekly World News**, and **Soap Opera Magazine** with a current aggregate weekly circulation of approximately 7.2 million copies. The company's periodicals are featured in approximately 180,000 locations in the United States and Canada.

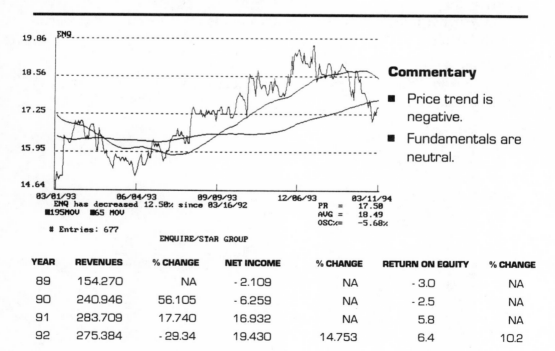

Commentary

■ Price trend is negative.

■ Fundamentals are neutral.

ENQ has decreased 12.50% since 03/16/92
■19SMOV ■6S MOV
PR = 17.50
AVG = 18.49
OSC%= -5.68%

Entries: 677

ENQUIRE/STAR GROUP

YEAR	REVENUES	% CHANGE	NET INCOME	% CHANGE	RETURN ON EQUITY	% CHANGE
89	154.270	NA	- 2.109	NA	- 3.0	NA
90	240.946	56.105	- 6.259	NA	- 2.5	NA
91	283.709	17.740	16.932	NA	5.8	NA
92	275.384	- 29.34	19.430	14.753	6.4	10.2

KNIGHT-RIDDER INCORPORATED

Symbol: KRI   Exchange: NYS

PRICE 3/4/94	RANGE	P-E RATIO	DIVIDEND	YIELD	BETA
58$\frac{1}{4}$	52$\frac{1}{4}$ - 63	21.74	0.35	0.1	1.3

LAST FOUR QUARTERS REPORTED

REVENUES	% CHANGE	NET INCOME	% CHANGE	RETURN ON EQUITY	% CHANGE
2451.347	5.23	148.089	1.37	12.33	5.86

Corporate Summary

Knight-Ridder, Inc. is an international information and communications company engaged in newspaper publishing, business news and information services, electronic retrieval services, and news, graphics, and photo services. The company is also involved in other newspaper businesses, cable television, and newsprint production through business arrangements, including joint ventures and partnerships.

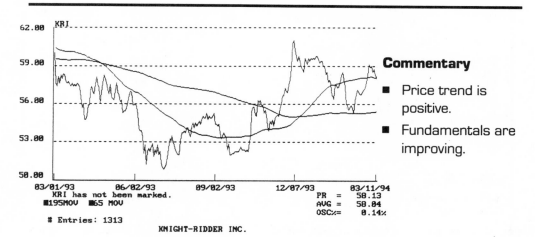

KNIGHT-RIDDER INC.

KRI has not been marked.
■195MOV ■65 MOV

PR = 58.13
AVG = 58.04
OSC%= 0.14%

Entries: 1313

Commentary

■ Price trend is positive.

■ Fundamentals are improving.

YEAR	REVENUES	% CHANGE	NET INCOME	% CHANGE	RETURN ON EQUITY	% CHANGE
89	2268.256	8.876	179.836	22.525	19.6	9.8
90	2305.162	1.627	149.045	- 17.122	16.7	- 15.1
91	2237.318	- 2.943	132.068	- 11.391	11.5	- 31.0
92	2329.529	4.121	146.086	10.614	12.4	7.5

MAGNATECH CORPORATION

Symbol: MAG   Exchange: OTC

PRICE 3/4/94	RANGE	P-E RATIO	DIVIDEND	YIELD	BETA
$7\frac{3}{8}$	$1\frac{3}{4}$ - 8	30.73	0	0	0.3

LAST FOUR QUARTERS REPORTED

REVENUES	% CHANGE	NET INCOME	% CHANGE	RETURN ON EQUITY	% CHANGE
19.227	178.29	1.184	330.55	17.31	229.79

Corporate Summary

Magnatech Corporation is in the business of communications, including video and audio tape production and duplication and satellite broadcasting of television signals. The majority of the company's business is generated in the area of audio tape production. The company was established in 1987 and is based in Ft. Lauderdale, Florida.

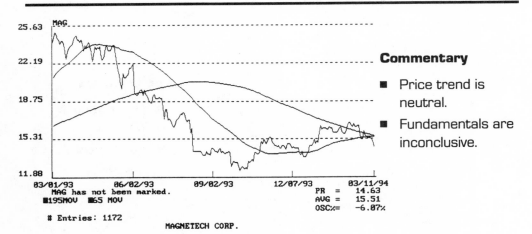

```
25.63  MAG
22.19
18.75
15.31
11.88
     03/01/93    06/02/93    09/02/93    12/07/93   03/11/94
     MAG has not been marked.              PR  =   14.63
     ■195MOV  ■65 MOV                      AVG =   15.51
                                          OSC%=   -6.07%
     # Entries: 1172
```

Commentary

- Price trend is neutral.
- Fundamentals are inconclusive.

MAGNETECH CORP.

YEAR	REVENUES	% CHANGE	NET INCOME	% CHANGE	RETURN ON EQUITY	% CHANGE
89	4.802	42.832	.0284	21.368	6.1	- 15.4
90	3.362	35.784	0.234	1.299	7.2	- 21.4
91	2.476	91.345	0.231	12.136	9.1	3.2
92	1.294	NA	0.206	NA	8.8	NA

Chapter 24

Florida Diversified Companies

The companies in this section didn't fall comfortably into any of the other categories, so I grouped them together. Don't look for any correlation between them, because there isn't any. Also, don't make a negative assumption about them just because they didn't fit into any particular group. Each company should simply stand on its own merits.

AIRSHIP INTERNATIONAL LIMITED

Symbol: BLMP   Exchange: OTC

PRICE 3/4/94	RANGE	P-E RATIO	DIVIDEND	YIELD	BETA
1/2	3/8 - 1 1/2	NM	0	0	1.3

LAST FOUR QUARTERS REPORTED

REVENUES	% CHANGE	NET INCOME	% CHANGE	RETURN ON EQUITY	% CHANGE
10.125	41.17	- 1.825	NA	- 26.69	NA

Corporate Summary

Airship International Limited owns and operates airships, commonly known as blimps, for the aerial advertising and promotional purposes of Fortune 500 companies. The company operates Skyship Series airships, the most technically advanced in the world, certified by the Federal Aviation Administration for day and night passenger flight. Airships offer exposure on a grand scale, providing live televised coverage of major sporting and special events.

AIRSHIP INTERNATIONAL LTD.

Commentary

- Price trend is flat.
- Fundamentals are neutral.

YEAR	REVENUES	% CHANGE	NET INCOME	% CHANGE	RETURN ON EQUITY	% CHANGE
89	2.362	- 21.267	0.051	- 83.113	3.7	- 90.0
90	4.693	98.688	- 3.356	- 6680.393	- 2314.5	- 62273.4
91	7.015	49.478	- 4.418	NA	- 168.2	NA
92	7.258	3.464	1.165	NA	12.5	NA

DSI INDUSTRIES INCORPORATED

Symbol: DSIC   Exchange: OTC

PRICE 3/4/94	RANGE	P-E RATIO	DIVIDEND	YIELD	BETA
7/16	3/8 - 11/16	43.70	0	0	1.7

LAST FOUR QUARTERS REPORTED

REVENUES	% CHANGE	NET INCOME	% CHANGE	RETURN ON EQUITY	% CHANGE
25.585	17.46	0.333	0.30	3.25	- 12.39

Corporate Summary

DSI Industries is the parent company for four major corporations located throughout the United States. The subsidiary companies conduct business in the areas of oil drilling, medical research, and investments as well as the running of botanical nurseries. The majority of revenues for DSI Industries are generated through Sunshine Botanical Nurseries and the Norton Company, which handles the company's oil drilling ventures.

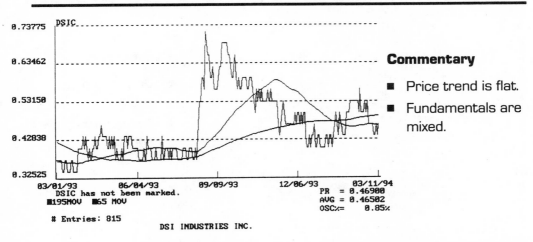

Commentary

- Price trend is flat.
- Fundamentals are mixed.

DSIC has not been marked.
■195MOU ■65 MOU

PR = 0.46900
AVG = 0.46502
OSC%=   0.85%

Entries: 815

DSI INDUSTRIES INC.

YEAR	REVENUES	% CHANGE	NET INCOME	% CHANGE	RETURN ON EQUITY	% CHANGE
89	0.657	- 9.003	- 0.277	NA	- 29.6	NA
90	0.728	10.807	- 0.076	NA	- 8.7	NA
91	9.462	1199.725	0.903	NA	11.4	NA
92	21.699	129.328	0.193	- 78.627	2.2	- 80.6

HEIST (C.H.) CORPORATION

Symbol: HST   Exchange: ASE

PRICE 3/4/94	RANGE	P-E RATIO	DIVIDEND	YIELD	BETA
$7\frac{1}{4}$	$7\frac{1}{4} - 9\frac{5}{8}$	29.00	0	0	0.9

LAST FOUR QUARTERS REPORTED

REVENUES	% CHANGE	NET INCOME	% CHANGE	RETURN ON EQUITY	% CHANGE
77.096	7.76	0.728	-56.04	2.95	-55.94

Corporate Summary

C.H. Hiest Corporation has been engaged in furnishing industrial maintenance services to the heavy industries like oil refineries and petrochemical
companies. Its services are currently performed in the U.S. and Canada. In
1978, this company started operations in the temporary help field. In
1989, the company acquired PBI, an installer and vendor of insulation for
commercial applications.

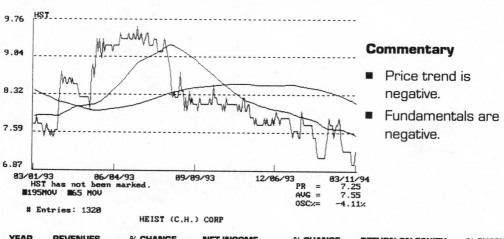

Commentary

- Price trend is negative.

- Fundamentals are negative.

HST has not been marked.
■195MOV ■65 MOV

PR = 7.25
AVG = 7.55
OSC% = -4.11%

Entries: 1320

HEIST (C.H.) CORP

YEAR	REVENUES	% CHANGE	NET INCOME	% CHANGE	RETURN ON EQUITY	% CHANGE
89	53.007	17.145	1.719	49.869	9.6	35.2
90	65.006	22.637	2.639	53.519	12.8	-33.0
91	70.082	7.809	2.021	-23.418	8.2	-35.5
92	71.398	1.878	1.270	-37.160	5.1	-38.2

HI GROUP INCORPORATED

Symbol: MH   Exchange: NYS

PRICE 3/4/94	RANGE	P-E RATIO	DIVIDEND	YIELD	BETA
8¼	7 - 11	8.68	0	0	0.6

LAST FOUR QUARTERS REPORTED

REVENUES	% CHANGE	NET INCOME	% CHANGE	RETURN ON EQUITY	% CHANGE
18.982	12.46	4.334	43.65	22.46	11.62

Corporate Summary

MHI Group, Inc. is engaged in the ownership and operation of funeral homes and cemeteries. The company's funeral homes and cemeteries, all of which are located in Florida, are separate business units that compliment and generate business for one another. The majority of the company's sales are made on a pre-need basis, that is, prior to death. Payment is made in equal installments over the life of the contract.

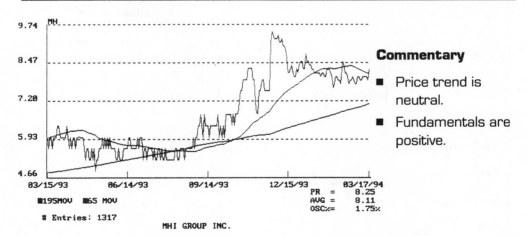

Commentary

■ Price trend is neutral.

■ Fundamentals are positive.

PR = 8.25
AVG = 8.11
OSC% = 1.75%

■195MOV ■65 MOV

Entries: 1317

MHI GROUP INC.

YEAR	REVENUES	% CHANGE	NET INCOME	% CHANGE	RETURN ON EQUITY	% CHANGE
89	9.406	15.638	0.313	- 41.165	4.9	- 56.0
90	12.586	33.808	- 0.623	- 299.042	- 8.5	- 273.6
91	16.115	28.039	2.074	NA	18.5	NA
92	16.789	4.182	3.516	69.527	20.8	12.5

SUN CITY INDUSTRIES

Symbol: SNI   Exchange: ASE

PRICE 3/4/94	RANGE	P-E RATIO	DIVIDEND	YIELD	BETA
$2^7/_8$	$2^3/_4$ - $3^1/_4$	NM	0	0	0.6

LAST FOUR QUARTERS REPORTED

REVENUES	% CHANGE	NET INCOME	% CHANGE	RETURN ON EQUITY	% CHANGE
64.350	2.95	- 0.137	- 374.00	- 4.54	- 381.62

Corporate Summary

The business of Sun City Industries is conducted through its wholly-owned subsidiaries which are engaged principally in processing and marketing shell eggs and the distribution of eggs, butter, cheese, poultry, and other dairy products. The company is based in Ft. Lauderdale, Florida.

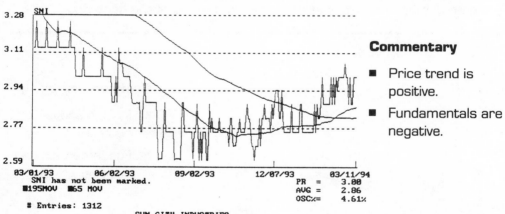

SNI has not been marked.
■195MOV ■65 MOV

PR = 3.00
AVG = 2.86
OSC%= 4.61%

Entries: 1312

SUN CITY INDUSTRIES

Commentary

■ Price trend is positive.

■ Fundamentals are negative.

YEAR	REVENUES	% CHANGE	NET INCOME	% CHANGE	RETURN ON EQUITY	% CHANGE
89	72.636	17.738	- 1.464	NA	- 44.6	NA
90	70.543	- 2.881	- 0.353	NA	- 12.9	NA
91	68.429	- 2.997	0.354	NA	11.2	NA
92	61.255	- 10.484	- 0.333	- 194.068	- 11.8	- 205.3

TODHUNTER INTERNATIONAL INCORPORATED

Symbol: TODH   Exchange: NMS

PRICE 3/4/94	RANGE	P-E RATIO	DIVIDEND	YIELD	BETA
15	8¾ - 15	14.29	0	0	NA

LAST FOUR QUARTERS REPORTED

REVENUES	% CHANGE	NET INCOME	% CHANGE	RETURN ON EQUITY	% CHANGE
66.016	3.36	4.835	61.44	18.54	- 7.04

Corporate Summary

Todhunter International Incorporated produces citrus-based brandy, distilled spirits, and fortified wine used as ingredients in a variety of alcoholic beverages, bottled coolers, and prepared cocktails and other beverages on a contract basis, and produces for distribution in the Southeast, a line of popularly priced spirits. The company also imports, bottles, and distributes alcoholic beverages in the Bahamas and produces vinegar and cooking wine.

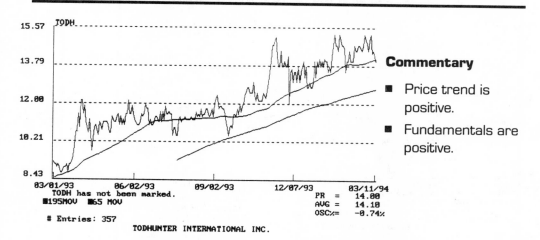

Commentary

■ Price trend is positive.

■ Fundamentals are positive.

TODH has not been marked.
■195MOV ■65 MOV

PR =   14.00
AUG =   14.10
OSC%=   -0.74%

Entries: 357

TODHUNTER INTERNATIONAL INC.

YEAR	REVENUES	% INCREASE	NET INCOME	% INCREASE	RETURN ON EQUITY	% INCREASE
89	NA	NA	NA	NA	NA	NA
90	NA	NA	NA	NA	NA	NA
91	61.270	NA	2.027	NA	16.2	NA
92	61.500	0.375	2.784	37.346	18.5	14.6

TRANSMEDIA NETWORK INCORPORATED

Symbol: TMNI   Exchange: OTC

PRICE 3/4/94	RANGE	P-E RATIO	DIVIDEND	YIELD	BETA
$18^3/_8$	$8^3/_{16}$ - $18^3/_8$	40.21	0	0	0.9

LAST FOUR QUARTERS REPORTED

REVENUES	% CHANGE	NET INCOME	% CHANGE	RETURN ON EQUITY	% CHANGE
40.190	42.61	2.884	43.13	NA	NA

Corporate Summary

The main business of Transmedia Network Inc. is the acquisition of "rights to receive" from its clients, which are then sold for cash to holders of the company's Transmedia Network, Inc. Executive Savings Card. "Rights to receive" are the company's rights to receive goods and services, principally food and beverage credits, in payment for purchasing inventory of rights to receive directly for cash or by financing the rights for other goods or services.

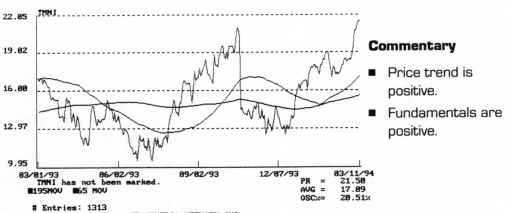

Commentary

- Price trend is positive.
- Fundamentals are positive.

```
22.05  TMNI
19.02
16.00
12.97
 9.95
     03/01/93   06/02/93   09/02/93   12/07/93   03/11/94
       TMNI has not been marked.            PR  =  21.50
     ■195MOV  ■65 MOV                       AVG =  17.09
                                           OSC%=  20.51%
       # Entries: 1313
```

TRANSMEDIA NETWORK INC.

YEAR	REVENUES	% CHANGE	NET INCOME	% CHANGE	RETURN ON EQUITY	% CHANGE
89	4.711	52.460	0.099	182.857	9.8	85.0
90	7.481	58.799	0.309	212.121	19.9	103.09
91	13.721	83.411	1.043	237.540	36.7	83.9
92	25.522	86.007	1.745	67.306	18.5	- 49.6

TRIARC COMPANIES, INC.

Symbol: DWG   Exchange: ASE

PRICE	RANGE	P-E RATIO	DIVIDEND	YIELD	BETA
$20^7/_8$	$15^1/_2$ - $31^3/_4$	NM	0	0	0.9

LAST FOUR QUARTERS REPORTED

REVENUES	% CHANGE	NET INCOME	% CHANGE	RETURN ON EQUITY	% CHANGE
1057.373	- 11.26	- 62.811	NA	NA	NA

Corporate Summary

Triarc Companies, Inc. is a holding company which, through its direct and indirect operative subsidiaries, is engaged in four primary businesses: fast food, soft drinks, textiles, and liquefied petroleum gas. The company's four main businesses are conducted through Arby's, Inc., Royal Crown Cola Co. (RC Cola), Graniteville Co., and the National Propane Co. The majority of the company's revenues are generated in the area of petroleum gas.

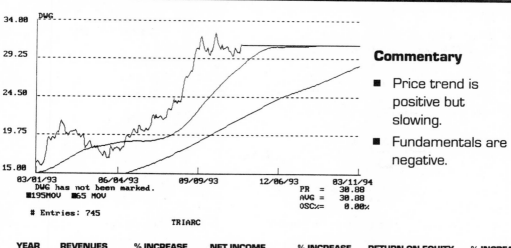

Commentary

- Price trend is positive but slowing.
- Fundamentals are negative.

YEAR	REVENUES	% INCREASE	NET INCOME	% INCREASE	RETURN ON EQUITY	% INCREASE
89	1175.099	7.097	- 2.601	- 319.865	- 2.2	- 398.8
90	1231.236	4.777	- 12.894	NA	- 11.8	NA
91	1215.323	- 1.292	- 17.556	NA	- 19.0	NA
92	1275.056	4.915	- 7.502	NA	- 807	NA

WACKENHUT CORPORATION

Symbol: WAK   Exchange: NYSE

PRICE 3/4/94	RANGE	P-E RATIO	DIVIDEND	YIELD	BETA
12¾	12¼ - 15¼	425.00	0.09	0.01	0.8

LAST FOUR QUARTERS REPORTED

REVENUES	% CHANGE	NET INCOME	% CHANGE	RETURN ON EQUITY	% CHANGE
659.676	9.04	0.188	- 97.64	0.38	- 97.78

Corporate Summary

Wackenhut Corporation is primarily engaged in the furnishing of security guard services for residential and commercial developments. The company also provides investigative services, job training under contract with the Department of Labor, the training of security guards and other emergency personnel, as well as the management of detention and correction facilities. Wackenhut is based in Coral Gables, Florida.

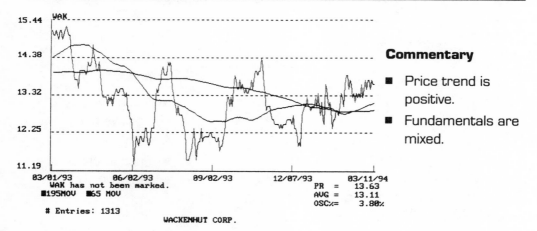

Commentary

- Price trend is positive.
- Fundamentals are mixed.

WAK has not been marked.
■195MOV ■65 MOV

PR = 13.63
AVG = 13.11
OSC%=   3.80%

\# Entries: 1313

WACKENHUT CORP.

YEAR	REVENUES	% CHANGE	NET INCOME	% CHANGE	RETURN ON EQUITY	% CHANGE
89	462.181	15.258	5.874	13.070	17.5	2.7
90	521.191	12.768	6.963	18.539	18.4	5.2
91	572.527	9.850	7.721	10.886	18.0	- 2.0
92	630.320	10.094	1.137	- 85.274	2.4	- 86.7

Summary and Recommendations

You have just completed the most comprehensive book available on investing in Florida. You now know the various investment options available to you. What remains is for you to select one or more of the options that best fits your personality and needs.

Are you a conservator or an aggressive investor? Active or passive? Income-oriented or growth?

Once you decide what kind of investment works for you, concentrate on getting more information. For example, each month we produce a newsletter that updates the material in this book. If you would like to review a copy, we will be happy to send you a current issue without charge. Write or phone: J.W. Dicks Research Institute, Inc., 520 Crown Oak Centre Drive, Longwood, FL 32750, 1-800-333-3700.

If you see a stock that you like, write to the company and ask them for their latest annual report. Take advantage of the fact that you live in their state and visit the company's headquarters. All public companies have an investor relations department, which is there to help you become comfortable with the company.

Throughout the book I have given you lists of names and phone numbers to contact for more information about a particular area of interest. Once you start the investigative process, you will find that one name leads you to another until you find a contact you are comfortable working with. When you do, you will have arrived. Like most things, investing is relational. You will ultimately be more successful at it when you invest in things you know and with people you like dealing with.

The grass may always be greener on the other side of the fence, but there is nothing like investing in your own "backyard."

Appendix

Symbol Used for quotes and listed in the paper.

Exchange Where the stock is traded:
NMS National Market System
NYS New York Stock Exchange
AMS American Stock Exchange
OTC Over The Counter

Price Current price on dated information obtained.

Range The price range for the last quarter.

PE-Ratio Price earning ratio. Negative ratios are listed as NA.

Dividends Any currently and for the last quarter.

Yield Income paid to stockholders annualized.

Beta Volatility factor compared to Dow Jones Industrial Averages.

Corporate Summary A brief description of the company as taken from its last annual report of 10-K.

Chart Is a price line chart showing the relationship to the price of the stock and its 65 and 195-day moving average.

Commentary Our summary of the current trends in the stock.

Box Information Annual reported information. Data retrieved by Standard & Poors Compustat Services on contract. NA stands for information not available from public filing.

All information has been obtained from sources deemed reliable. Investors interested in a company should obtain updated information before investing.

Glossary

Bankruptcy Sale: The process (frequently auction format) by which a trustee appointed by the court liquidates the assets of a debtor.

Beta: A number, actually a coefficient, which represents the volatility of a security. The higher the figure, the more volatile the security; the lower the figure, the less volatile. The determination is made by comparing the security's beta to that of the market as a whole, typically represented by the number "1."

Call Date: A call is the right of a bond issuer to pay off the bonds before the maturing date. This privilege allows an issuer to sell new bonds at a lower interest rate. The call date is the date the redemption may take place.

Certificates of Deposit: An interest-paying debt security usually issued by a bank. Maturity lengths of CDs vary from weeks to years. Interest rate quotes vary with the broad movement of interest rates within the economy. CDs issued by banks are government insured up to $100,000.

Coupon Rate: The interest rate the issuer of a bond agrees to pay.

Deficiency Judgment: A legal judgment sought by a creditor (usually a mortgagor) against a borrower for any claims left unpaid by a foreclosure sale.

Department of Housing and Urban Development (HUD): Federal agency whose purpose is to provide low-to-moderate income housing through subsidized or special loan programs.

"Designer" Certificates of Deposit: CDs which offer features to make them more competitive: Penalty-free withdrawals and interest rates favorably tied to a particular indicator (e.g. the Prime Interest Rate) are just two examples of such features.

Discount Broker: A stockbroker or brokerage company which executes transactions on negotiable securities at a significant discount to those charged by full service brokers. Typically, discount brokers do not provide investment advice, analysis, or any other type of comprehensive financial service.

Discount Mortgages: First and second mortgages which may be bought as investments. The investor pays an amount below what is actually owed to the seller, creating the discount. The seller receives what he deems to be an acceptable lump-sum payment for the mortgage and the investor takes over as the recipient of the monthly payments.

Discount: The amount **below** the face value by which a debt security (bond) sells. Bond sellers which find themselves selling at a discount do so because the interest rate earned by the bonds is lower than what would currently be available to potential buyers elsewhere in the market.

Dividend: Distribution of earnings to shareholders, typically paid quarterly.

Executor: An executor is the person charged in a will with the responsibility of administering an estate and distributing the assets contained therein.

Federal Deposit Insurance Corporation (FDIC): The Federal agency which guarantees, up to specific limits, the money on deposit in banks.

Federal National Mortgage Association (FNMA): Government-sponsored corporation which purchases mortgages from lenders and resells them to investors. Known by the nickname "Fannie Mae."

Federal Savings and Loan Insurance Corporation (FSLIC): Similar to the F.D.I.C., the F.S.L.I.C. guarantees the money on deposit in savings and loan institutions.

Foreclosure: A legal process whereby a mortgage holder (usually a lending institution) may seize the property of a delinquent mortgagor (borrower). The property may then be sold to pay off the claims of the mortgage.

Full Service Broker: A stockbroker who buys and sells negotiable securities for clients and charges a commission. Typically, the full service brokerage provides advice and analysis on securities to clients, which helps to justify the full commissions they charge clients for transactions.

Fundamental Analysis: Determining present or future value of a security by using financial information on the company selling the security. Relevant information would include net profit, returns on equity, price to earnings ratio, dividend payout and the percent change in these factors during previous time periods.

Incremental Investing: A method of purchasing securities whereby the total purchase planned is made in increments over a period of time. This buying procedure allows the investor to evaluate his decision **without** committing all of his capital at one time. The purchasing method significantly helps to mitigate risk during uncertain market conditions.

Liquidity: The relative ability of a security or piece of property to be converted into cash.

Load: The cost including sales commission charged to buy an investment. The cost is usually charged at the time of purchase and is known as a "front end" load. If the cost is charged at the time of sale it is known as a "back-end" load.

Maturity Date: The date at which the principal of a bond comes due for payment to the investor.

Money Market Funds: Bank money markets are fully-liquid bank accounts paying interest on their balance. The amount paid is determined by the instruments which back them i.e., treasury bills, commercial paper, and "jumbo" CDs (CDs with a face value of at least $100,000). These accounts are government insured up to $100,000. Mutual fund money market accounts are similar to those offered by banks. However, they usually pay a higher rate of interest than the bank versions because they are not insured.

Mortgage: A debt instrument securing a loan on a piece of property.

Moving Average: A tool of technical analysis. The average price of a security or index calculated over a predetermined period of days, weeks, months, or even years. The average "moves" because as each new piece of data is added, the oldest is dropped. When the average price is represented by a dot on a graph, a technical analyst can connect the dots to create a line showing the movement trend.

Municipal Bond: A debt security issued by a state or municipality.

No-Load: The term used to characterize investments (typically open-end mutual funds) which charge no sales commission.

Premium: The amount **above** the face value by which a debt security (bond) sells. Sellers of bonds which pay a rate of interest higher than the current rates will usually realize this premium as buyers are willing to pay more to receive the better rate.

Price-Earnings Ratio (P-E Ratio): The price of a stock dividend by its earnings per share. Used by investors to help determine how much they are paying for the earning power of a company. High P-E ratios typically belong to smaller, growth-oriented companies with great expectations of high earnings, and thus are more indicative of higher risk.

Probate: The legal process by which the will of a decedent is presented to a court for administration and disposition.

Real Estate Owned: A term referring to the real property repossessed by a lender and targeted for liquidation.

Real Estate Investment Trust (REIT): An investment company which manages a portfolio comprised of real estate interests, to include ownership of mortgages and/or real property. Shares of a R.E.I.T. are issued to investors, and frequently these shares are traded on an exchange. It is a method passive investors may participate in real estate with a small amount of capital. R.E.I.T.'s are also more liquid than more traditional types of real estate investment.

Real Rate of Return: The return an investor realizes from an investment **after** it has been adjusted for taxes and inflation.

Resolution Trust Corporation (RTC): Government agency set up in 1989 which is responsible for selling the assets of Savings and Loans determined to be insolvent by the Office of Thrift Supervisor.

Second Mortgage: A loan recorded after a first mortgage. Typically initiated when a homeowner or other real property owner needs more money.

Stop/Loss Order: An order to a broker from a customer which dictates the price at which a security will automatically be sold. Typically used to protect profits or prevent further losses.

Tax Lien Certificate: A certificate issued by municipalities which represents one year's worth of unpaid property taxes. They are sold at an auction, with investors bidding on the interest rate. The winning bidder is the one who bids the lowest rate.

Tax Sale: The actual sale of the property represented by a tax lien certificate. The certificate holder may request such a sale after holding the certificate for a minimum of 2 years. The sale is conducted by the county in an auction format.

Technical Analysis: The forecasting of the future price of individual stocks, industries, and markets through the evaluation of historical price movement and volume. Technical analysts typically use charts to put such movements in perspective.

Veteran's Administration (VA) Loan: A mortgage loan awarded to a veteran of the U.S. Armed Services. The loan is guaranteed by the Veteran's Administration, thereby reducing risk to the lender. VA guarantee permits the lenders to provide higher loan to value loans at favorable terms.

Volatility: The tendency of a security or market to rise and fall significantly in value.

Yield to Call: The yield on a bond which is calculated with the assumption that it will be redeemed ("called") by the issuer at the first available call date. *See call date.*

Yield: As it pertains to a stock: The percentage rate of return as represented by the dividend paid. As it pertains to a bond: The actual rate of return which accounts for purchase price and time remaining until the bond matures.

Other Titles of Interest from Bob Adams, Inc.
AVAILABLE AT YOUR LOCAL BOOKSTORE

Low Risk Investing
How to get a good return on your money without losing any sleep
Paperback, 352 pp., $9.95

In *Low Risk Investing*, Williamson clearly and concisely explains the many sound alternatives for achieving a good return on your money with minimal risk. He rates each investment vehicle for security of principal, stability of income, total return, tax consequences, and as a hedge against inflation. Williamson also defines each investment, outlines its advantages and disadvantages, and details how the instrument is bought and sold.

100 Best Mutual Funds You Can Buy, 1994 edition
Trade paperback, 300 pp., $12.95

Updated yearly! Williamson systematically re-evaluates every one of the over 3,000 mutual funds on the market todetermine an authoritative ranking of the top 100. Each fund is analyzed for total return, risk, quality of management, current income, and expense control. Includes money market funds.

If you cannot find these titles at your bookstore, you may order them directly from the publisher.

BY PHONE: Call 1-800-872-5627 (in Massachusetts 617-767-8100). We accept Visa, Mastercard, and American Express. $4.50 will be added to your total order for shipping and handling.

BY MAIL: Write out the full title of the books you'd like to order and send payment, including $4.50 for shipping and handling to: Bob Adams, Inc., 260 Center Street, Holbrook, MA 02343.

PLEASE CHECK AT YOUR LOCAL BOOKSTORE FIRST